LIVING TOMORROW'S COMPANY

The Centre for Tomorrow's Company

The Centre for Tomorrow's Company has been created to build on the work of the RSA Inquiry Tomorrow's Company.

It is a direct response to the continuing interest sparked by the publication of the findings of this business-led Inquiry in 1995.

The Centre's purpose is to inspire and enable British businesses to compete with the best through applying the *inclusive approach*.

The Centre is business-led and its main impact is on four groups who are crucial to competitiveness.

- Businesses – a broadening membership of companies which share the inclusive approach and lead by example.
- Investors – a growing band of fund managers, analysts and pension professionals who need a wider range of measures by which to assess companies.
- Tomorrow's wealth creators – who will be provided with research and learning material that helps them understand what makes companies successful.
- Public policy makers – influencing the debate on competitiveness and governance and strengthening policies which build a stronger economy through stronger companies.

The Centre operates on a not-for-profit basis.

For details contact:
The Centre for Tomorrow's Company
19 Buckingham Street
London WC2N 6EF
Telephone: 0171 930 5150
Fax: 0171 930 5155
E-mail: ctomco@ctomco.demon.co.uk

LIVING TOMORROW'S COMPANY

Mark Goyder

Gower

Published by
Gower Publishing Limited
Gower House
Croft Road
Aldershot
Hampshire GU11 3HR
England

Gower
Old Post Road
Brookfield
Vermont 05036
USA

Mark Goyder has asserted his right under the Copyright, Designs and Patents Act 1988 to be identified as the author of this work.

British Library Cataloguing in Publication Data
Goyder, Mark
    Living tomorrow's company
    1. Success in business
    I. Title
    650.1

    ISBN 0 566 08020 6

Library of Congress Cataloging-in-Publication Data
Goyder, Mark
    Living tomorrow's company / Mark Goyder.
    p. cm.
    Includes index.
    ISBN 0 566 08020 6
    1. Entrepreneurship. 2. Success in business. 3. Social responsibility of business. 4. Management. I. Title.
HB615.G69 1998
658.4–dc21   97–31503
                CIP

Typeset in Garamond by Bryn Morgan and printed in Great Britain by Biddles Limited, Guildford.

Companies involved in the RSA Inquiry Tomorrow's Company

Sponsors (Participating companies)

Anglian Water Plc
Bain & Company
Baring Venture Partners Limited
S J Berwin & Co
Blue Circle Industries PLC
Cable and Wireless plc
Cadbury Schweppes plc
Coopers & Lybrand
Countrywide Communications Group
  Limited
F.I. GROUP PLC
Guinness PLC
The Harry Crook Foundation
IBM United Kingdom Limited
John Lewis Partnership
Kleinwort Benson Investment
  Management Limited
Manpower PLC
Midlands Electricity plc
The National Grid Company plc
NatWest Group
N M Rothschild & Sons Limited
WH Smith Group plc
THORN EMI plc
Unipart Group of Companies
Whitbread Beer Company

Past sponsors

British Gas plc
The Henley Centre for Forecasting Ltd
Ocean Group plc
Saxton Bampfylde International plc
South Western Electricity plc

Founder Members of The Centre for Tomorrow's Company

AMPI Trust
Anglian Water Plc
Arlington Securities plc
BAA
Birmingham Midshires Building Society
British Telecommunications plc
The Co-operative Bank plc
The Government Purchasing Agency
John Lewis Partnership
Jungheinrich Great Britain Ltd
Marshall of Cambridge Ltd
NatWest Group
Pertemps
Porsche Cars Great Britain Ltd
Scottish Homes
Unipart Group of Companies
United Utilities PLC
Whitbread Beer Company
Willett International Ltd
WPP Group plc

CONTENTS

ix

LIST OF TEXTBOXES, FIGURES AND TABLES

Textboxes

Figures

Tables

FOREWORD

While this is a book about business, it is not exclusively a book for business. Because its mission is, implicitly, to explain why businesses exist, it should be of interest to anyone who benefits from their existence.

Almost everybody is a customer of, supplier to, employee of or owner of a business of some sort. Absolutely everyone is a direct or indirect recipient of those services paid for by taxes levied on the businesses themselves or those employed by them. Without the facility provided by businesses to marshall, reorganise and redirect resources to create new wealth, most benefits enjoyed by our society would still be waiting to happen. This book invites business leaders to recognise these truths and accept the exceptional accountability it puts on them. Fortunately, by taking the broader, more measured view of success, significant mutual benefits accrue to shareholders, managers and all other constituencies without managers needing to feel even slightly martyred. Indeed, their sense of accomplishment can be significantly heightened. This recognition by leaders and managers of businesses of the benefits of management-in-the-round is described in the book by the single word 'inclusiveness'.

The birthplace of *Living Tomorrow's Company* was the Royal Society for the encouragement of Arts, Manufactures and Commerce some five years ago. Known more colloquially as the RSA, its full title conveys a certain degree of inclusiveness. Indeed, in this age of increasing specialisation and vested interest, the RSA prides itself on playing a highly unusual – possibly unique – role in British society by crossing the frontiers of constituencies, disciplines and ideas. The breadth of our programme is large, covering manufactures, commerce, design and technology, education, the arts and the environment. A project that requires knowledge, experience, skills or an outcome that can all be found or satisfied within merely one of these areas is of no interest to the RSA. We have no desire to compete with others better qualified. However, if any two or more constituencies of British endeavour can contribute to, or benefit from, a project then the RSA is ready to be the medium or catalyst for an exchange of ideas and formulation of recommendations for action.

In 1992, a debate had emerged in the UK on the role of business and its effect on British culture. Who should be the real beneficiaries of success? Were the spoils being distributed in an equitable way? Were sources of capital, and their hired help, top management, being disproportionately rewarded? The fact that the debate was felt necessary, of course, was the result of a series of spectacular financial successes – and failures – in the 1980s. Many of the apparent successes were the result of privatisation. Despite the fact that conspicuous and broadly based business success had not been experienced in the UK since Edwardian times, the Great British Public – led nasally and characteristically by the media – felt that values in British society were now uncomfortably out of balance.

A recent Chairman of the RSA Council, Professor Charles Handy, had already stimulated a discussion within the walls of the Society by addressing the question, 'What is a company for?'. Mark Goyder had recently joined the RSA as Programme Director, after 15 years operating experience in British industry. With the support of the RSA Council, he organised a series of dinners at which over 70 business leaders were challenged to give their vision of the company of the future. Twenty-five agreed to participate in the Inquiry and support it with the sponsorship of their companies.

Mark Goyder led the staff team on the Inquiry, working closely with its Chairman, Sir Anthony Cleaver. The Inquiry's findings were published in June 1995, and the final report rapidly became a best seller, continuing to sell over 150 copies a month over two years after publication. As a result of the final report there was now a real momentum. The business community wanted help and support in putting Tomorrow's Company into action. Far-sighted members of the investment community saw the opportunity to develop a new and better range of investment criteria. Within a few months, Mark had resigned from his post at the RSA, and the Centre for Tomorrow's Company had been born, as an independent charity. Allan Willett became its first Chairman and Mark its first Director.

The overriding outcome of the Tomorrow's Company inquiry was an invitation from the RSA to British-based businesses and their leaders to make the journey towards inclusive management practices where customer, suppliers, employees, the community at large, as well as shareholders and other providers of finance can become fellow travellers. In this way each and everyone will have a better chance of enjoying the continuous rewards of tangible and intangible success through achievement of mutually compatible objectives. Also, such sustainable success can only provide Britain with a greater proportion of world-class businesses committed to excellence. The

Centre for Tomorrow's Company, now independent of the RSA, carries the responsibility of leading those who wish to travel along the path to inclusiveness.

As I travel around the globe, I read dozens of business books. *Living Tomorrow's Company* is, in my view, unique. It is exceptionally well written – and its invitation to make the journey to Tomorrow's Company is open to all. If our businesses can be led and managed throughout the world in a fashion that makes us all proud to be beneficiaries of their rewards, then the birth of Tomorrow's Company will indeed prove to have been historic – and the RSA will certainly be proud of any role it might have played in providing the maternity ward and the mid-husband!

Dick Onians
Chairman of Council
Royal Society for the encouragement of Arts, Manufactures and Commerce

PREFACE

This book is about the survival and success of businesses in an age of human abundance and social limits. The territory it deals with is, simultaneously, the easiest and the hardest territory for entrepreneurs, investors, managers, and business leaders as they gear up for an unpredictable future. The case for the inclusive approach, which is the subject of this book, is simply stated – and sometimes because of that easily ignored. It puts people and relationships at the heart of sustainable business success – a view to which nearly all of us pay lip service but few of us apply in practice.

To apply the inclusive approach fully involves a frontal challenge to the unthinking way in which many of today's managers, investors and commentators routinely talk about value, profit, ownership, and their duty to their shareholders. If they read this book they will have a fresh language and a practical starting point for making the journey to Tomorrow's Company.

The RSA Inquiry, Tomorrow's Company, which published its findings in 1995 and the Centre for Tomorrow's Company which it spawned, have always spoken to four particular audiences – business leaders, investors, educators, and public policymakers. This book aims even wider. Many people inside and outside business may regard business as an unstoppable juggernaut on which they can have no influence. They should read what this book has to say about the importance which openness and listening have played in the success of a business. They might even follow the example of entrepreneurs who have felt as unhappy as they have, and started a business of their own to show how it can be done. We all have our own ideas about the business future which we would like to see. We can all do more to shape that future than we might currently realise.

We have all become used to thinking of problems in boxes. What I do with my personal pension is not usually allowed to connect with what I feel about the way decisions are taken in the boardrooms of businesses in which I have a stake. And yet, as Chapter 8 shows, the two are connected.

In the attempt to make practical sense of the role of business in a changing world, the book draws on two main sources. The first is the experience and shared thinking of a group of UK-based business leaders, brought together to form the Tomorrow's Company Inquiry, and followed up by the companies who formed the Centre for Tomorrow's Company in 1996. The second is my own experience and beliefs, formed from experience in business, community work and political life and heavily influenced by the work of my father, George Goyder, who started writing about these issues in the early 1940s. My father had the foresight to warn the then government in the UK in 1949 that nationalisation would not be the way to capturing the hearts and minds of the people working in industry. He was also the first person – in 1961 – to introduce the idea of the social audit. He continued to refine his thinking about the future company up to his last book *The Just Enterprise*. My father was an inspiration to me and to many others. He died just as I was completing this book and I dedicate it to him and to my mother in acknowledgement of their love and example.

This book is not a 'how-to' manual or a guide to business perfection. None of the companies quoted as examples later in this book claim to be an ideal role model in every regard. Like human beings, all companies will be stronger in some areas than others. All will have ups and downs in their financial performance during the lifetime of this book! One of the main conclusions of the Inquiry was that each business has its own journey to make. Each needs to work out for itself its own unique direction and strategy. People who are looking for an immediate practical guide are invited to turn to Chapter 6 and Appendix 1 – or to contact the Centre for Tomorrow's Company!

It is, however, intensely practical. Business people, investors, business educators and policy makers for business cannot hope to make good decisions on their journey unless they have a reliable map to guide their thinking. This book is aimed at providing some sort of map for just such people, whether they be aspiring chief executives, bewildered middle managers, nervous trustees of the company pension fund, or public officials with a brief to improve a region's competitive performance.

It is time we all had a better understanding of the role we play, passively or actively, in shaping the business world. The truth is that all of us can make a difference to the way business will evolve. All of us, too, can contribute to the health of Tomorrow's Company. This book is intended to show how.

Mark Goyder

ACKNOWLEDGEMENTS

I would like to thank Charles Handy, Martin Findlay, Dick Onians, Sir Anthony Cleaver, Christopher Lucas, Sir Adrian Cadbury, Michael Frye, Eva Beazley, Claire Conington, Neil Hartley, Peter Smith, Sir Geoffrey Chandler, Robin Buchanan, Ron Emerson, Crispin Tweddell, Alan Benjamin, George Binney and everyone involved in originating and managing the RSA Tomorrow's Company Inquiry including the whole Inquiry Team, the RSA Council, my RSA staff colleagues, the RSA Fellows and networks, and the thousands of people all over the world whom we consulted.

I would like to thank too, Allan Willett, Nick Obolensky, Kate Young, Bob Andrews, Carlota Bedwell, Hilary Sutcliffe, Alan Barrell, Philip Sadler, Stuart Hampson, Prue Leith (Martin Findlay and Dick Onians again!) together with the patrons, Honorary Members, Founder Members, and many other supporters for their part in the creation of the Centre for Tomorrow's Company, and the contribution to the ideas in the book. Thanks are also due to Veronique Renard and Sarah Beety for their help in preparing the text. I would like to thank also Dan Edington, Paul Myners, John Neill, Mike Jackson, Keith Orrell-Jones, Peter Mutter, Philip Goldenberg, Bill Eyres, David Grayson, and many more who helped with reading the text and assisting with case study research material.

I would like to thank Sarah Curtis for encouraging me to write the book, Kate Young for suggesting the title, and the RSA and CTC for giving me some time to write it.

At crucial stages of my thinking I have been refreshed by the opportunity to share ideas with the 'Tomorrow's Corporation' seminar at the Aspen Institute in Colorado, for which I am indebted to Michael Higgins and James O'Toole, and at the Cranlana Institute in Melbourne, for which my thanks are due to Peter Sheldrake. Andrew Thompson persuaded me to visit and study the Silicon Valley phenomenon, and I thank him, the people I visited, including Professor Jerry Porras, and Sir Colin Marshall of British Airways for that opportunity.

My wife Conca has the credit for patience, endless proofreading, timely encouragement and keeping my feet on the ground. She indeed has been 'Living Tomorrow's Company'.

Above all, as I look back over the past five years I would like to celebrate the unstoppable energy and conviction of an unnamed number of people who are in their own ways all determinedly making Tomorrow's Company live.

Mark Goyder
Hawkhurst, Kent
May 1997

1 JANE MILL'S VIEW FROM THE FUTURE

ON ACCOUNTABILITY

> *To prevent the weaker members of the community being preyed upon by innu-merable vultures, it was needful that there should be an animal of prey stronger than the rest commissioned to keep them down. But as the king of the vultures would be no less bent on preying on his flock than any of the minor harpies, it was indispensable to be in a perpetual attitude of defence against his beak and claws. The aim, therefore, of patriots was to set limits to the power which the rulers should be suffered to exercise over the community; and this limitation was what they meant by liberty.* John Stuart Mill[1]

The year is 2059. It is exactly two hundred years ago that John Stuart Mill wrote his famous book *On Liberty*. That book told how and why society put an end to the unaccountable power of its rulers. The process took centuries. First, there were immunities to protect subjects. Next, rulers were required to obtain the consent of a parliament before taking action. Eventually people saw that the only way to have control over rulers was for the community to choose them, hold them accountable and remove them if necessary.

A descendant of Harriet and John Stuart Mill is writing on 'Accountability'. Jane Mill charts the changes in the relationship between government, people and business:

> There was a time when people yielded unqualified freedom to those who ran businesses.
>
> Then, because of excesses in their behaviour towards society and the people who worked for them, (national) governments introduced controls. These covered pollution, hygiene, health and safety, and working hours. In the twentieth century some governments turned to nationalisation as the way to make indus-try more accountable to society. But the European experience of nationalisation after the Second World War proved them wrong. Large corporations run by state appointees under the guidance of politicians proved less efficient and even less accountable than large corporations run by shareholder appointees. Meanwhile the list of society's restrictions on business grew, with the encouragement of trade unions, until they provoked an inevitable backlash. Governments moved to curb the power of unions, and to ease the total burden of regulation, red tape and restrictive practice.

At the same time as national governments introduced these regulations, businesses became international. Companies like BP, General Motors, and Microsoft had turnovers in excess of all except the largest governments, and enjoyed a greater power over investment, education, and infrastructure. They were challenged by non-governmental organisations to justify the impact of their commercial activities, whether this involved persuading breastfeeding mothers to buy baby milk, or co-operating with oppressive governments to demolish ecology and communities in order to generate hydro-electric power. A small number of activists could buy shares in a bank or an oil company, and cause public embarrassment at its Annual General Meeting. The public attitude to business had become cynical: even long-established businesses with strong ethical histories were assumed to be interested only in profit and not in human beings. At a time when many businesses were being sold back to private shareholders, this cynicism was reinforced by a fashion for enhanced pay and pension packages for a few very senior executives.

But, in the midst of all the many regulations and immunities, until the late twentieth century most business people used to accept that the rights of ownership gave businesses only one accountability – to their shareholders and no-one else. These enormous baronies were still seen by insiders as accountable only to those who 'owned' them, whether the owners turned out to be private individuals or a collection of investment institutions.

Many people around business recognised that, as with the primitive rulers of states, there was no logic for the absolute power of shareholders. The entrepreneur, starting a business with his or her own money, was taking nearly all the risk and was entitled to nearly all the control. The big institutional investor owning 2 per cent of a big corporation might have difficulty selling its stake, but could not be said to be taking as large a risk.

In J. S. Mill's account of the development of political accountability, the change came as a result of bitter conflict over centuries. In the corporate world the change is already happening in the 1990s, and it is hastened by a form of natural selection. Businesses which fail to adapt to changing public expectations damage their reputation, jeopardise the value of their brands, lose customer and employee loyalty and destroy public confidence – with serious consequences for their share price.

As is shown in Chapter 4 the pressure on companies grows stronger with the changing attitudes of each succeeding generation to pollution, health, equality of opportunity and diversity in the workplace, and with the accelerating speed with which unfavourable publicity can ricochet around the world. It becomes harder to sustain a compartmentalised view of the world. Global warming, carbon emissions, the hole in the ozone layer are everyone's problem: the largest businesses were among the first to recognise that if they failed to take steps to measure and control their environmental impact, they could be destroying their own ability to trade in future. By 2020, social issues will have taken on the same importance, and tomorrow's shareholders will expect businesses to take steps to invest in the health of the communities in which they operate as a simple matter of risk management.

All over the world competent leaders of business now recognise that unless they are seen by the community to be meeting the needs of that community, in future as well as present generations, at the same time as they make a return for their shareholders, they risk both additional regulation and a loss of reputation which would affect those profits. They now face the classic difficulty which has always confronted those who attempt to lead people through unfamiliarity to necessary change: there is no ready-made language to describe the task. Some of the words used to argue for change merely serve to confirm their denial of the future.

Most contributors to the debate so far have attempted to use the rather crude language of 'stakeholder theory' – a slogan which is understandably rejected by many managers and investors. To trade shareholder accountability for 'stakeholding' is, in their view, to sacrifice clarity for blancmange. It appears to replace the narrow, but clear, accountability of business to its shareholders with an accountability to everyone – an accountability so broad as to be valueless.

There is a particular irony in the timing of the popularity of the word 'stakeholder'. It had its origins with the frontiersmen of the USA. It referred to the territorial claim that settlers would stake. It reflects an age in which a new, more settled order was gradually being imposed after a turmoil of conflict and change. Yet it is becoming fashionable in countries like the UK just when the opposite is happening! Settled assumptions about organisations and people's relationships with them are being torn up. Soon, less than half of the people of working age will have a full-time job, and the chances of that full-time job being permanent have been reduced for everyone, even for public servants. A new generation is coming to adulthood which must expect to have to create its own employment opportunities. Already half of them say they would prefer to be self-employed. Many more mature people have had to come to terms with a life which combines one or more part-time jobs with unpaid activity. Employment uncertainty is all around us. Those who lack the necessary mixture of new skills, adaptability and mobility face long-term unemployment. A new proverb will become the cliché of the 2020s: 'Security is only achieved by those who welcome insecurity'.

All this need not be a threat to a person who continually adds new skills to his or her repertoire. Every individual has to choose whether to treat that reality as threat or opportunity, and every society has to extend its hand to those who end up as victims of that volatility. But one thing is certain: this is not a world of settled boundaries and there is little territory to which any of us can claim a stake. 'Stakeholder theory' is less pervasive than it deserves to be because it is an attempt to use yesterday's language to describe the world of tomorrow. We need a new language of business.

As businesses come and go, the best and most enduring of them will recognise that categories like 'customer', 'employee' and 'investor' are no more than masks which described particular human needs. They are useful masks, but there is a danger in taking them too far, since people ultimately do not live their lives in compartments marked 'customer', 'citizen', 'investor', 'employee'. What matters is reputation, character and trust. People make an all-round judgement of a company, which then informs their behaviour towards it. They do not separate out what they know about it as a customer from what they know as a shareholder. If the business is to prosper and grow in this world of overlapping relationships, it will need an inclusive view (which is introduced in Chapter 2 and described in Chapter 6). It will need to be sensitive to all the relationships that can make or break its future. Like any mature person, the business will need to understand the total effect it has on others, and be sensitive to their expectations.

We can now return to Jane Mill, and her description of the changing accountability of business.

> This left a problem with the traditional doctrine of shareholder supremacy, which was now looking as dated as the old doctrine of the divine right of kings. There was accountability to shareholders, of course, for the long-term generation of shareholder value. But the doctrine that this was the only kind of accountability, or that this accountability by itself gave the business its reason for being, began to fade as people, relationships, reputation and knowledge became the critical assets of the business.

> What was the logic of telling co-workers that the company owed them no accountability when without them, the company could deliver little value to the shareholders? What was the logic of behaving as though the business was only accountable to shareholders, when chief executives were finding that they had to spend a part of every week explaining and justifying the company's environmental, employment and safety policies to communities of all kinds?

In Tomorrow's Company far-sighted business leaders will stand the problem on its head. They will stop thinking about accountability as a restriction of their freedom. They will start to see it as an enhancer of their freedom. They will acknowledge that no business can survive unless it continually passes the market test of identifying and meeting some human need. They will realise from the force of the evidence quoted (described in Chapter 3) that the businesses which survive and prosper longest will be those that meet such needs most competitively, while at the same time behaving in a way that wins the widest trust in their activities. Accountability in a wider sense will be seen as the necessary accompaniment to efficiency.

Tomorrow's business leaders will have learned to think *both/and* instead of *either/or*. For example they will stop thinking of 'community' as a cost, and start thinking of it as the one relationship in which all the different human expectations of a business come together.

They will also stop thinking about shareholder value as something which they only discuss with their shareholders. They will begin to impress on all their partners the crucial importance of generating shareholder value, and the crucial part they have had to play in creating it. But at the same time they will impress on all their partners, including their shareholders, the point that value for shareholders can only be sustained if people can see how the business is adding value for the community as well. After all, if a business has got the community right, it is unlikely to have got its employees, its customers, its suppliers or its investors wholly wrong. By the early 2020s businesses will be regarding it as unthinkable to report on shareholder value without also reporting on the social value they have created.

With this thinking in place, the language will slowly catch up with the reality. For example, in fifty years time, the term 'employee' will seem as obsolete as the term 'domestic servant' seems to us! It will eventually become less fashionable to say that business is solely about making money. Already younger businesses are beginning to talk more about creating value for customers, co-workers, associates, business partners, communities and shareholders throughout the world. This will help younger people making their career choices: the time will come when they no longer feel that by going into business they are 'selling out' their principles. In spite of their international outlook businesses will become strongly identified as a part of the society or societies in which they operate. They will naturally put down roots in communities at the same time as they educate those communities about the perils and discontinuities of competitive business. The most successful and enduring companies will instinctively talk about success in two parts – the creation of shareholder value and the creation of social value, freed from the late twentieth-century assumption that a business has to choose between the two.

Those who are slow to abandon the old habits of thinking will find that this inclusive approach, far from undermining returns to investors, turns out to be crucial to survival in an increasingly turbulent world.

TOMORROW'S FEATHER DUSTER

Of course, many businesses will not survive at all. It will not be enough to design brilliant new forms of home entertainment, revolutionary applications in artificial intelligence or superb nutritional advances in microbiology. Great empires now grow, flourish and are toppled within a single decade, overtaken by the next wave of technology and market change. One American businessman put it to me with characteristic brutality: 'Today's peacock is tomorrow's feather duster'.

Across the world millions of new businesses are born every year, and of the half of them which survive beyond two years, many are content, without further expansion or ambition, to provide useful work in selling the experience of one or two individuals.

As will be shown in Chapter 5 the businesses which will go on growing, to endure and generate great wealth all around them will be those which combine two qualities. They will have all the traditional characteristics – financial rigour, focus on shareholder value and disciplined measurement, but they will also be adaptable to their very fingertips. They will be exceptionally well connected – not in that nineteenth century social sense – but in touch with the change that is all around them. They will be sensitive to the needs of their present and future clients and business partners, and with present and future marketplaces around the world. They will be sensitive to the aspirations of their present and future business partners, co-workers and associates. They will combine a deep understanding of the particular market niche they currently occupy, with a sophisticated awareness of the wider world and its ability to catch them by surprise. To remain this flexible and this aware, they will become highly effective at building lasting relationships, and brilliant at giving people choices. Some of the best business success stories will be companies which succeed in turning a purely transactional business into a relationship business.

THE PARADOX OF PERMANENCE

Success for such businesses, as for individuals, will be summed up in the paradox of permanence. While they can only survive through constant adaptation, they will also recognise that they need something solid and unchanging. They will have values and personality that endure. They will even have a 'hard core' of people who stay with them, but these people will only have achieved this permanence through constant adaptation.

Alongside adaptability, trust will be a key to permanence. Companies will have earned their lasting place in a dizzy, complex and critical world because, somewhere deep down, people feel they have integrity. Products will be changing far too quickly for businesses to be differentiated on the quality of their products alone. Businesses will stand out from the pack because, in all the relationships which are crucial to their success, people know what they stand for and can identify with them. It will also be those businesses which have this integrity which find that they are most successful at crossing cultural boundaries – an important ingredient to twenty-first century success.

A culture of challenge will help businesses win and keep trust. No self-respecting business will pretend that it is perfect. Their leaders will expect to be questioned on any discrepancy between word and deed. Like twentieth-century politicians, twenty-first century business leaders will become used to being stopped in the car park or street, and held accountable by employees, customers and citizens. Those who want to remain credible and trustworthy will not hide behind opaque windows and carefully prepared statements. The next generation of business leaders will grow up in this atmosphere of challenge, and thrive on dialogue.

At the same time, as competition becomes more intense, the assumptions of people in and around business are changing. They will no longer expect to spend their whole lives inside large padded corporations. A majority of those who work in business will expect in due course to move on from a life dominated by organisations to an extended third age in which they strike a different balance. The task for leaders will be to engage the interests of this more footloose generation – by being simple, direct, entrepreneurial, trustworthy and even entertaining!

GLOBAL CLOGS TO CLOGS

There is another factor which will hasten these changes of attitude. It is a global version of the 'clogs to clogs in three generations' syndrome, as described below by Jane Mill in 2059.

> As economies became economically more successful, they also became more comfortable. They spent more and saved less. The children of the entrepreneurs went to university and qualified for the law and other professions. In time the tigers who had terrified the West took on some of the fat-cat features of the mature economies which they had overtaken. They became comfortable and overweight. New tigers overtook them. A few regions in a few countries broke the trend and managed to sustain their economic improvement over more than two decades. These were countries where wealth creation was driven by something more lasting than the simple motivation of getting rich and then getting out. It was affirmed, and accepted by the culture around it, as a valid contribution to society, and so, quite naturally, succeeding generations sustained the momentum. Global competition itself had become the ultimate accountability, selecting for long-term success those societies and those businesses which had a sustainable ethic of wealth creation imprinted in their genes.

If the economies and businesses we care about are to equip themselves for survival and success, it will be important that the time-honoured practices of investment, corporate governance and accountancy change to reflect the diversity of measurements demanded by both the shareholders and the stakeholders of a successful company (these areas are the subject of Chapters 7 and 8). It will become a priority for any chief executive to demonstrate to investors the robustness of the company's ethics, the dynamism of its programme of innovation, and the speed with which its people could learn and adapt to new circumstances. We can expect eventually to see a common language grow up to describe this – still irritatingly full of jargon and acronyms but less obscure than the incomprehensible 'management speak' of the late twentieth century.

Business schools can be expected to teach in a different way, taking on a structure that looks more like that of the workers' educational associations which flourished in preceding centuries. In twenty years' time the portentous MBA (Master in Business Administration) will have begun to fade in the more advanced economies. It will be gradually replaced by more flexible and international ways of learning the skills of leading an organisation. People will plan their own programmes, choosing the modules which suit them with the help of a long-term tutor, who would typically be a former chief executive. In Europe it will become a normal qualification for a top job that the person concerned had spent a total of at least two years working outside their own industry, often in the investment world, in education or in what is left of the Civil Service. Today, top jobs in business usually go to the person with the deepest experience of that industry. By 2020 the usual practice may well be to make appointments in pairs or even threes, to achieve a deliberate balance between inside, specialist knowledge, and a wider understanding of the changing world, and to free people to move between their paid work and their continual broadening and development.

Governments – meanwhile – will have to change their idea of what it means to be accountable, and what it means to be successful. They will recognise that they must become much more sophisticated in the choices which they offer to their citizens. In all sorts of ways – some of them more appropriate than others – government has been turning to businesses to deliver sensitive solutions in areas where blanket policy was no longer appropriate. There is an irony here. Business is in the process of learning that success will not be achieved by keeping eyes only on their shareholders. Governments are beginning to suspect that to achieve any impact with limited resources and infinite expectations, they will need more sensitivity and feedback than is provided by the ballot box. The rigid twentieth-century government machine measured success in terms of money spent or saved, and operated through narrowly focused departments. And it was based on the assumption that accountability began and ended with the ballot box. These departments traditionally had their eyes on annual budgets and their ears filled with the clamour of the industries they sponsored and the traditional lobby groups that surrounded them. Often, different departments had contradictory objectives, and the task of government came to be viewed as reconciling these. We may expect to see great departments of state decimated as ruthlessly as have been the great corporate headquarters before them. Power will be spread out to regions, districts and parishes, and to an array of new delivery agencies and social entrepreneurs. Accountability and regulation will be provided through a sophisticated measurement and auditing framework which is concerned as much with values and quality of life as with value added and quantity of output or spending. In the next thirty years the inclusive approach which this book describes will have as much relevance to government as to business.

There will be daunting risks that threaten the survival of the most apparently successful businesses and economies and some of these are described in Chapter 9. There will be the risks that come from the sense of social exclusion, and risks that come from the damage done to the more fragile parts of the ecosystem. This will reinforce the importance of the social audit. Businesses and government know that in future they will be measured on many dimensions. An international company will be challenged in Paris on the integrity of its actions in Thailand. It will see externally verified reports on its social and environmental impact. Life will be simpler for those businesses which take the initiative and commission their own social audit.

Businesses which are to survive and succeed in this age of limits will have first to rid themselves of the prejudices and blockages that distort our thinking about success. That is what the next chapter is about.

2   A ROMANCE AND AN ADVENTURE

Economic man offers a misleading caricature of human nature because he only evaluates means and does not consider the legitimacy of ends . . . In practice, individuals have sufficient imagination and empathy to consider the consequences of their actions for others, and to compensate for these by purely internal rewards and punishments . . . Mark Casson [1]

How selfish soever man may be supposed, there are inevitably some principles in his nature which interest him in the fortune of others, and render their happiness necessary to him, though he derives nothing from it except the pleasure of seeing it. John Stuart Mill [2]

ENLIGHTENED SELF-INTEREST

It is over one hundred years since the Cambridge physicist J. J. Thomson discovered the existence of the electron. In the course of that one hundred years our lives have been transformed. Before Thomson's discovery 'everyone knew' that matter could only be reduced to atoms: beyond atoms, matter was thought to be indivisible. Thomson opened the door to the world of electronics: a new order whose potential we are still fully to understand (as we shall see in Chapter 4).

There is an open door to business opportunity through which many of the cleverest people in business never walk. We don't have to wait for a great scientific discovery to break down successful business behaviour into its constituent parts. We already know all we need to know to rediscover the connection between business success and human motivation in all its varieties. The only thing that stands in our way is the shadow thrown by *homo economicus.*

HOMO ECONOMICUS – HIS PART IN OUR DOWNFALL

Homo economicus is profit-maximising economic man. He was invented by economists to help them understand how the market works, and to develop and then test some economic principles which would help them to predict what happens in the economic world.

To make any kind of generalisation in the economic laboratory, you have to simplify and concentrate on those parts of economic behaviour that are predictable. But some investors and some managers have allowed our friend *homo economicus* to escape from the laboratory. Instead of being a thin cartoon character, they have seen him as a model for real life. And, just as when children try to act like TV heroes, the real life results are messy and misconceptions arise.

TWO MISCONCEPTIONS

The problem arises from two particular misconceptions: one has an effect on the way business people see society; the other has an effect on the way business people describe their purpose.

The invisible hand

Adam Smith is often referred to as the high priest of capitalist individualism. He describes the 'invisible hand' of the market, through which thousands of individuals pursuing their self-interest are able at the same time to contribute to the public good through the efficient operation of the market. But it should be remembered that Adam Smith pictured an economy which worked through everyone pursuing their self-interest inside (and subordinate to) a society in which people helped each other. In other words the self-interest he had in mind was 'enlightened self-interest'. 'All members of society stand in need of each other's assistance . . . where the necessary assistance is reciprocally afforded . . . the society flourishes and is happy.' This is true of individuals, of households and of regions and nations and even trading blocks. We may live in a competitive world, but at the same time we depend on each other. That's where the word 'enlightened' comes in.

Enlightened self-interest means taking some responsibility for the consequences of your own actions. While you pursue your own interests and do so aggressively, you never forget what effect your behaviour is having upon other people. It means that even while you are behaving as 'economic man' you remember that you and the people you are dealing with are more than just economic man. As a citizen, you recognise some standards which you believe everyone needs to follow if there is to be a healthy climate for people like yourself to do business.

Business, in this view, cannot opt out of its responsibilities as a citizen. It cannot sub-contract to some 'invisible hand' or to legislation and government, the responsibility for ensuring that the consequences of its market-driven actions are acceptable.

Greed is good

Enlightened self-interest is a long way from the thinking of Milton Friedman, who asserted in the 1960s that the only responsibility of business was to serve its shareholders. It is further still from the 1980s' neo-capitalists caricatured in the film *Wall Street* whose villain, Gordon Gekko, declares that 'Greed is good.'

Greed and selfishness are real and we see examples of them every day. But we also see examples of principled behaviour, of generosity, trust and partnership. There is human variety, conditioned by how people are, how they have been brought up, and what their priorities are and what experiences they have had. In the economics of real life people do not follow the crudest stereotypes of profit maximisation. They sense a value in codes of behaviour that restrain them from fully indulging their immediate self-interest. They often learn to trust each other. They frequently take a pride in going well beyond what the contract requires.

There is a widespread prejudice that businesses are only in existence to make a profit for their owners and that any deviation from this purpose is unnatural and a distortion of the market. Like the misunderstanding about 'the invisible hand' this prejudice started with the escape from the laboratory of some understandable but necessarily limiting assumptions that economists have made about economic behaviour. There is nothing wrong with constructing economic models on the assumption that everyone has the same profit-maximising ambitions. Some caricatures are very helpful in the construction of theoretical models of behaviour. The danger lies in taking what is simply a set of assumptions and elevating them into a set of natural laws which all business people are expected to obey. 'Let us assume this is how everyone behaves,' has in some minds become 'This is how everyone behaves all the time.'

In marketing, companies do not limit their appeal to the economic part of their customer's make-up. Look at their consumer advertising: it is designed to appeal to a whole range of emotions – the desire to be secure, to be popular, to be a better parent or provider. When businesses sell their products and services to customers they are uninhibited in identifying them with the whole range of human emotions. Yet, when chief executives and their close colleagues are invited to talk about their businesses, they often seem to regard it as a sign of weakness to talk about what they do in any but the narrowest of economic terms. Business is about making money, some say. Some even think that they are being true to their capitalist ancestors when they declare that 'people are only motivated by two things – fear and greed'. They would be surprised to hear that great capitalist Henry Ford say: 'Business must be run at a profit, else it will die. But when anyone tries to run business solely for profit, then also the business will die for it no longer has a reason for existence.'

There is nothing wrong with investors judging their investment in exclusively financial terms. That – with some qualifications to which we will return in Chapter 8 – is what they have invested their money for. No, the problems arise when half-truths are claimed as whole truths, and exclusive statements of purpose replace inclusive ones. 'We are here to create value for our shareholders,' quickly becomes corrupted into 'We are here *only* to create value for our shareholders.' Exclusive messages are bound to end up as dishonest messages, because the company itself has to contradict them, and the audiences overlap. The same people are often customers, and employees and shareholders. A bank or supermarket chain which declares undivided and exclusive devotion to shareholders may confuse customers who are simultaneously being told how much the company cares for them! In spite of this there are many chief executives who still fear that if they express their commitment to shareholders in anything but exclusive terms, they will be judged to be taking their eyes off the task of making a return for the shareholder, and will risk undermining investor confidence.

WHY PEOPLE START BUSINESSES

This exclusive preoccupation with the shareholder is anything but entrepreneurial. People set up businesses for all sorts of reasons: an engineer may be looking for a way of making a new pump he has invented; an impresario may simply be looking to bring new acts onto the stage; a financial services expert may be attracted by the sheer elegance of a new investment vehicle he has designed. Some individuals start businesses to get rich. But very few people start businesses in order to make money for people whom they do not know!

Marriott Corporation was founded by J. Willard Marriott, Senior. He was once asked if he had founded the company to make a million or to build an empire. He responded:

> No, not at all. I just had three general ideas in mind, all equally important. One was to render a friendly service to our guests. The second was to provide quality food at a fair price. The third was to work as hard as I could, day, and night, to make a profit . . . I wanted to grasp the rewards of growth: jobs for more employees, money to take care of my family and to contribute to good causes . . . The service business is very rewarding. It makes a big contribution to society. A good meal away from home, a good bed, friendly treatment . . . It's important to make people away from home feel that they're among friends and are really wanted.[3]

Marriott created a company that stood the test of decades. We shall see in Chapter 3 that theories about 'profit-maximising economic man' are not much help in explaining the most enduring stock market successes of the twentieth century.

But *homo economicus* still casts his shadow over our thoughts and, with a few honourable exceptions, is reinforced in many of the most distinguished institutions of business education. In his account of a year at Stanford Business School, Peter Robinson describes how he and his fellow business students are put through course after course of spreadsheets, formulae and quantitative analysis.[4] Halfway through the year, he finally comes across a teacher called Font 'whose understanding of business rose above the technical disciplines to acknowledge the existence of human soul'. Font's classes were poorly attended. He based his teachings on those of the economist Joseph Schumpeter. In Robinson's description, we learn more of this.

'As you know from your courses here at the business school' Font said, 'most economic models are static.' The typical model saw human activity as mechanical and repetitive, always settling at an equilibrium between expenditures and receipts. 'The problem', Font said, 'is that this bears almost no resemblance to reality.'

By contrast, in Schumpeter's view the important events in any economy were sudden and discontinuous, innovations that overturned the settled patterns rather than reconfirming them.

'Here in Silicon Valley', Font said, 'you can't drive to the grocery store without seeing two or three high-tech start-ups that weren't there the week before. Is that static equilibrium? Not a chance. It's Schumpeter's process of dynamic change.'

Behind the sudden, disruptive innovations stood the entrepreneurs who introduced them. According to the usual models, entrepreneurs only wanted to maximise their profits. 'But according to Schumpeter', Font said, 'the puny motive of profit maximisation barely explains anything at all. Just listen to Schumpeter in this passage . . .

'There is the will to conquer, the impulse to fight, to prove oneself superior to others, to succeed for the sake not of the fruits of success, but of success itself. Finally there is the joy of creating, of getting things done, or simply exercising one's energy and ingenuity.'

Font set the book down and looked at us. 'Capitalism', he said, bringing the class to a close, 'is not in my view a matter of counting coins. Capitalism is a romance and an adventure.'[5]

Whether new or established, large or small, the best companies capture something of that romance and adventure: they inspire people by transcending the prosaic content of everyday operations. But to do that takes empathy, imagination and leadership – three qualities not given enough attention in the teaching of business, let alone economics.

THE QUALITIES OF THE ENTREPRENEUR

Without a commercial instinct and an eye for profits, few business entrepreneurs would last long. But there are three other qualities which are at least as important in explaining the success of the entrepreneur, and we hear much less of these from the conventional economist's view of motivation. The first is empathy – the ability to put yourself in someone else's shoes. This is crucial in understanding what customers are not being offered today, but might be offered tomorrow. Like Virgin Atlantic Airlines, many a new business idea comes from a frustrated customer who cannot find the service he or she is looking for, and decides to introduce it. The second is imagination – the ability to invent in your mind solutions which others had not envisaged

Textbox 2.1 Leadership – a summary

1. Leadership makes a difference. Leadership does make a difference to the performance of individuals, groups and organisations. It does so at the individual level by creating commitment. Leadership also improves the performance of groups and organisations by team building, and by generating pride in collective achievements.

2. Leadership is a three-way process. Leadership can be defined as a process of influence which brings about changes in people's attitudes and/or behaviour as a consequence of interaction between leaders and followers in a given context. For the influence to succeed connections must exist between the needs, expectations and values of the followers, the words and actions of the leaders and the particular circumstances of the situation in which leadership is being exercised.

3. Leadership effectiveness exists at two levels. Effective leadership can be defined at two levels. The first level is when leadership is deemed to have been effective once the attitudes and/or behaviour of followers have been significantly influenced. The second level is when, as a consequence of that influence, the group is enabled to achieve goals which otherwise would not have been capable of achievement.

4. Leadership and management are distinct. Managers are concerned with formal logical processes such as planning and controlling. They have to allocate financial and material resources as well as manage people. Leaders are concerned exclusively with people. Management development and leadership development are not the same and it is important to understand the difference.

5. Leadership is widely distributed. The study of leadership has been distorted by over-concentration on truly great world class leaders. The thousands of 'working leaders' provide a better source of lessons for those who wish to be more effective as leaders in their everyday work situations.

6. Leadership is not just about change. Leadership is also involved just as often in maintaining traditional values in the face of challenges from those who wish to bring change about or in enabling groups of people to endure hardships.

7. Personal qualities do matter. When deciding whether or not to accept the ideas or suggested courses of action made by others we are, of course, influenced by the judgements we make about them. Are they honest, reliable, pleasant to deal with, courageous, intelligent or wise? There is such a thing as charisma, difficult as it is to define. It is as powerful as it is exceptional and most 'working leaders' manage very well without it.

8. Behaviour matters more. There is strong evidence to suggest that it is more important to behave consistently and predictably than it is to adopt any particular style. Leader behaviours which are generally cited as contributing to effectiveness include:
• developing and articulating a vision;
• listening;
• empowering;
• role modelling;
• problem solving;

Textbox 2.1   Leadership – a summary (continued)

- walking the job;
- demonstrating confidence;
- representing and protecting the group.

9. The situation is all-important. The effectiveness of leaders and of styles or patterns of leadership is contingent on the situation and in particular on:

- national culture;
- whether it is face-to-face leadership or 'institutional' leadership;
- whether or not a sense of crisis exists at the time;
- how experienced and competent the followers are.

10. Learning to lead requires three essential ingredients. These are:

- opportunities to practise leadership by being given early experience of real responsibility and challenge;
- a high degree of self-awareness achieved through a good quality mentoring and feedback;
- opportunities, under guidance, to reflect on values and to develop a well-integrated set of values to serve as a template for use when making difficult decisions or choices. This issue of values is a neglected feature of most leadership development programmes in business and industry.

12. Tomorrow's leaders will need to be different. Changing social values will increasingly render the traditional 'hero' figure obsolete. The leaders of tomorrow will need to be less assertive, less dominant, less surrounded with the trappings of power. They will be more feminine, less masculine in approach. They will act as stewards of the organisation's future, showing concern for all the stakeholders, seeing leadership as service rather than as controlling. They will accept the need to continue learning and to achieve 'personal mastery'. Above all they will master the art of asking the pertinent questions rather than trying to supply the answers.

Source: *Leadership* by Philip Sadler (Kogan Page 1997)

– for example, the people who imagined a user-friendly bank without branches and invented First Direct. The third is leadership – defined by John Gardner as

> . . . the process of persuasion or example by which an individual or leadership induces a group to pursue objectives held by the leader or shared by the leader and his or her followers.[6]

Without leadership the entrepreneur cannot create and continually develop organisations which deliver a new product or service. Without leadership the entrepreneur cannot hope to inspire colleagues to unprecedented levels of achievement in delivering solutions to the customer.

Bonus schemes and financial rewards can reinforce people's commitment, but leaders are able to improve the performance of a team or organisation or community by reaching deeper than their economic selves. Leaders point out to people what they have in common, appealing to that part of their make-up that wants to belong and contribute, and help a group to realise together a potential that they would never achieve as competing individuals.

William Blake spoke the language of a leader when he said 'I must create a system or be enslaved by another man's.' Leaders are never content with the formulae they inherit. They look behind the economic mask to the people with whom their organisations have relationships. While others are faithfully following the logic of today's marketplace, leaders introduce a new logic that shapes tomorrow's.

Business school is supposed to train business leaders. Too often in the past our business educators have stopped short of describing what lies behind the economic mask. Read Peter Robinson's experience of Operations, as taught in one of the world's best business schools. He has described how he struggled through units of finance and data analysis, all of them taking human behaviour as unvarying and profit maximising. Now he is doing the final examination on Operations:

> All term Operations had struck me as a particularly frustrating course. It was always posing big, important questions, only to reduce them to bitty word problems. Look at this one question from the essay part of the final. 'It is generally felt that piece rate compensation for factory workers . . . is inconsistent with the Toyota production system. Why?'

> After cramming the night before I knew the answer. Toyota used a quality control system known as TQC or Total Quality Control, devised by the American, W. Edwards Deming, but put into effect first and most widely admired in Japan . . . TQC gave workers the freedom to halt an entire production line whenever they discovered a defect. But if the Toyota workers were paid by the piece they would be reluctant to halt the line since doing so would cut into their pay.

> But *why* did the Deming quality control ideas take deeper root in Japan than in the United States? Why were the Japanese so much better at making things than we were? Operations never even attempted to answer these questions.[7]

THE NEED BEHIND EVERY RELATIONSHIP

Behind every business relationship lurks, somewhere, a human need which that business is striving to meet. Businesses only last if they are good at meeting human need – not merely in the customer relationship, but in all the other relationships as well.

As you push your trolley around Marks & Spencer on a Friday evening you are a customer. The people in front of you in the queue for the till are customers. But they are also employees – the chances are that some of them work for a company which supplies the store. They are also investors or – as some would have it – 'owners'. Several will be members of a pension fund, perhaps one whose fund managers have selected this retailer's shares, or perhaps hold a 'tracker fund', a balanced portfolio of all the FTSE 100 com-

Textbox 2.2 Five ways conventional economics gets humans wrong

The frustration Robinson feels with Operations is the frustration many – including some economists like Mark Casson – feel with economics. Casson has pointed out at least five ways in which conventional economics gets human beings wrong.

1. People do not have stable preferences which the economist must take as given: with different leadership, they can respond in different ways.

2. Utility – the economist's word for what people value when they are making economic decisions – has an emotional as well as a material part to it, and the emotional part can be influenced by leaders.

3. Information is much more limited than the economists admit: consumers don't know everything there is to know about how a product will perform, for example, so in making a buying decision they rely heavily on generalisations like the reputation of the company. A company can lose more through the publicised dishonesty of a few employees than it may have gained through the technical quality of its product.

4. People can't spend their whole lives comparing products and changing accordingly. There are moments of choice but many times when you are stuck with your choice.

5. Everyday life is not a series of 'market trades' enforceable by contract. People work together in teams, meet by chance in pubs, and of course behave differently towards people they already know through other contact.

panies including this one. Most of those in the queue will have life insurance policies, and some of the policies will have retailing among their investments. Some of the shoppers, too, will be parents, some even governors, of the schools from which Marks & Spencer draws its employees and with which it participates in education business partnerships and initiatives designed to prepare pupils for working life. Practically everyone in that queue is either a taxpayer or a recipient of benefits from the same local authority or national government upon which the company depends for regulation and to which the company contributes taxation. Even if they have not all helped to pay for the road along which the store's delivery lorries thunder, most will have sat in cars or buses waiting while the lorries perform that difficult reversing manoeuvre outside the store. All of them are citizens.

No human being is merely a customer, or just an investor, or citizen or supplier. We shift constantly between all these roles, and prefer to be treated as whole human beings rather than as mere inputs, outputs or units of production. Marks & Spencer has some 15 million customers and over 40,000 employee shareholders. At the annual general meeting – which is supposed to be for their shareholders – the company addresses shareholders who may also be customers, suppliers, neighbours, or regulators. It is impossible to disentangle the links. And why should they want to?.

18

Businesses have to deal with human beings, and not simply with their relevant economic compartments. Of course, customers need to be satisfied or delighted first as customers. But part of their customer response is their response as ordinary human beings.

While people acting as investors expect to be treated as investors, and offered a competitive return on their investment, it would be natural for them to have some interest as human beings in knowing how that economic return was earned, and at whose expense. This does not mean that Marks & Spencer should ever forget the reason why you are in that queue on a Friday evening. It is just that, however much you may have been brought there by the textbook reasons of price, value, quality, variety and convenience, you are still, even on a Friday evening in a long queue, human enough to smile and feel better when the checkout operator looks you in the eye, and is kind to your troublesome six-year-old who ought to be in bed by now.

THE MIXTURE OF MOTIVES THAT MAKES A BUSINESS TICK

'I could think of easier ways of earning a living', say some frustrated entrepreneurs. A business which only deals with people as rational economic actors, and fails to deal with them as human beings, will rarely be sustainable. For capitalism to work well, it has to include the diversity of motivations in the combination that are right for the business in question. Profit maximisation is a necessary element – but it is rarely, if ever, sufficient.

Why is the checkout operator taking the trouble to treat you as a human being? Perhaps because it is in his or her nature. Perhaps it breaks the monotony. Perhaps the training has emphasised this and there is pride in a job well done. Perhaps the company surveys customer attitudes and pays a bonus accordingly. A little of all of these, probably. But even if they are one of those 40,000 employee shareholders they're not doing it to create more owner value, although the desire to treat customers well may be reinforced by the knowledge that the success of the business will be reflected in the value of those shares. Equally, if the store is Waitrose – a part of the UK-based John Lewis Partnership – it may reinforce the checkout operator's friendliness to customers to know that he or she is one of the partners among whom all profits after re-investment will be shared.

It is striking how different capitalism begins to sound as soon as human beings are introduced as the ultimate beneficiaries of all this economic activity.

'We are here to make money for our owners', can be used as an alibi for all kinds of impersonal, insensitive behaviour by businesses – closing plants, not paying suppliers on time, exploitative employment conditions. It is a half-truth. It describes a necessary condition of success. It is vague. It does not say over what timescale the success it to be delivered. There are even people who believe that the measure of success is the current share price. There are others who would interpret the 'here to make money for owners' statement over one, two, three or seven years. It is like the rhetoric of politicians at party conferences. They can win huge applause for saying, 'We commit ourselves to a comprehensive health service, free at the point of delivery.' It begs all the difficult questions like 'When?', 'How?' and 'Who pays?'.

It would be more complicated to say 'We are here to make money for our owners, who are expecting and are entitled to an economic return, but who are themselves human beings who would expect us to treat our customers, suppliers, employees and neighbours much as they would hope to be treated by companies they deal with as customers, suppliers, employees, etc.' But making such statements does bring you much nearer to the full range of human wishes than does mere 'owner value'.

The real reason for being in business is to meet some mixture of many needs. The word 'meet' is significant. Arranging to meet one or more people involves some mutual effort. Someone has to travel, someone else to host the meeting. A meeting could not happen unless each party made some effort to think about the convenience and need of the other.

The same is true of meeting needs in economic life. To achieve lasting sales, for example, one must deeply understand the needs of the person to whom one is selling. The minute he or she becomes convinced that you are doing it purely for the cash, without any concern for the benefit you are offering, you have undermined the relationship. Honesty may indeed be the best policy, but a man who practises honesty for this reason only is not an honest man.[8] Shareholder value, expressed with a proper awareness of the time it takes to create the value, and the human being behind the shareholder, is a useful concept for focusing all the activities of a business. It becomes even more useful when it is used as a common language, throughout the business to make it very clear what success looks like. Stripped of this proper awareness, shareholder value can also be, as Dr Johnson said about patriotism, the last refuge of the scoundrel. It can become a substitute for thought, an alibi for management (not shareholder!) self-interest, or even a megalomaniac's charter.

INTRODUCING THE INCLUSIVE APPROACH

Nothing is so important to a business as the motivation of its people. In a mature economy people are rarely driven to work by the need to avoid starvation, and money alone will not buy above average performance. It is the motivation of people that makes the difference. Inside and outside the organisation, what inspires commitment is the sense that the people with whom you work value, and what you are doing is of value to others. It is how people feel valued and what value they feel they are adding that makes the difference between average and excellent performance. If people are to perform well they need to feel involved in a project that is bigger than they are, and a cause worth putting heart and soul into.

The purpose of the company has to satisfy this human need to be valued and to be creating value. The success of the company depends on the conviction which its own people convey to all those with whom it deals. In practice, this means including in the company's purpose all the human needs that the business is meeting, so the people who encounter the company genuinely feel the company's concern for meeting their needs. There must not be a synthetic surface of customer concern concealing contempt for all except the shareholder. Greed may be a motivator – it is rarely a unifier. If people are to be united in a task, and if the company they represent is to speak convincingly and coherently through the actions of them all, they need both a goal and a leader that make them look beyond themselves.

As the company's board reviews its purpose, it is forced to think about what needs the company serves – in all its relationships. Inclusiveness is a 'both/and' not an 'either/or' approach. The commitment is made to generate a fair and sustainable return to the investors. This is a precondition for meeting all the other needs that the company must meet. But if the board thinks that the process begins and ends with describing how it will meet the needs of its shareholders, it is tying a ball and chain round the ankles of the company. Every relationship is an opportunity. Every human need which the company serves is a key to improved performance. The better the company understands and meets the needs of customers, suppliers, employees, and all those whose needs it serves as whole people, and not as economist's puppets, the more chance it has of uniquely exploiting its strengths in the marketplace. As Mill said, 'He who does not understand the other's case understands little enough of his own'.

This is the power of the inclusive approach. It means seeing every relationship as an opportunity to add value. It means a deep understanding of the nature, the needs, and the values of the people on whom the business depends. It is described in more detail in Chapter 6.

RELATIONSHIPS ARE THE KEY TO SUCCESS

In the inclusive approach leaders at any level in the organisation – from boardroom to cash register – will therefore constantly be asking a number of questions, all of which relate to identifying those relationships crucial to the future of the business.

For each relationship, all leaders will ask:

- Who is really behind this relationship? (For example, a component manufacturer supplying one of the car industry's major sub-contractors will look beyond the immediate customer to the car manufacturer, and beyond the car manufacturer to the car buyer, if he or she is fully to understand the factors affecting the success of that relationship.)
- What is the end-user really looking for from this relationship? (A fund manager serving the needs of a group of savers needs to understand in full colour what the savers he or she is serving are looking for from their investment, and not be content to treat them as clones.)
- How far are the needs of the end-user and the needs of this company aligned?

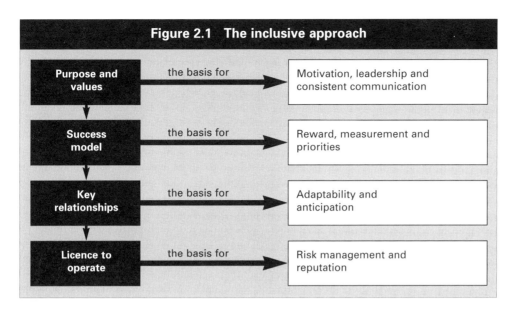

Figure 2.1 The inclusive approach

- How can we improve the alignment so that we can genuinely create a relationship founded on shared destiny?

  The same thought process, conversely, is a reliable guide to help organisations who represent customers, suppliers, employees, investors, and the community in its various forms, to shape their approach to a business with which they deal.

- What is the company looking for in this relationship? How does it square with what we are looking for? Can we, and should we, increase the alignment between the two?

For both parties, in other words, the basis is enlightened self-interest – with a focus on the future and the acknowledgement of the value of the trust built up in the past.

Each business is faced with the challenge of finding its own purpose in its own unique way. A company needs to be clear about purpose, and capable of inspiring the optimum level of commitment and support from customers, suppliers, employees, investors and community. Yesterday's company may regard these relationships as unalterable facts of life. Tomorrow's company recognises that all relationships have to be worked at. And the basis for a strong relationship is mutual self-interest, mutual trust and a sense of shared destiny across the whole range of issues that motivate people.

It all seems so obvious! Yet we persist in our dependence on slogans or 'silver bullets'. We seem to have a deep need to think 'either/or' in spite of all the evidence that the big prizes go to those who think 'both/and'.

MEANS AND ENDS

The most heated arguments are those which represent the apparent clash of two truths which need not be in conflict. The apparent clash between stakeholder and shareholder is a good example.

Many of those who claim to be opposed to 'Tomorrow's Company' and the inclusive approach take this position because they believe that 'it takes your eye off the ball'. In other words, a focus on the needs of customers, employees, suppliers and the community as the creators of value for shareholders dulls the concentration of business managers. They should be focused on results.

There is an important half-truth in this criticism. To focus on relationships and to ignore results would be disastrous: perhaps not as irreparable as ignoring relationships and focusing on results. But it is a dangerous mistake to treat a half-truth as if it were the whole truth.

This is often done by those who specialise in new formulae for measuring shareholder value – the apostles of Economic Value Added (EVA), Value Based Management (VBM) or Total Shareholder Return (TSR).

All of these are methods of helping a company to focus clearly on results. They force the chief executive and the board to think clearly about success. They are a reaction against the inadequacies of other, less satisfactory, formulae – such as Return on Capital Employed (ROCE). These take no account of the cost of capital and the alternative uses to which the same capital might be put – what economists call the opportunity cost. But it is through the understanding, the commitment and the effort of people that the ambitious targets which are set as a result of using these methods will be achieved.

This is where leadership comes in. Without a leader shareholder value remains a mystery known only to the chief executive and a few cronies. A leader communicates this with urgency and captures people's imagination.

Keith Orrell-Jones, the chief executive of Blue Circle (one of the companies involved in Tomorrow's Company Inquiry), a major international manufacturing group headquartered in London, told me in 1996 of his own experience. Measured in the traditional way, Blue Circle's cement-making subsidiary was doing well, making 20–25 per cent return on capital employed. But there were pitfalls in the traditional way of measurement. The cement plants had been built many years ago, and their capital value had been heavily depreciated. The business was showing an apparently healthy return on an unrealistically undervalued asset. No account was being taken of the replacement cost.

The first task Orrell-Jones faced was to agree with his cement manufacturing managing director that the new measures of success were fair, and that the business faced a far steeper climb than it had previously recognised. Then they had to make the same case to the workforce as a whole.

Once the urgency of the change had been accepted, Total Shareholder Return (TSR) became a common language throughout the business. People knew what results had to be achieved, and worked to a common success model. There have been dramatic changes at Blue Circle. A shift which used to be run by 25 people now can be run by seven. The alternative to this reduction in employee numbers would have been the extinction of the whole business. The depth of changes made is typified by the lorry drivers. They came up with a whole range of ideas to reduce costs, some described by Orrell-Jones as 'highly imaginative'. The resulting increased flexibility has led to a new five-year pay deal incorporating a security of employment provision.

Businesses need an approach to defining and measuring success that relentlessly exposes waste, and strengthens competitiveness. The power of habit and inertia is strong. In the absence of good leadership any organisation drifts towards average performance. Total shareholder return is a powerful analytical tool. But behind such tools, there have to be human reasons why people would be willing to abandon traditional practices. There have to be leaders in whom they believe; values which convince them.

The mistake which the more fanatical advocates of EVA or TSR make is to believe that they have discovered the whole truth. They suggest some useful ingredients and then try to suggest it could be a total diet. They treat the company as the means to the shareholders' ends and forget about the human needs the company must appeal to if it is to inspire commitment and loyalty.

The high priests of VBM talk about 'the governing objective' by which the company will be managed.

> A Chief Executive committed to the governing objective is more likely to ask 'If we implement the strategies that will create value for our shareholders each and every year, what might the company look like in ten years?' rather than, 'What is our vision of the future and therefore, what should the company look like in ten years?' This is an extremely important difference in perspective. The shareholders are not interested in what the company *per se* will look like in ten years. They do not care how big its sales or assets will be, they do not care what business it will be in, whether it will be global or local, or even whether it will be an independent entity. Shareholders really want to know, or be able to forecast one thing: How much wealth will the company create in the future. And that very simple, unadorned question must be the chief executive's focus as well.[9]

Here we see a classic case of means elevated to ends, of a success model that may be appropriate for some companies in some situations, inflated to become a universal engine of dehumanisation. It is true – and obvious – that the prime concern of shareholders is with the company's continuing ability to create wealth. It is true – and equally obvious – that a chief executive who fails to deliver those returns over a reasonable timescale has failed. It is untrue – and dangerously misleading – to draw the conclusion that the chief executive should put on the blinkers of the shareholder, and stop thinking about what the company should look like in ten years time. This is the classic fallacy of people who know the price of everything but the value of nothing. The result of such thinking would be to encourage the business to ignore its unique history and values, and concentrate on a series of tactical moves based on immediate competitor pressures. There is a high risk to leaders who focus on immediate improvement without any coherent sense of building an organisation capable of enduring through inspiring the people who work in it and around it. There is already ample evidence, more of which will be quoted in Chapter 3, to demonstrate that this kind of thinking is a recipe for under performance.

A recent study of over 1,600 US companies which adopted variants of the approaches of this kind found that 50 per cent reported reduced profits and only 10 per cent an overall gain.[10] This is not suprising. They were all changing in the same direction – focusing on core businesses, cutting out activities that achieved less shareholder value creation. They were not doing anything to make themselves different, or preparing themselves to respond quickly to the unexpected. They were cutting out the very people who might have been on hand to help as midwives to new development. According to one study, US industry in the nineties has already spent $10 billion on downsizing. It is hard for businesses to stand aside from the pressures to create shareholder value, unless they do have the rare ability to reinvent themselves.

Chief executives are chosen for their ability to lead, and create new opportunities for their businesses, not to follow a formula and programme their minds around the attention span of the mythical and impersonal shareholder. If they were, then it would be easy to write chief executive software and save a very expensive remuneration package!

These men and women are chosen to lead a unique organisation, and to capitalise on its unique strengths while combating its particular weaknesses. You cannot expect a shareholder to have a radically new vision for the company. You can expect that of the chief executive – the role is about more than playing the hand of cards you have been dealt. It is about managing an ever changing hand at the same time as you design and invent new cards and new rules. Every business will find its own reason to exist, but every lasting business will find a reason that is rooted in meeting the needs of a number of what are often described as its stakeholders.

STAKEHOLDERS – A CONFUSING ALTERNATIVE

The alternative which we are usually offered to shareholder or owner value is 'stakeholder theory'. Stakeholder is a word which carries strong emotion, but an often contradictory meaning. To many people the stakeholder concept is one which applies both at the (micro) level of the company and at the (macro) level of society. John Plender, whose book *A Stake in the Future* was subtitled *The Stakeholder Solution* has recognised this:

> The stakeholder concept operates at several levels. At the level of the firm, it asserts the need to recognise the value in a much wider set of relationships than those acknowledged by the principal-agent model of capitalism, with its heavy emphasis on property rights . . . It is the job of the manager to foster [those relationships] in the long-term interests of the company and the wider interests of society.
>
> At the level of the nation, a stakeholder economy is one which derives competitive strength from a cohesive national culture, in which the exercise of property rights is conditioned by shared values and co-operative behaviour . . . No absolute definition of a stakeholder economy is possible, since all countries have some cohesive and some less cohesive elements in their national cultures . . .

Finally, at a political level, stakeholding offers a language in which the criterion of inclusion represents a central yardstick.[11]

Nor is that an end to wide range of different uses of the world 'stakeholder'. Even among those whose restrict themselves to the level of the business, there are huge variations. 'CBI rejects stakeholder solution' announced a newspaper headline in the UK recently.[12] On closer reading it turned out that the Confederation of British Industry had just published a paper arguing against two-tier boards! At the other extreme the term is used with conviction by companies which espouse employee share ownership but refuse to recognise trade unions. It is not surprising that many in business regard the word with some suspicion!

Even excluding the use of the word to denote an approach to politics, there are at least three quite different views concealed behind the word. There is the appeal to a 'stakeholder economy' or even a 'stakeholder society', a society whose arrangements for sharing the fruits of success are such that everyone feels that they have a stake in its success. Alongside, and overlapping this 'macro' view, there are, then, two quite different 'micro' versions of the stakeholder company. In the first of these views, 'stakeholder' is taken to mean everyone except the shareholder. In the second, 'stakeholder' is used to mean everyone including the stakeholder!

The stakeholder view of the company – two micro versions
Excluding the shareholder

Here the term stakeholder is used to define all those business relationships other than that between the company and its shareholders. The argument is that since customers, employees and the local community have invested effort, or custom in the store, and are affected by the decisions it takes, the business should not simply be run for the shareholders, but should in some way be run with their interests also in mind. This is hardly controversial, until you reach the question of accountability. It is suggested that managers of companies should be accountable not simply to shareholders, but to customers, suppliers, employees and the community.

The trouble with this approach is that it still divides people up into their different parts and emphasises the rights they can expect from the company, rather than giving managers a unified way of thinking about how to deal with each of them. The use of the term 'stakeholder' does not make it clear how a company should weigh the claims of different stakeholders or be accountable to them. At one level, you therefore have a harmless doctrine which points to a number of important relationships that a business ignores at its peril. This is understandably caricatured as 'being nice to everyone'.

If the stakeholder approach is to mean more than being nice, it has to have some teeth. The 'other groups' have to be identified in some practical way. The company has to give an account of its actions to the stakeholders, and the stakeholders have to have the opportunity to give the company their views. A way has to be found of doing this which protects the freedom of the enterprise to make decisions, to change fast and compete properly without being a victim of 'paralysis by analysis'.

The two-tier board is sometimes presented as a solution to this problem. Stakeholders, it is argued, can be represented at the senior board, and have their formal input. Members of the junior or 'management board' can be free to make their business decisions within a policy framework laid down from on high.

But the problem remains obstinately unsolved. Consider the practicalities of the two-tier board. Which stakeholders are represented on it? Who chooses them? To whom are the stakeholder board members accountable? The test comes when a business has to choose between the conflicting claims of stakeholders. Who comes first? At least the traditional shareholder view offers a clear answer – the interest of the shareholder – even if this view sometimes confuses the immediate shareholder and the long-term shareholder. As global competition puts pressure on costs, many people, particularly in the higher-wage economies, will have to be squeezed out, sometimes through compulsory redundancy.

All these problems were encountered by the worker directors who sat on the boards of British Steel and other UK nationalised companies. Some were accused of 'selling out' – of seeing problems through management eyes. Others were accused of continuing to act as trade unionists – of not seeing problems through management's eyes. The experience shows the poverty of any approach which expresses the duties of directors in terms of particular interest groups – whether shareholders or stakeholders. Under UK law, a director's duty is to the company. Directors and boards have to act as stewards for the long-term interests of the company, not shop stewards for any interest group – an issue which is explored further in Chapter 7.

Like 'owner', stakeholder is often used in a one-sided way. It expresses the relationship in terms of a claim by the stakeholder on the enterprise, and a duty by the enterprise towards the stakeholder. This may serve as a salutary reminder to businesses that many people who are not shareholders have invested effort in the business and deserve due recognition. But the word 'stakeholder' does not say what that recognition should be. It does not offer the leaders of a business a clear basis for leadership. Its value, like that of the term 'ownership' is more rhetorical than practical. When there is a takeover battle raging, and the defending management do not want to surrender their control of the company, it is very convenient to cloak the defence in crisis of undying loyalty to 'stakeholders'.

The stakeholder view of the company – two micro versions
Everyone a stakeholder . . . even the competition

There are some participants in the debate who have recognised these weaknesses and attempted to rectify them. They use the word in a more comprehensive way, and they include shareholders inside their definition of stakeholders. In *The Stakeholder Corporation: A Blueprint for Maximising Stakeholder Value*, David Wheeler and Marian Sillenpää of The Body Shop distinguish between 'social' and 'non-social' stakeholders, and divide each into 'primary' and 'secondary'.

> Stakeholders are individuals and entities who can be influenced by, or can impact upon, an organisation . . .
>
> Primary social stakeholders include
>
> - shareholders and investors
> - employees and managers
> - customers
> - local communities
> - suppliers and other business partners

> Secondary social stakeholders embrace government and other civil society and include
>
> - government and regulators
> - civic institutions
> - social pressure groups (e.g. trade unions)
> - media and academic commentators
> - trade bodies
> - competitors
>
> Primary social stakeholders are those who have a direct stake in the organisation and its success. Secondary social stakeholders may be extremely influential . . . but their stake is more representational than direct. Consequently, the level of moral accountability to a secondary stakeholder tends to be lower.
>
> Primary non-social stakeholders include
>
> - the natural environment
> - future generations
> - non-human species
>
> Secondary non-social stakeholders include
>
> - environmental pressure groups
> - animal welfare organisations[2]

This division proposed by Wheeler and Sillenpää is at least a basis for thinking separately about different relationships. Indeed, the five primary social stakeholders are practically the same key relationships used in the inclusive approach by the RSA Inquiry *Tomorrow's Company*. David Wheeler and Marian Sillenpää even describe theirs as a 'stakeholder inclusive approach'. The problem is that while the list is exhaustive, it is in danger of becoming exhausting. It extends not only to shareholders, but also to competitors and non-human species. It is hard to see it being used as a basis for simple and inspiring communication to practical managers.

There are, in practice, two stages to reviewing relationships in an inclusive approach – and these are described in Chapter Six. This kind of exhaustive list is valuable when an organisation is engaged in the first stage of mapping all its relationships. It can become a liability once you start to make choices, set priorities and simplify measurements. The main danger lies in a failure to focus attention on a few really important relationships.

'Just because I go into a newsagents and buy a Mars Bar, I don't feel that makes me a stakeholder in the Mars Corporation', said one business leader.

Used without qualification, stakeholder is a misleading word. It makes very different business relationships sound the same. It does not differentiate between an employee with thirty years of service and the casual buyer of a newspaper. It may make more sense in geographically static businesses in traditional communities that are slow to change. It makes much less sense in a fast moving global economy in which large companies are buying in services and hiring people across continents without ever seeing them.

A new language

Many of the arguments advanced under the stakeholder label are compelling. It is a pity that they have to use a term which has become loaded with contradictory meanings, sometimes exclusive and adversarial (as in, 'Stakeholder excludes shareholder') and sometimes exhaustive but confusing (as in, 'Everyone a stakeholder').

We need a new language to describe the relationships of Tomorrow's Company, a language which is richer in its description of the human variety of business and its relationships than is captured either by 'shareholder value' or 'stakeholder' in its different forms.

Measured over a long enough period, the concept of shareholder value provides a clear focus. The danger is that it may tempt managers to confuse the short-term interest of the shareholders with the long-term interests of the enterprise, and to forget that shareholder value is generated by stakeholders.

Managers with a stakeholder perspective never forget that they depend for their success upon meeting human needs in a wide range of relationships. Their risk is that they lack a simple yardstick of success. A stakeholder perspective can serve as an alibi, and a distraction from the requirement to create measurable value.

By themselves, neither shareholder nor stakeholder perspective inspire a business. If life in your company is to be a 'romance and an adventure' inspiration has to come from something deep within the personality of the business and the people who make it unique.

3   VALUE AND VALUES

Business people are creative human beings. They work hard, they worry; they have families and mortgages; they care about the future of their community and their country.

Like actors, or service personnel, or trade unionists or lawyers or planners or housing managers or any other group of human beings, business people have faults – some are vain, some are greedy, some may even be bullies. Equally they have merits – inspiring leadership, impressive loyalty and dedication, the ability to improvise, the insistence that there has to be a solution and that it is no-one else's responsibility to provide it, the realism bequeathed by the bottom line.

But, in the UK at least, business people have become the object of cynicism. This cynicism is unnecessary. It is largely unjustified. It may drive away from business the very able people whom business needs. And the business world has no-one to blame but itself.

This is not a question of poor public relations, or even a throwback to the genteel hostility of the upper classes to the world of 'tradesmen'. If you dig down to the roots what you find is tangled thinking about business and its values.

Take four words: business, company, enterprise, firm. Do they all mean the same thing? If they are different, what is the significance behind the differences?

The origins of the four words are different. And behind the differences lie deeper differences in approach to wealth creating activity.

THE ENTERPRISE AND THE BUSINESS

In the beginning, there has to be an enterprise – 'a design of which the execution is attempted, a piece of work taken in hand'. The dictionary tells us enterprise means starting something new, and taking a risk to do so. It takes some courage and creativity to be an entrepreneur – to see and to take a business opportunity others either had not seen or had not taken. Without the enterprise there would be no talk of companies or firms and no need for analysis and accounting. The pure entrepreneur does not simply evaluate and compare existing business opportunities: she or he takes risks to create new ones. Enterprise starts with the imagination – and any society which wants to survive will celebrate its entrepreneurs, particularly those who aim high enough to create a globally competitive business. 'The trouble with you British is that you are too civilised', said an eminent engineer to me in Hong Kong. 'You've forgotten what it means to start a business out of the back of a mini van.' I could see what he meant: there is a tendency for most of the newspaper discussion of business in the UK to be about long-established businesses and the merry-go-round of executive hirings and corporate reconstructions.

But the statistics are only as sound as the categories they count. And here we come to the crucial distinction between a company and a business. Once an entrepreneur has created an enterprise, that enterprise can be classified by the business opportunity to which it is a response. 'Business' represents one of those sprawling entries which make dictionaries such distracting places to visit. Its origins are simply in busy-ness. In its early use the word could also imply 'mischievous or impertinent activity' or 'anxiety' or 'care and attention'. Later in the sixteenth century it came to mean 'occupation'. And only in the eighteenth century did it come to mean transactions, and in the late nineteenth century 'a commercial enterprise as a going concern'.[1]

But there are two other important meanings to untangle from the word 'business'. First, in an environment which sees many changes of corporate control, it has become useful as a description of the underlying activity which may survive many mutations of ownership. My first serious job in 'business' was in a GEC subsidiary called Elliott Automation. In around twenty years the company passed from the hands of its founders into English Electric, from English Electric into AEI. From AEI into GEC. From GEC to Fisher Controls. From Fisher Controls into Plessey. And, then, back to GEC with the take-over of Plessey by GEC. The underlying business was the same business: the same engineers designed products for the same markets, and felt the same frustration over delays in getting them from design into production; the sports and social club carried on much as before and the food in the canteen didn't get better or worse. The business carried on while the ownership and control of the company changed. And, as Richard Onians points out, that makes the statistics provided by Companies House and the accounting firms on company registrations and deregistrations a misleading indicator of the state of business development: 'Without a business a company is a mere shell, a plaything of lawyers or accountants'.[2]

Second, business is used as an aggregate term – 'the business community', 'business interests', 'the reputation of business'. This is a reminder of another crucial distinction that is sometimes missed – the difference between the success of the whole economy of a region or country or trading bloc, and the health of individual enterprises within it. The individual businessman or woman is concerned with individual survival. But that does not mean that it is healthy for the economy as a whole that every business survives. An effective market system is one that operates appropriate natural selection, allowing the best businesses to prosper and the worst to be gobbled up or to starve. The problem for the market economy is how to encourage entrepreneurs to create businesses in the first place and how to ensure that the market rewards those businesses that will ultimately make the strongest contribution.

Individual entrepreneurs will have their own – often unarticulated – definition of what they mean by success. Some will be content to stay small. Some may not be concerned with the survival of the business beyond their lifetime, or even beyond a fixed timescale. Some may never want to know that they have the makings of a world-class business. The issue most face is how to secure the continuance of their business as a going concern so that they can then go on to achieve their own chosen version of success. The uniqueness of a business might lie as much in the design of the organisation as in the product or process. Few seem to have realised how much there is to be gained by thinking through what kind of organisation and what kind of relationships they want to create. Too many entrepreneurs find themselves running a firm: only realising later that their long-term success will depend upon building a company.

THE FIRM *VS* THE COMPANY

> Company. Either from *con* and *pagus*, one of the same town or *con panis*, one that eats of the same mess.[3]
>
> Company. A body of persons combined or incorporated for some common object.[4]

A company is a band, a group of people with a common objective. Its Latin origins are about sharing. In its original use the word suggests a view of business that starts with people and relationships, and sees them as the key to enduring financial success. Only later, through the creation of the joint stock company, does the word come to be used more to describe a thing separate from the people who formed it. Interestingly, the dictionary also points out that company can mean 'the partner or partners in a firm whose names are not included in the style and title, usually written "Co"'.

So the firm is a thing, and the company is (originally) the people. The origins of the word 'firm' are also Latin. *Firmare* in late Latin meant to confirm by signature. The firm was literally the imprint – the style or name under which a commercial house conducts business. Although it came in due course to be particularly associated with unincorporated organisations such as professional partnerships, and although there are more uses of the term such as: 'the family firm', in its original use the word suggests a view of business as a bundle of contracts. When economists speak of 'the theory of the firm' they traditionally describe labour alongside land and capital as the commodities that the manager is seeking to deploy. Whereas the concept of the company started as a gathering together of people, the notion of the firm is of the visible, commercial identity to which individuals are bound by contract. People working together under clear leadership towards a common task define a company; a firm hires labour. Throughout this chapter, and throughout the book, this distinction between *company* and *firm* will be used. It is central to the argument for the inclusive approach.

The company has personality: one firm is more likely to be like another. The company – like any band of people – has dynamism: people can adapt as the task changes. Because a company adds value through having personality, it is perfectly logical to keep a company going long after the business rationale for the original enterprise has passed. Those who see simply a thing called a firm would be more likely to argue that once the original mission has been fulfilled the firm should be folded up and the money returned to shareholders. It is easier to talk about shareholders owning a firm: as soon as you start acknowledging that a company stands or falls by the abilities of the people who work in it, the idea of a distant shareholder enjoying the absolute right to dispose of the company starts to undermine the sense of loyalty.

The concept of the firm reflects a one dimensional view of human nature. It confines people to the economist's caricature – *homo economicus* – whom we met in the last chapter. The firm hires labour. It is one more commodity, along with capital and land, that the business manager has to deploy. The performance of that labour is dependent on its price. If loyalty is recognised, it is secured by financial incentives.

This view is strongly present in the USA, where many investors believe that unless the chief executive of a business and the key directors stand to make a fortune out of their successful performance, they will not have the motivation to do a good job. And it has been echoed in many of the more extravagant pay deals being negotiated by the heads of the privatised utilities in the UK. As a result, it is the view of the firm, and not the view of the company, that is now strongly identified in the minds of the public. Remuneration and incentive are, in the public mind, polite words for hire and bribe. Rationalisation, restructuring and down sizing are euphemisms for fire and sack.

> S.G. Warburg employees are set to receive some £60m in deferred payments to secure their loyalty to Swiss Bank Corporation, after its £860m acquisition of the UK-based investment banking business formally came into effect yesterday. The fund is designed to retain staff and 'lubricate integration' said Mr Maurice Ospel, chief executive of SBC Warburg the combined investment bank which begins operations today, just two months after SBC and Warburg announced they were in talks. The move comes as SBC Warburg prepares substantial redundancies . . . About 1,000 of the combined group's 11,000 employees seem likely to go.[5]

This is a long way from the notion of a company as a group of people united by a common task. Or, if there is a common task, it is seen by the public as being nearer the caricature described in John Grisham's thriller *The Firm*, where we see a talented and honest, if naive, lawyer whose life is taken over by the law firm for which he works. Here a senior colleague is telling him how to succeed in the 'money factory':

> 'Don't ignore the billing', he warned. 'That's the first rule of survival . . . The competition among the partners is intense but good-spirited. They're all getting

rich, right? . . . It's very motivational . . . Bonuses can be earned by partners for exorbitant billing'.[6]

Business – from this perspective – is about making money. The *firm* is a machine. People are a commodity it consumes. 'If they could get 10p more an hour they would go down the road.' Loyalty is about how much you get paid. 'If I wanted to do good I would have become a social worker.' 'The only social responsibility a business has is to make a profit.' 'It's the share-holder's money and the management have no right to put it to any purpose except the shareholders' profit.' These are some of the common expressions that reflect the influence of *firm* thinking.

The difference between people who think *company* and people who think *firm* is rather like the difference between people who think *home* and peo-ple who think *house* about the place where they live. Some people move into a house and immediately imbue it with their style and personalities: there is a distinctive character about the decor and the arrangement of rooms and pictures and hanging baskets, and the fireplace that reflects their personali-ties and their tastes. There is an assumption of continuity. Money is spent that could not be wholly recovered in the event of an early sale but adds to the individual character of that home. Others, particularly those who expect to be moving on again in a few years, make a much simpler payback calculation. They accept what they inherit by way of carpets and colour schemes, and avoid spending on longer-term schemes knowing that their time will soon come to sell.

The difference is, in many ways, one of taste and circumstance. There is no point in trying to persuade someone who thinks *house* to think *home*. People's views are shaped by their experiences. If you spend your life being moved from one posting to another, you may feel little incentive to create a home. If you spend your life analysing businesses solely in terms of their price earnings ratio and their net asset value you are likely to be rather bemused by someone who talks about them in terms of their human quali-ties. The irony is that it is precisely those human qualities which will in the end play the largest part in shaping the financial performance which you are watching so closely – just as, to many buyers, it may actually be the sense of 'home' which makes the difference between buying and not buying a partic-ular house.

Every business is in part a bundle of transactions and in part a bundle of relationships. Some business activity lends itself more obviously to empha-sis on transactions – as I reflected ruefully when being treated with contempt in a French motorway service station that I knew I was unlikely to visit again! What each business has to decide for itself is what mixture works best, given its circumstances. The shocking reality is that many businesses never con-sider their options. They never even explore the potential benefits of behav-ing more like a *company* and less like a *firm*. They are slaves to a rigid orthodoxy they have inherited and never questioned. They know with cer-tainty that if you want to know how well the firm is doing you can do so by looking at the accounts. They have no doubt that if you want to make more profit you concentrate on forcing suppliers' prices down and sales prices up. And that if you want to improve the performance of your directors the most important thing to do is to come up with a really irresistible remuneration package. That, to their common sense view, is what business is about.

And so we have two widely held but conflicting beliefs about business. First, the *company*, that it is all about customers, employees, suppliers, communities, investors and the leadership that points them all in the same direction: if you get these very human things right, the economic rewards will follow. And, second, the *firm*, that it is about economic man – the right incentives, the right deals and the right price.

The rational perspective contains important economic principles. There is nothing wrong with them and indeed to neglect them is to put the business at risk. The danger lies in the over-confident belief that they are somehow the key to business success. Past history, present experience, and what we can see of the future all point to the same conclusions. People who think they are running *firms* will be beaten by people who are building *companies*.

Table 3.1 The company *vs* the firm	
THE COMPANY	THE FIRM
has personality in its own right	is the property of the shareholders
is a bundle of values and relationships	is a bundle of contracts
sees itself as an adaptive organism	sees itself as a machine

	IN THE COMPANY	IN THE FIRM
Assets are	stewarded	sweated
People are	its greatest asset	a cost
Profits are	how we survive	why we exist

WHAT MAKES FOR LASTING SUCCESS – THE HISTORY

There is no laboratory in which scientists could test what makes companies successful. That is, what makes business so exciting: the choices have to be made by leaders on the basis of their own experience and limited information. The RSA Inquiry *Tomorrow's Company* was a statement of conviction of a group of business leaders. The Inquiry team's findings were based on their experience and their own interpretation of the world around them. But there is a growing body of evidence to encourage those leaders who choose to see business in terms of the *company*, and not the *firm*.[7]

Just as the Inquiry was being launched, John Kotter and James Heskett published *Corporate Culture and Performance*. In a series of studies of company performance over an eleven-year period, they found that:

Firms with cultures that emphasised all the key managerial constituencies (customers, stockholders and employees) and leadership from managers at all levels outperformed firms that did not have these cultural traits by a huge margin. Over an eleven-year period, the former increased revenues by an average of 682 per cent v. 166 per cent for the latter, expanded their workforces by 282 per cent v. 36 per cent, grew their stock prices by 901 per cent v. 74 per cent, and improved their net incomes by 756 per cent v. 1 per cent.[8]

The key to their thinking was that it was through strong relationships with these constituencies that firms would be able to adapt. The implication was that, in a world that is changing at an increasing rate, companies which did not have a strong emphasis on the key constituencies and leadership would come under even greater pressure.

The keys to long-term survival

In the early 1980s, as part of a long-running debate on diversification, the Chairman of Shell asked his Head of Planning to show him examples of companies which were older than Shell, which were relatively as important in their industries as Shell was in its own, and which during their history had successfully weathered some fundamental change and survived with their corporate identity intact. The Shell planning team found companies like Dupont, in the USA, Mitsui in Japan, and, oldest of all, Stora in Sweden, a pulp and paper company which started out as a copper mine more than 700 years ago.

What did these companies have in common? The Shell team found four answers.

1. Conservatism in financing. 'They had an understanding that money-in-hand meant that they had options at moments that suited them. Capital availability means flexibility.'

2. Sensitivity to the environment about them. 'The leaders of these companies were outward looking and part of their surrounding world. As a result they were sensitive to changes and developments in that world. They saw early, concluded quickly; therefore were able to take action quickly. These companies were mostly connected to their communities in ways which promote intelligence and learning.'

3. A sense of cohesion and identity among employees. 'The Shell researchers found a concern and interest in the human element of the company which was quite surprising for the times in which their histories played out. Also, employees and management seemed to have a rather good understanding of "What this company stood for" or "What this company was about". And "What it was about" was something with which these people were happy to be identified.'

4. The common characteristic was tolerance at the margin. 'Companies which have changed successfully have made full use of decentralised structures

and delegated authorities. The companies have not insisted on relevance to the original business as a criterion for selecting new business possibilities, nor upon a central control over moves to diversify.'[9]

These conclusions complement a recent study, *Built to Last* [10] of 18 of the USA's most visionary enduring hundred-year-old companies. The authors, Jim Collins and Jerry Porras, wanted to study the sources of long-term business success. They knew how quickly the current selection of apparently healthy and profitable businesses could turn into an industrial casualty list. They wanted to study success over many decades. But they were also convinced that leadership was crucial to long-term success. And, as they started to think about long-lasting companies that people admired, they noticed that it was not always possible to identify outstanding individuals at the helm of these companies. It appeared to them that 'visionary leadership' was not brought from outside these companies by charismatic leaders, but imbued in the whole organisation. They then searched out more companies who showed this quality of visionary leadership by asking the people who they felt were most likely to be able to distinguish it – business leaders themselves. From their responses Porras and Collins were able to select 18 visionary companies, all of whom had distinguished themselves by being acknowledged leaders in their industries, had made an indelible imprint on the world they lived in, had multiple generations of chief executives and had been through multiple product life cycles. The resulting study, published shortly before the findings of the *Tomorrow's Company* Inquiry, is called *Built to Last*.

These companies, say the authors, had been more than simply enduring, and more than simply successful. They had been through bad times but shown extraordinary resilience. In their study Porras and Collins wanted to avoid the trap of linking successful companies with a number of banal characteristics that were also to be found in less spectacular companies. They called this the 'discover buildings trap' which they expressed in terms of the following question and answer:

'What do all these companies have in common?'
'Why, they all have office buildings.'

To avoid this they compared the visionary companies not simply with the stock market average, but also with a 'control group' of companies that had themselves been successful. And when they came to compare the three sets of results, they were amazed.

> Suppose you made equal $1 investments in a general-market stock fund, a comparison company stock fund, and a visionary company stock fund on January 1 1926 . . . Your $1 in the general market fund would have grown to $415 on December 31 1990 – not bad. Your $1 invested in the group of comparison companies would have grown to $955 – more than twice the general market. But your $1 in the visionary companies stock fund would have grown to $6,356 – over six times the comparison fund and over 15 times the general market.

The authors of *Built to Last* describe a number of myths which were shattered in the course of their research. These included:

Myth 2: Visionary companies require great and charismatic visionary leaders. *Reality:* 'Some of the most significant chief executives in the history of visionary companies did not fit the model of the high profile charismatic leader. Indeed some explicitly shied away from that model . . . They concentrated more on architecting an enduring institution than on being a great individual leader. They sought to be clock builders, not time tellers . . .'

Myth 3: The most successful companies exist first and foremost to maximise profits. *Reality:* 'Contrary to business school doctrine, "maximising shareholder wealth" or "profit maximisation" has not been the dominant driving force or primary objective through the history of visionary companies. Visionary companies pursue a cluster of objectives of which making money is only one – and not necessarily the primary one. Yes, they seek profits, but they're equally guided by a core ideology – core values and a sense of purpose beyond making money. Yet paradoxically, the visionary companies make more money than the purely profit-driven comparison companies.'

Myth 4: Visionary companies share a common subset of core values. *Reality:* 'There is no "right" set of core values for being a visionary company. Indeed two companies can have radically different ideologies, yet both be visionary. Core values in a visionary company don't even have to be enlightened or "humanistic" although they often are. The crucial variable is not the content of a company's ideology, but how deeply it believes its ideology and how consistently it lives, breathes, and expresses it in all that it does.'

The right difference

Andrew Pettigrew and Richard Whipp have written a detailed comparative study of the performance during the 1980s of pairs of companies in the car industry, publishing, and merchant banking. They stress that every company is different. Context is all-important. In the same industry or the same company a decentralised approach was appropriate at one stage in the decade and inappropriate at another. They came to the conclusion that the companies which were the most successful shone in five ways:

1. They analysed and interpreted their external environment well.
2. They had effective leaders.
3. They knew how to link strategic and operational change – how to turn big plans into effective practice across organisations.
4. They saw people as the prime asset and were good at human resource management.
5. They held the organisation together while simultaneously reshaping it.[11]

There is no one right approach. Each company must find its own route to greatness. And lasting profits do not come by short-cuts: they come by the conscious design and building of a company which knows what it stands for, and is capable of inspiring the people who work in it to produce ever better results without the requirement for a heroic chief executive.

The reactive trap

W. Chan Kim and Renee Mauborgne spent five years studying more than 30 companies around the world in an attempt to discover what drives high growth in revenues and profits. Their answer was that high-growth companies were not differentiated by the age or outlook of their managers, nor big investments in the latest technologies, nor the favourable nature of the environment in which they were competing. They found that:

> The less successful companies were stuck in the trap of competing. Their strategic logic centred around building competitive advantages. They benchmarked the competition and focused on outperforming rivals. The result was a perpetual cycle of offering a little more for a little less than competitors. The competition, not the customer, set the parameters of their strategic thinking.[12]

Kim and Mauborgne point out that when companies' thinking is driven by the competition, it puts them in a reactive frame of mind; it makes them imitate when they should innovate; and it clouds their understanding of what customers want. One of their examples is the battle between IBM and Compaq in the 1980s. The two companies sought to out-perform each other in producing a higher specification PC.

The best companies in the study paid little attention to matching or beating the competition. They sought to make the competition irrelevant by offering a quantum leap in value. Kim and Mauborgne suggest four questions businesses should ask themselves if they are to achieve high growth.

1. What factors that our industry takes for granted should be eliminated?
2. What factors that our industry competes on should be reduced well below the standard?
3. What factors that our industry competes on should be raised well above the standard?
4. What factors should be created that our industry has never offered?

This is a manifesto for lateral thinking. It associates high growth with an emphasis upon what makes the company unique, and low growth with an emphasis upon how well the firm is competing by the established measures. It takes empathy, imagination and leadership to force an organisation to ask these questions about tomorrow while continuing to deliver cash flow today. To a *company*, the quest for uniqueness and adaptation is natural. For a *firm*, the temptation is always to squeeze more return out of the established formula.

Prisoners of orthodoxy

There is nothing wrong with the desire for focus, rigour, and financial results. But for too many business leaders and investors, they have stood in the way of deeper thought about the origins of success. Those who see the world in 'firm' terms might react in a number of ways to a company seeking to display the qualities listed earlier in the Shell study by Arie de Geus. Some of these reactions are displayed in the box below.

Textbox 3.1 'Firm' reactions

CONSERVATISM IN FINANCING ...MONEY-IN-HAND... CAPITAL AVAILABILITY MEANS FLEXIBILITY

Shareholders are becoming increasingly restless with the management of ABC plc for its failure to deal with its cash pile. Pressure is growing for an increase in dividends. Said one fund manager: 'It's the shareholders' money and if this management isn't going to put it to work then we'll have to remind them who owns this company.'

SENSITIVITY TO THE ENVIRONMENT

'ABC plc has a great reputation for being involved in the community. But what worries me is who the hell do the board think they are. They're not there to play God in the community. They have one job and one job only. They're there to make money for the stockholders. They've taken their eye off the ball. If more of their remuneration were based on the share price perhaps they wouldn't worry quite so much about being good neighbours.'

A SENSE OF COHESION AND IDENTITY AMONG EMPLOYEES

'Why is this firm wasting shareholders' money on country house retreats to discuss philosophy? What right have the employees to be consulted on whether it opens its doors on a Sunday? It's things like this that get in the way of running a business. Any shareholder could tell them their purpose is to sharpen up the bottom line performance. I don't care what the company stands for as long as it's making good money.'

TOLERANCE

'There is not enough focus or discipline in this business. We should be getting out of all these non-core activities and introducing some focus.'

Building lasting foundations

The available evidence tells us that great companies are built on the foundation of lasting vision and deeply held values, and that there is a strong correlation between issues concerning people, including relationships, and sustainable business success. The question arises: 'If it is so clear that this is traditionally where shareholder value has come from, why do so many investors and so many boards appear to neglect it?'

The economist John Maynard Keynes observed that, 'Practical men, who believe themselves to be quite exempt from any intellectual influences, are usually the slaves of some defunct economist.'

Theories or mental models are very powerful. They can shape the way apparently strong people think, and their influence can outlast their realism.

Textbox 3.2   Manufacturing winners

Professor Amin Rajan, in an RSA lecture in 1996 reported the conclusions of two research studies.

Rajan concluded that there were the following five key ingredients of successful companies.

1. Their leaders are visionary, enthusiastic champions of change who have communicated their business goals throughout the company and generated the necessary commitment at all levels.
2. They have flexible, motivated employees capable of performing multiple tasks at differing levels of responsibility.
3. They learn from their customers, competitors, suppliers and academia.
4. They have a culture of innovation that seeks continuous improvement in products and working methods.
5. Their business processes and practices seek to achieve low cost product customisation while retaining a clear edge in price, quality and service. They have inverted traditional manufacturing logic by securing for batch production all those advantages commonly associated with mass production and standardisation.

Rajan concluded:

> These companies have a style that reconciles the diverse needs of customers, shareholders and employees. Through strong face to face contacts their leaders generate a sense of excitement and mutual trust which enthuses managers and employees to go that proverbial 'extra mile' for one another, creating the essential motivation for high productivity.[13]

Investors and boards have been conditioned by 'firmist' thought processes. They only feel comfortable – forgive the pun – on *terra firma*. They have not broken down solid concepts like shareholder value and business results into their constituent elements – elusive particles like creativity, inspiration, values, reputation and risk. The measures they apply, and the questions which they ask, do not prompt the people in whom they invest to build companies: they reinforce those who run firms.

Everyone who starts or runs a business is free to choose what sort of business they want it to be. A sole trader who buys and sells commodities and rarely deals with the same people twice, could, in theory organise a perfectly satisfactory business on the principles of the firm. Some may choose to treat their people like commodities.

It is hard to imagine many circumstances where such an approach would work for long. Even a trader in commodities needs trust to simplify transactions. And one has only to write down the cruder assumptions associated with 'The Firm' to expose them as unsustainable inside the law:

> I have set up this business to make as much money as possible. I don't particularly care how, as long as it is legal. I don't want to share this money with anyone else: I will pay people at whatever rates the market compels me to pay them. I will get my supplies at the lowest possible cost and if I can find a better value supplier I will happily drop my existing supplier, however long he has been working for me. I don't want a relationship with my customers: I want

their money. I reluctantly pay my local taxes but that is all the involvement I want with the community round here.

Not many of these proprietors would be willing to have such a statement printed and circulated throughout their premises. Most would recognise that its publication would make business much more difficult. Customers are less willing to spend money with companies who, they feel, do not really care about them. Indeed when the jewellery retailer Gerald Ratner proclaimed in a speech at the Albert Hall that some of his company's products were 'crap', his shops were overwhelmed with returned bracelets and sherry decanters. A planning application is less likely to succeed if the local authority feels that the business accepts no responsibility as a local citizen. Businesses need people to buy from them, work for them, supply them, invest in them and trust them. On its own, profit-maximising behaviour does not achieve any of those conditions for corporate growth, any more than eating and drinking by themselves create the conditions for personal growth.

But what of the future? Does this all remain true in the age of the virtual company? Does it matter that companies have a clear and lasting identity when competitors can rush out a 'me-too' product in weeks? Surely, it might be argued, in an age of impermanence, the days of the company are numbered and the day of the firm has arrived. People will be employed on short-term contracts, to perform specific tasks, and then they will be conveniently disemployed. More and more of us will be self-employed. More and more of our relationships will be casual.

In the next chapter these issues are explored. The conclusion is that you still need permanence in an age of discontinuity. In fact, you need it more.

4 THE RULES OF THE GAME ARE CHANGING

I was in a plane, ten minutes from its landing at Gatwick Airport, and suddenly I could see below me the landmarks around my home. Frustratingly, I could not quite identify our house. It is the same with technology. Its impact on our jobs and lives is starting to become clear. But in terms of the shape of our future economy and society, technology hasn't quite landed yet. For example, no-one can tell us for certain what use we will end up making of artificial intelligence, or micro-biology or even the exponential growth in our capacity to process information and transmit it across the world. No-one can tell us. All we know is that the change is accelerating.

TECHNOLOGY IS CUSTOMISING OUR WORLD

After the Industrial Revolution, in 1780, it took Britain 58 years to double real income per head. At the end of the twentieth century, China did it in ten years. A greeting card that plays 'Happy Birthday' holds more computing power than existed on earth before 1950. In 1960 a transatlantic telephone cable could carry only 138 conversations simultaneously. By 1996 a fibre-optic cable could carry 1.5 million conversations. A computer manufacturer revealed to me recently that the life cycle of their latest model was now around 80 days. People and organisations adapt much more slowly than technologies. We have some catching up to do, a point Nicholas Negroponte makes dramatically:

> Did you ever know the childhood conundrum of working for a penny a day for a month, but doubling your salary each day? If you started this wonderful pay scheme on New Year's Day, you would be earning more than $10m per day on the last day of January . . . Using the same scheme, we would earn only about $1.3m if January were three days shorter (i.e. February). Put another way, your cumulative income for that whole month of February would be roughly $2.6m, instead of the $21m you earned in total during January. We are approaching those last three days in the spread of computing and digital information.[1]

Perhaps Peter Drucker is right, and the appropriate comparison is not with the Industrial Revolution, but the invention of the printing press which led to the first information revolution. Says Drucker:

> By 1465 – not much more than ten years after Gutenberg's invention – the number of printed books was six to ten times as great as the number of manuscripts . . . An illuminated manuscript of the Bible cost three years' rent on a fair sized estate. Then the printed bible came along, costing a week's wages.[2]

As a result of the second information revolution, Drucker predicts that the nation state and the traditional city will disappear, but the main impact will be on education. The Open University showed over a generation ago how technology could be used to overcome distance. Tomorrow we can expect sophisticated learning packages which enable us to learn in teams (dispersed around the city or the globe), explore, discover, share insights, and simulate examinations or real-life hazards (as pilots already do through virtual reality).

JEANS AND GENES

The new technology offers us the opportunity, once we get our minds round it, to tailor everything to our personal requirements. Tomorrow's companies are being created around decentralisation. Intelligence is being moved from corporate HQ to the work team or the home. As customers we will soon have the capacity to programme our equipment to edit all the available material and select, according to our preferences, a personally tailored TV or newspaper. We can choose where and when we buy without going out to a shop. We can already get our measurements taken and held by a jeans retailer and order future pairs by phone for delivery anywhere in the world - provided we haven't put on too much weight. The same is true of work: technology offers many individuals the opportunity to work from home, although, at the same time, it offers the same flexibility to the customers of that work. For those who are fastest to adapt, distance and time zones cease to be an obstacle to providing a service. Those who get left behind will be punished. Software engineers in Surrey may be able to work from home, but along with bank and airline staff they will also be in danger of losing work to rivals in India or rural Ireland. With one person, a mobile phone and a laptop, aggressive competitors from Asia can compete across Europe without the need for elaborate European headquarters. Meanwhile, the homes in which we hope to work and live will take on more of the characteristics of the office or factory, with sophisticated control panels for regulating the central heating, the oven, the communications systems, perhaps even the recycling of the water from our washing machines. In medicine we are now presented with the prospect of selecting not only the sex but the genetic make-up of our offspring – with all the ethical complications that accompany that choice.

Businesses will have to organise themselves so that everything can be tailored to the individual. We already experience this when we ring up the more highly organised insurance company and they know where we are calling from, when we last spoke to them, and what the claims department said to us only last week.

There are several paradoxes here. As cars have more chips in them, Joe Public no longer dares to put his head under the bonnet. We all become more dependent on the techno-expert who can rescue the system after it has crashed. And if the system in question is one on which the traffic flows of central London depend, we had better have good back-up.

Equally, the insurance company will only be able to take advantage of all that knowledge it has about me if it does so sensitively. If I ring up my credit card company and the person the other end says 'Hello, Mr Goyder, what's the weather like in Hawkhurst?', or 'How was your holiday?', that's fine by me, although it may offend some. But just imagine how I might feel if I rang up and the response was 'O, hello Mr Goyder, what's your excuse this month for not paying your minimum repayment on time? If you carry on spending at the present rate you will be over your credit limit long before Christmas'. I would feel overlooked and invaded.

THE DEMISE OF THE MANUAL

Information is power. The more people have, the more sensitive they will need to be in using it. The more organisations let go of the power, by employing people at a distance and expecting them to be close to the customer, the more they will be relying on what is going on inside people – their intrinsic motivation, and their values, not their formal targets, and the policy manual.

If the credit card company finds it cheaper to employ its credit control people from home, how does it know that the customers are being spoken to in an appropriate tone? How are people to be motivated to do a good job under those circumstances especially when they are not sure of their security of employment?

It won't be done by following the policy manual. It is much more cost effective if people do it naturally because the organisation they work for has a clear sense of what it stands for, and where the company is going, if it has won people's commitment, earned their trust, and offered them trust in return. People in the front line will need a deep understanding about the business. They will be accountable for performance and they will be measured so that they can clearly see and improve the value of the contribution they are making. How do you maintain that trust and that shared sense of values? You find ways to bring dispersed people together, to underpin it. And, of course, you measure by asking customers about their experiences.

The paradox is, as Charles Handy has pointed out, that in a networked society human values like trust and togetherness become more important precisely because of the increased distance and the increased risk.

A RACE WITHOUT A FINISHING LINE

The car maker Toyota have been running a programme that will halve their fixed costs in seven years. One Matsushita plant at Utsonomiya produced 17,000 TVs with 2,000 people in 1968. Eighteen years later it was producing 1.84 million TVs with 1,120 employees – very crudely, producing 100 times more with half the people.[3]

Malaysia built a motor industry from scratch in ten years. A few years ago the discussion was about countries like Malaysia, Indonesia and Thailand being used by the Japanese as lower-cost centres for production. By the late 1990s Malaysia was finding that it was no longer a low-cost centre, and was looking to innovation and the high levels of knowledge and skills of its work-force to compete while moving production offshore to China or Vietnam. Soon enough the most successful of these countries will find their labour costs too high and push up-market to higher value goods, while yet cheaper centres of production emerge.

In the 1990s the world's car manufacturers turned their attention to China. This is not surprising. Even at the beginning of the 1990s there were more middle-class consumers in China than the whole of the population of the UK. A generation later, the Asian market for accounting, auditing, consultancy and other professional services will be as large as the world market was in 1996.

Microsoft became the most powerful company in the world in less than ten years. Yet Microsoft's continuing dominance depends on its ability to anticipate and ride the next big wave of change. Microsoft's own people admit that they misread the importance of the Internet. They were left with literally a few days to reposition Microsoft before it was eclipsed by other Internet providers. Thinking Machines Corporations was an impressive super-computer company which disappeared after ten years. The solution which it pioneered – parallel computer architectures – was no longer needed because of the speed with which others were able to piece together low-cost mass-produced personal computers.

Speed was the factor most often mentioned by chief executives in the Tomorrow's Company Inquiry. Jerry Kaplan founded a company called GO in 1987 to commercialise the use of a pen rather than a keyboard to operate a computer. At its peak, Kaplan's share of the company was worth $10m, but the speed with which Apple, Microsoft and IBM brought out their own tech-nology killed GO within five years. I remember talking to one of the founders of Intuit, another Silicon Valley company which produced 'Quicken' and which is a competitor of Microsoft, about the sense of urgency when it became known that Microsoft was working on a rival product. Founders, accountants, everyone, became involved in the day-and-night working to win the race with Microsoft and get the new product to the market in 90 days. (They succeeded.) Of course, all of those people saw that their jobs were on the line and many of them had a financial stake in the business. But money, fear of unemployment and the employment contract are not by themselves going to motivate people to turn such somersaults in the interest of their com-pany. My impression was that what motivated them was pride, a belief in and sense of ownership of their product and their capability, mutual loyalty, and the desire to beat one of the biggest names in the business.

WE ARE ALL COMPETITORS

You do not have to be an international company to feel the effects of international competition. The providers of bed and breakfast in Cornwall or the Isle of Wight may not have seen themselves as operating in a global market until a combination of cheap air travel, better information, and changing tastes made overseas holidays, and not the British seaside fortnight, the holiday norm. They might at least have imagined they were safe where their older customers were concerned. They were wrong. In 1996, SAGA, a specialist older people's holiday company, announced that it was abandoning the Isle of Wight and confirmed that more and more of their customers wanted to watch orang-utans in Borneo. A few years ago, they explained, they might take 800 people a week to the Cornwall seaside resort of Newquay. But there had been so few bookings that year that they had dropped it entirely from their brochure.

You do not have to be an international company to take advantage of the improved information. One Norfolk farmer was surfing the Net and discovered that USA wheat futures had tumbled. He sold his stock immediately, ahead of a fall in UK prices, and saved himself over £500.[4]

CAPITAL MARKETS – THE RISKS INCREASE

Capital too is becoming more footloose. Between 1982 and 1992 world financial assets more than tripled, from $11 trillion to over $35 trillion. Foreign investment quadrupled between the early 1980s and the mid-1990s. Daily transactions through the world's payments and settlements networks were around $10 billion in 1975, $1 trillion in 1985, and $6 trillion in 1995.[5] It might be thought that this would make investment a more impersonal business, and in one sense that is true of derivatives or currency trading. But think of the kind of judgements that investors in businesses are now having to make. Biotechnology companies are valued in £s billion although they have yet to show a product or a profit. The £45 billion available each year in the UK from savings, insurance policies and pension funds are increasingly being poured into businesses whose only assets are their knowledge, ideas and the apparent capability of their people to turn those ideas into commercial revenue. In one sense global investment is highly impersonal: people trading in currency or derivatives seem a long way removed from real businesses with real customers. It is true that many people who work in the City of London are not directly involved in putting capital into tangible businesses. Their function is to lubricate the system and help other people manage their risk whether that means insurance against or betting on the unexpected. Yet here too, we find that thanks to integration of technology and speed of transactions, the risks multiply. As a result, the integrity of the people handling this trade becomes more important than ever.

MAKING VALUES MORE IMPORTANT THAN EVER

The world derivatives trading business is an example. By 1994 the global derivatives business was worth $16 trillion.[6] Derivatives are an investment at one stage removed from reality – they enable you, for example, to bet on the future value of the Japanese Nikkei stock exchange index. They can be used to help companies manage the risk of holding particular stocks or currency. They can also be used for speculation. They introduce massive new risks for financial institutions. Nick Leeson, the rogue trader responsible for the collapse and subsequent take-over of Barings, was trading in Nikkei options. Leeson's was not the only case. Since then heads have rolled at NatWest Markets and in the investment world at Jardine Fleming and Morgan Grenfell.

Investigations into such cases tend to speak of 'failures of internal control'. The implication is that if only there were more inspectors or 'compliance officers' these abuses would not happen. Much less attention is paid to the promotion and reinforcement of a clear code of behaviour. These are fiercely competitive businesses where results are everything: unless people are given explicit guidelines which tell them where the limits are, it is inevitable that the most determined operators will convince themselves that it is an acceptable risk to cut corners and break rules.

Proper checks and controls are important. But companies which only rely upon these will be left behind by competitors who have learned how to compete without compromising trustworthy behaviour. Tomorrow's Company will find it impossible to manage the risk in these marketplaces by the methods which were described in the last chapter as being appropriate to the Firm ('We're all getting rich, right. It's very motivational.'). It will have clearly stated the values that it stands for. It will make such values a part of its appraisal processes. Its bonus payments will reflect not only how much profit a trader contributed, but how faithful he or she had been to the code of behaviour. It will promote adventurous and entrepreneurial people – but only if they share those values. And it will create an atmosphere in which the majority of honest employees quickly challenge behaviour that is inconsistent with those values.

WORK: THE DEMISE OF 9–5

Although the examples quoted here may come mostly from the UK, the pattern of work is changing everywhere. Work is becoming less full-time. The number of people in full-time jobs in the UK has declined below 60 per cent of the total 25.5 million people in employment.

Work is becoming less permanent and more flexible: by the mid 1990s, 80 per cent of companies in the UK employed temporary or part-time workers; 65 per cent contracted out; 60 per cent used flexible work patterns; 22 per cent used home-based workers; 11 per cent used teleworkers.

Across the globe there are already over 20 million teleworkers, and this number is forecast to increase to 200 million by 2016.[7] According to Charles Handy only one third of British workers now work a normal nine-to-five day.

The nature of work itself is becoming less manual. It is estimated that by the year 2000, the UK will have 10.5 million managers and technical employees, compared with only 7 million manual workers, reversing the situation of two decades ago. Between 1950 and the mid-1990s, 5 million manufacturing jobs disappeared in the UK. In the same period 8 million new jobs have been created in services.[8] Manufacturing is expected to account for only 10 per cent of employment within 30 years.[9]

Work is becoming more independent. The number of self-employed doubled in the UK between 1981 and 1995. Of men under the age of 45, 50 per cent would prefer to be self-employed.[10] Work is, too, becoming less male. The proportion of women in the UK workforce is expected to rise from 46 per cent in 1994 to 52 per cent by the year 2001.

Workforces everywhere are becoming more diverse. In Birmingham 20 per cent school leavers comes from an ethnic minority background. There is a high price to be paid by companies which mishandle this diversity. The share price of US oil giant Texaco fell 5 per cent after a racial discrimination court case, and the resultant outcry from civil rights groups.[11]

THE DEATH OF DEFERENCE

Businesses must expect to come to terms with customers and employees who are more demanding. But the new demands are of two types. People care about the quality of the product they are paying for, but they also care about the quality of life on the planet around them. Businesses must expect to be challenged and criticised on both fronts. Speaking a few months after Shell's volte-face over Brent Spar, C. A. J. Herkstroter, President of Royal Dutch Shell commented:

> The public reacted in a way that we did not expect . . . Finding ourselves in the middle of these tensions, we have discovered that we have to place a new emphasis on listening and exchanging views. To gain a greater understanding of the changes we have found that we have to communicate more, both internally and externally . . . We have found that the increased expectations have not been accompanied by an equivalent increase in trust. In fact just the opposite. There has been a loss of trust in companies, just as there has been a loss of trust in government, in traditional religious institutions and in international institutions . . . In industry we may have – 'unwittingly' – contributed to these developments through our failure to provide adequate information for an informed public debate. We were, perhaps, excessively focused on internal matters . . . [12]

What people want out of life is gradually changing. This change is far harder to capture than changes in our technology. Its effect on business is multiplied because it affects every relationship a business has, simultaneously changing the expectations of customers, employees, suppliers, investors and the community.

Between 1970 and 2000 half the population of Europe will have died and been replaced. The European Values Study has attempted to chart the change in attitudes that this is bringing about.[13] It summarised the change in two words – secularisation and individualism. The influence of all traditional forms of authority is shown to be declining right across Europe. People are not accepting their creed or their code from established authority: they are working it out for themselves. At the same time there is more emphasis on the identity of the individual, the potential of the individual and the rights of the individual. The growing numbers willing to contemplate self-employment are one by-product of this change in outlook.

The study found – among other generational shifts in attitude – more emphasis on quality of life, greater priority given to freedom over equality, more emphasis on individuals providing for themselves, a search for greater personal involvement in one's work, less confidence in democratic institutions, almost universal support across Europe for green and human rights movements, less tolerance of immigrants or of neighbours whose behaviour is considered unacceptable.

Generalisation is dangerous, but this would once again seem to imply that, in Europe at least, we are moving towards a world in which:

- Customers and communities will have a lower level of tolerance for companies whose business is based on behaviour they regard as unethical or environmentally harmful.

- Employees will be more demanding (and respond to opportunities to be self-directing). They will find paternalism less appealing. At the same time many of them will feel threatened by change, and therefore unwilling without exceptional motivation to sacrifice family and quality of life to the demands of an organisation which might well no longer need them.

- Many of the established rules and reference points are being swept away: leaving a leadership vacuum. Organisations which traditionally commanded respect and loyalty – such as the civil service or big companies – no longer do so. Organisations which manage, against these odds, to inspire loyalty will have a crucial advantage.

- It will become harder for businesses to disregard public sentiment in the hope that 'no-one will know'. People feel it is their business to know and the media will make sure that they do. Companies will have to assume that every decision they take may have to be explained in public.

The BSE crisis in the UK offers a telling example. A risk to consumers was identified. The public was given reassurances – but not the full picture. Inadequate precautions against the risk were taken by the beef industry. As a result, when the full picture emerged, there was a collapse in customer confidence, which devastated not only the British beef industry, but that of most other European countries. A well-informed and critical public of customers will react swiftly and devastatingly where a company or industry has forfeited its trust. Reputation and confidence are the fragile vessels which carry billions of pounds of shareholder value. The sums involved dwarf the small deviations in operational performance which investment analysts follow so closely.

RICH AND POOR: THE WIDENING GAP

Robert Shapiro, Chairman of Monsanto, interviewed in 1997, said:

> Today there are about 5.8 billion people in the world. About 1.5 billion of them live in conditions of abject poverty . . . world population will just about double by sometime around 2030. Without radical change, the kind of world implied by those numbers is unthinkable. It's a world of mass migrations and environmental degradation on an unimaginable scale. At best it means the preservation of a few islands of privilege and prosperity in a sea of misery and violence . . . Our nation's economic system evolved in an era of cheap energy and careless waste disposal, when limits seemed irrelevant. None of us today, whether we're managing a house or running a business, is living in a sustainable way. It's not a question of good guys and bad guys. There is no point in saying, 'If only those bad guys would go out of business, then the world would be fine.' The whole system has to change. There's a huge opportunity for reinvention. We are entering a time of perhaps unprecedented discontinuity. Businesses grounded in the old model will become obsolete and die.[14]

Thirty years ago threequarters of the world's wealth was created by just 20 per cent of its population. That figure has now increased to 85 per cent.[15]

In 1950, 32 per cent of the developed world lived in urban areas. The figure is expected to rise to 40 per cent by 2000 and 57 per cent by 2025. By 2000 it is expected that there will be 20 'mega-cities' with populations of more than 11 million people.

Migration will inevitably grow in importance. Since 3 billion people are going to be added to the world's population (a 40 per cent increase) in under two generations, and since 90 per cent of the additional population will come from outside the OECD countries, it is inevitable that people in poor countries which border richer countries will seek to move.

Pressures on public expenditure have become a major issue for governments. This has been compounded by the growing proportion of the population in most developed countries who are over 65. Hamish McRae tells us that in 1960 the UK was, with France, the oldest of the industrial nations, with 12 per cent of its population over 65. By 2020 that proportion will have risen to 16 per cent, with a much higher concentration of over 85's. But because of what is happening in other countries, the UK will by this stage, with the USA, have become the youngest of the industrial countries. At the same time

Japan will have become the oldest. McRae speculates about what this means for countries like the UK. He sees increases in the retirement age to 67 or 70, students working part-time while doing their degrees, more women working, with continuing strains on the stability of the traditional family unit, and more retraining to 'recycle' the redundant skills of 40-year-olds.[16]

The knowledge economy offers amazing opportunities to those entrepreneurial enough to grasp them. There is, in principle, nothing to stop any school sixth former becoming the next Bill Gates. There is no doubt that the gap in income and wealth between those who get on the escalator and those left behind will grow. In the UK, the Institute of Fiscal Studies reported that the richest 10 per cent of households had (in 1997) as much income as all households in the bottom 50 per cent and poverty had increased on all measures. By 1993 70 per cent of income in the bottom 50 per cent of households came from means tested benefits.[17]

Britain has been the most extreme example of inequality in the developed world, with a gap between the richest and poorest in 1996 as big as that of Nigeria. But, worldwide, the United Nations was warning in 1996 that the gap between rich and poor had doubled in fifteen years.[18]

This will have an impact on companies. Many of their revenues will be tied up with the fortunes of the large cities which may be experiencing the social strain caused by a combination of migration and employment insecurity. For example, a few years ago the Chairman of Dixons reported that his company was having to spend an extra £20m to combat the effects of ram raiding. In the Los Angeles riots it was noticeable that one retailer whose premises were least damaged was Macdonalds – a company that had invested heavily in education of its own people and in its surrounding neighbourhoods. In riots in Brixton, Marks and Spencer survived unscathed.

'Healthy high streets depend on healthy back streets.' For reasons that will be developed in Chapter 9, the time is coming when major businesses will be putting as much professional effort into reporting their impact on the health of those backstreets, as they are putting into measuring and reporting their environmental impacts.

ENVIRONMENT: WATER WARS AND WONDER WHEAT

The impact of growing population upon finite resources means, simultaneously, new strains and new opportunities. At worst, it could mean 'Water wars' as neighbouring nations fall out over their rights to dam or divert vital water supplies. At best, it could mean the growth of whole new industries built out of the need to improve nutritional efficiency of our food, or to enhance the ability of our crops to resist drought.

The USA – currently the largest economy in the world – has around 570 car owners per thousand of its population. China has one car owner per thousand, is already on the point of becoming a net importer of oil, and is likely to turn, increasingly, to the much dirtier option of burning coal. What happens to the atmosphere if car usage really takes off – if the Chinese consumer gets a taste for American consumerism? Something has to give. Imaginative car manufacturers are not assuming that the future lies in making more of the same kinds of car. The real prizes will go to those who offer transport solutions that combine consumer flexibility with environmental sustainability.

The additional greenhouse gases, global warming, melting of polar ice caps, and the changes in weather caused by deforestation, all have the capacity to add to the unpredictability of the world in which business is operating. There will be increasingly strident objections from people and pressure groups who want to see business and government do more, and faster, to protect the environment. The pressure of change will come in different forms: sometimes as regulation, sometimes as environmental breakdown, (like further oil shocks, or the shortages of water experienced across the UK in recent summers) sometimes as protest and sometimes as changed buying behaviour by customers.

CONCLUSION

The 'tomorrow' which is described in these pages is an age of technological abundance and environmental limits. It is an age offering the individual flexibility and opportunity, and yet one in which those who miss out will be left further behind than ever. It is an age in which technology can do almost anything, but in which governments and nation states may feel powerless. It is a time of powerful global capital, and yet also a time when the success of investments is determined by human factors like values, creativity, and motivation.

It is impossible to tell what all this may mean for the lives we lead and the kind of surroundings we live in. It is possible to paint different scenarios and to look at how the way we run companies in years to come will affect the outcome – an issue which is revisited in Chapter 9. One thing, however, does seem clear. This is not a time of clear boundaries or fixed compartments. Adaptability, sensitivity, and speed of reaction will be at a premium. Reputation and values will be vital. Organisations which are sensitive and tolerant of diversity will do better than those which are rigidly focused on any single objective or criterion of success. This is the approach to which *companies* aspire and which *firms* despise – a continuity of values and relationships. We cannot own the future: we will have to earn it.

5 THE TWO SURFACES OF SUCCESS

So what makes a business successful in the midst of such change? The answer is like Velcro®. A successful business will combine two surfaces with different textures. One surface has the gritty texture of competition and cost reduction – the hard surface –

- winning in unforgiving markets
- clarity, discipline and simplicity
- rigorous measurement against the world's best
- relentless cost focus
- restlessness and continuous change

The other has the pliant texture of collaboration and value creation – the soft surface –

- self-expression
- sensitivity to others
- being true to oneself
- interdependence, creativity, openness and tolerance of diversity needed to encourage creativity
- loyalty

To be successful tomorrow a business must be able to recognise the importance of each surface. It must resist the 'either/or' thinking that divides us into artificial camps like 'shareholder *vs.* stakeholder' or 'hard *vs.* soft' or 'tough *vs.* sensitive'.

It is the toughness of the competition that makes it important that your business is sensitive and has its own unique personality. How a company treats the opportunities and risks within every stakeholder relationship will determine its ability to generate value for shareholders. And, when it comes to measurement, the softest areas (creativity, empathy, teamwork) require the hardest work.

RELATIONSHIPS OVERLAP

The easiest way to think about the qualities businesses will need is to take them relationship by relationship. With one exception, this chapter is about the effect of the changes on the employee relationship, the customer relationship and so on. While this is a convenient breakdown, it is artificial, for the reasons which were explored in Chapter 2. Never ignore the overlap! The examples which accompany this chapter illustrate the success of companies in achieving outstanding levels of performance from people across the usual boundaries defining employees, customers, and suppliers.

Loyalty is a vital ingredient to success in any business relationship. For example, the evidence suggests that it costs five times more in service businesses to go out and recruit a customer than it does to retain the one you've got. In their 'Excellence Model' MORI have distinguished between customers whose loyalty can be described as 'commitment' and customers willing to be 'advocates' of a company or its products. MORI point out that in 1996 the UK electrical retailer Dixons were spending £62m on advertising while Marks and Spencer were spending next to nothing.[1] But then M&S customers do the company's advertising for them: whereas 1 per cent of Dixon's customers advocated their products to others, 15 per cent of Marks and Spencer's customers were advocates.

But loyalty works across the boundaries of relationships too. Frederick Reicheld's book *The Loyalty Effect* shows how businesses which manage to build employee loyalty do better at customer loyalty as well. Long-term employees are better at finding and recruiting customers, and retaining them.[2] Evidence from MORI gives support to the common sense proposition that employees who feel satisfied in their work are more likely to speak out in favour of the employer, and the employer's products. In MORI's survey 41 per cent of those who declared themselves very satisfied with their job would speak favourably about the company's product or service, without prompting, and another 40 per cent would speak favourably if asked. Conversely 31 per cent of those who were very dissatisfied would speak unfavourably about their company's product or service without being asked, and a further 13 per cent of the very dissatisfied would speak unfavourably if asked. A full 50 per cent of the very dissatisfied employees would speak unfavourably about the employer (as opposed to its products) without being asked.

Relationships never did exist in watertight compartments: our friends talk to our neighbours; our children talk to the postman; and we may even meet the bank manager at the school parents' evening. The same is true of business. You are what you show yourself to be in all your relationships. There is no way of controlling the overlap.

But if that was true in the past it will be even more true in the future. As individuals, we already have information coming at us from many directions – from friends, from gossip in the High Street, from telephone, e-mail and the Internet, from TV and radio news, quiz shows, satire and investigative journalism. Every year there is an increase in the variety of communication sources. Just as the newly arrived fax machine prevented oppressive regimes of Eastern Europe in the late 1980s from imposing news blackouts, so will e-mail and the Internet and electronic publishing reduce the ability of companies to present themselves to us in the superficial wrapping of their own choice, hard as they may try.

A company's reputation, or the reputation of its brands, will depend upon the sum total of its behaviours – the way it has treated complaining customers, cash-starved suppliers, anxious employees and concerned communities.

The degree of overlap will vary – and this will determine the speed with which a reputation is established or demolished. I once worked in a Kent paper mill, by far the largest employer in the town. Most of our products ended up on printing presses or box-making plants hundreds of miles away – so our behaviour towards our customers did not overlap very much with our behaviour to our employees. But it was impossible for me to walk down the local High Street without bumping into a dozen of the people I worked with. The mill's relationship with its employees and its neighbourhood was almost synonymous, and if a manager made a mistake or the chairman had a private meeting with a Union representative it would all be discussed by off-duty employees and their families in the street the next day.

Large retail businesses have no choice. They have to be transparent and consistent in their dealings with shareholders, employees, customers and suppliers. They have to choose how they propose to hold dialogues with stakeholder groups. They cannot expect to treat shareholders as a watertight compartment.

The company whose communication with these groups is not rooted in consistent values will expose itself to lack of credibility, loss of confidence and damage to its reputation.

There are a few businesses left in which the overlap is small. There are businesses which depend on one-off transactions, and businesses whose only concern is offering a convenient commodity for a competitive price – say a bureau d'exchange in a small airport to which most of us will never return. There are businesses where the investors, customers and employees barely meet. But the world is getting rapidly smaller, and there are many entrepreneurs waiting to pounce: in the jungle of global competition, businesses which thought they were purely transactional are easy prey to rivals who can offer customers a reason for loyalty. It is only a matter of time before that impersonal bureau d'exchange is confronted by a more imaginative competitor whose staff are multilingual and offer tourist information as well as currency, or by an Internet provider who enables the traveller to order currency from home or en-route and have it delivered to him or her personally on arrival.

The communications revolution does more than destroy the boundaries between relationships. It also reduces the time delay. In the paper mill what the employee found out on the night shift might be spreading round the High Street by the following lunchtime. The information revolution presents a company like British Airways (BA) with the same problem on a global scale. Customers using the Internet can find out about improvements to services, reorganisations, or changes in the Air Miles arrangements the minute they are announced – well ahead of some of the people employed to answer their queries. If BA are not equally sophisticated in bringing these changes to the attention of their 50,000 employees, their front-line people may be in the uncomfortable position of hearing the news first from their customers. So BA have to become a highly efficient broadcasting company just to stay ahead with employee communication!

THE COMMUNITY AND TOMORROW'S COMPANY

Community is an imprecise term. It can cover everything from global warming to a stone thrown at the warehouse window. The community can mean the planet, the country in which you operate, the local neighbourhood, and the whole sum of individual people, near and far, on whom the business has an impact. In the past, community may have been viewed by many businesses as an afterthought. This is now changing. The community relationship is central to every business. Within that vague umbrella term lie many threats, and countless opportunities. Intelligent, aware businesses actively manage their community relationship so that they minimise risks and make the most of opportunities. However small your business, it is worth understanding how all those changes 'out there' can suddenly enhance, or undermine, your freedom to trade

The community and risk management

Environmental policy has become and will remain one of the most important areas of community policy. A few years ago, I was with a group of American investors and managers, listening to a presentation by Polaroid which described the systematic way in which they had set about the cleaning up of pollution in Boston Sound ahead of the deadlines set by the regulatory authorities. One or two of the investors present were amazed: how, they asked, could Polaroid possibly justify spending shareholders' money on doing something over and above the legally required minimum?

This precipitated a lively debate about the significance for shareholders of the company's licence to operate – which is introduced in this chapter and described in more detail in the next. Two years later I was interested to read that Polaroid was one of the highest scoring companies in a survey by ICF Kaiser. The study looked at 327 of the largest US public companies, and concluded that the introduction of environmental programmes, and their communication to the investment community, reduced share price volatility and could make their shareholders up to 5 per cent better off as a result.

> Adopting a more environmentally proactive posture has, in addition to any direct environmental and cost-reduction benefits, a significant and favourable impact on the firm's perceived riskiness to investors, and accordingly its cost of equity capital and value in the marketplace.[3]

One of the hazards of trading across Europe is the tendency of farmers and fishermen in France to blockade roads or cut off the Channel ports. Several times a year such action catches thousands of British lorries in a huge bottleneck and prevents haulage businesses and those whose goods they deliver from functioning normally. Often the businesses involved seem mesmerised by these events, which are of course largely beyond their control. That does not explain why, hours or even days after such troubles start, lorries are still seen making for the Channel ports and getting stuck in giant queues all over Kent.

These events are not unpredictable: it would be perfectly possible for the businesses involved to monitor the negotiations whose breakdown leads to such action. The best information, though, would be available to those businesses which took the trouble to treat the Channel ports as their community. Imagine how useful it would be as a major European distributor if you were on first-name terms with all the decision makers from the police, through the port administrators, to the representatives of the groups most likely to use these tactics. Such relationships could mean advance information, and the chance to implement a contingency plan which maintained the flow of supplies. They might develop into reciprocal support arrangements so that lorry drivers from France who were isolated in the UK, and those stuck in France, received food, accommodation and other help. Community relationships are central to the way businesses will manage both their risks and their opportunities in the future.

A community relationship has a multiplier effect on all the other impacts of a business. 'A good community programme is good for our reputation – and a good reputation is good for business' is how Sir Iain Vallance, the Chairman of British Telecommunications put it. A strong reputation, earned in this way, is like a deposit at the bank of public goodwill. When Marks and Spencer successfully resisted charges made by a TV programme that they were using overseas suppliers who exploited child labour, there were very few among their customers who lost faith in the company. Imagine how much damage such adverse publicity would have had upon a company that was already in trouble with the British public, such as Yorkshire Water or SouthWest Trains. When Shell had an oil spillage in the River Mersey a few years ago, the judge in the subsequent case actually said that he was imposing a minimal fine because of the company's impressive record of corporate citizenship. And when Grand Met was in the battle to take over Pillsbury in the USA, it was able to turn the tables on its opponents because it had a more impressive record of community involvement than the management of the company it wanted to take over.

Opportunity from community

A good reputation can protect a company from its mistakes: equally, a good reputation serves to reinforce the strength of its brand. Research which analysed customer reaction to 82 brands across six countries including the UK, North America, and China, showed that Campbells, the soup manufacturer, enjoyed the strongest customer loyalty. Brand loyalty measurement goes deeper than simply assessing market share: it probes the underlying feelings customers have towards the brand, which influence their loyalty and future propensity to buy new products of the same brand. And the research showed that alongside the obvious factors like the ability of the product to meet the customers' needs, an important factor was 'deeply-held confidence in the company as much as its product'.[4]

Research also shows that more and more companies are now saying that they are involved in community investment and corporate giving because it builds employee commitment and customer loyalty.[5]

The community relationship can never be disentangled from the employee or the customer relationship. Some of the strongest returns on community investment have been in the area of employee development. Arlington Securities is a leading company in the provision of business parks. Its Company Secretary is Sarah Lyne. She started with the company as a PA/secretary. Every year Arlington run a Community Challenge for the under-26s, to raise money for charity. She became organiser of the community challenge, and that is where her own learning and development took off.

This in turn reinforces the significance of the MORI research already quoted: if you have a group of employees who are 'very satisfied' in their work, four out of ten of them will, without any prompting, recommend their employer's products. But if you have a group who are dissatisfied with their job, only four in 100 will make such a spontaneous recommendation, and a third of them will spontaneously talk *unfavourably* about the company's products. Satisfied employees are better ambassadors for the business and its products and reputation. Dissatisfied employees will actively discourage people from buying its products. Satisfied employees are satisfied because they feel valued, have development opportunities, and feel that they will be treated fairly, whatever may happen to the company. The company's involvement in the community adds to the variety of those development opportunities, and to the opportunity people have to be ambassadors for the company and its products.

But effective corporate citizenship is not simply about transmitting the company's messages. It also helps to sensitise the organisation to be more receptive to messages from outside. It pays any business, of any size, to keep its eyes open and its ear to the ground. It pays to know who can stop you trading. It also pays to be connected to the subtle shifts in attitude when they first emerge as fringe fashion or student protest, so that you are ready to exploit the opportunities that present themselves when fringe becomes mainstream. In Chapter 6, the B&Q example is quoted: here a business which set out to improve its environmental responsibility in the sourcing of wood found significant marketing benefits because it enabled the business to identify with a new and important generation of customers.

There is plenty of research evidence to reinforce the point that community means opportunity through openness. Take innovation. Recent MIT research concluded that eight out of ten ideas that have led to 'Breakthrough' products or services originate from routine discussions during coffee breaks, a chance encounter between colleagues in the corridor, or even being at home with the family.[6] A well-thought out community policy simply multiplies the number of chance encounters that could lead to innovation. A few years ago I heard how the Hackney Schools Curriculum and Industry Project gave children from primary school the opportunity to design a window for production in stained glass by a local company. Alongside the satisfaction and learning for the pupils of seeing their designs realised, and the gain for the school of having the window installed, the company learned to adapt their approach to the use of different materials and design inputs. And, in the process, commented the company, some of their staff had to learn a new flexibility of approach.

Here is how the Chairman of Monsanto, Robert Shapiro, expressed the link between 'community' and the future of his business:

> Years ago, we would approach strategic planning by considering 'the environment' – that is the economic, technological and competitive context of the business, and we'd forecast how it would change over the planning horizon. Forecasting usually means extrapolating recent trends. So we almost never predicted the critical discontinuities in which the real money was made and lost – the changes that really determined the future of the business. But every consumer marketer knows that you can rely on demographics. Many market discontinuities were predictable – and future ones can still be predicted – based on observable, incontrovertible facts such as baby booms and busts, life expectancies and immigration patterns.
>
> Sustainable development is one of those discontinuities . . . You can see it coming arithmetically. Sustainability involves the laws of nature – physics, chemistry, and biology – and the recognition that the world is a closed system. What we thought was boundless has limits, and we're beginning to hit them. That's going to change a lot of today's fundamental economics, it's going to change prices, and it's going to change what's socially acceptable.[7]

So corporate community involvement is many things. It is a way of keeping your ear to the ground; to be open to unexpected influence; to be ready to learn from the chance encounters that involvement in education, environment, or the arts may offer. But it doesn't stop there. It is the opportunity to make the soil into which you will be sowing more fertile - for example by co-operating with relevant schools or colleges to generate a flow of talented job applicants. And finally it is the chance to make a contribution to human betterment for the uncomplicated reason that you have the opportunity to do so. As was argued in Chapter 2, without an element of such idealism the edge is taken off the whole programme. Parents, teachers and pupils will not feel so inclined to co-operate in an education business partnership with business partners who are only 'in it for what they can get out': the most successful partnerships, inevitably, are those which are genuinely win-win.

The community relationship used to be simpler. A philanthropic entrepreneur ran a chocolate factory or a steel mill. He had a sense of *noblesse oblige*. In return for taking a lot out of the community he felt it right to put a lot back. He would support local good causes. There was a sense of 'casting your bread upon the waters' – a belief that by doing the right thing the company would secure important goodwill. But impact would rarely be measured.

The changing view of community

'We used to chuck charity over the wall,' said one IBM UK manager about the company's policies in the early 1980s. Then, under a new Chief Executive, Anthony Cleaver (who, as Sir Anthony Cleaver, was later to chair the RSA Tomorrow's Company Inquiry), a more rigorous view emerged. In 1987 Cleaver expressed the view, in a lecture to the RSA, that the company depended for its prosperity on five major groups – shareholders, employees, customers, business associates and the wider community. And he actually used the term taken up six years later by the Tomorrow's Company Inquiry: 'We require a licence to operate from society as a whole.'[8]

'We had to stop people talking about charity', said one IBM manager. IBM staff claim to have invented the phrase 'community investment'.

Writing in 1994, IBM's Corporate Affairs Director, Sarah Portway, exemplifies the Velcro organisation applying rigorous discipline to the practice of 'soft' principles like mutuality and social responsibility.

> When we speak of a return on our investment we are placing an internal discipline on ourselves to identify, at the outset, . . . what objectives we are seeking, and to . . . measure the extent to which we gained the return that we set out to achieve.

Portway explains that IBM set three major objectives for its overall community investment programme:

1. To contribute towards a favourable social and economic environment for IBM's business.
2. To be recognised by selected target audiences as a leader in corporate community involvement.
3. To promote the morale and motivation of employees.[9]

And a 1993 study of IBM's community policies by the Joseph Rowntree foundation showed the benefits which voluntary organisations felt they had received from this businesslike approach. They liked being challenged to think clearly about their mission and their methods. They gave particularly high scores to a specially designed Creative Management Skills course which IBM ran for their managers.[10]

Cynics will comment that the publication of this report coincided with a declaration by IBM of record losses. IBM will reply that the sophistication of its links with community organisations, and of Skillbase, the company it set up in 1990 to help its retirees to obtain consultancy work, proved crucial in helping many experienced staff made redundant on generous terms to find a new role, whether paid or voluntary. Indeed, between 1992 and 1994, the organisation shrank from 18,000 to 12,000 without any compulsory redundancy, a tribute to the adaptability of IBMers and the transferability of their skills.

Table 5.1 Total 1996 GrandMet community spend based on the London Benchmarking Group's template for reporting community involvement*

Activity	Abbreviated Definitions	INPUT Programme Costs in £000
1 Charity	**Responding to appeals from the community**	
Donations	Cash given to national and local appeals	1,513
Social Sponsorship	Support to causes or events with name recognition, but the activity is not part of a company's marketing strategy, it is to benefit the charity	2,025
Secondments & Consultancy	The service of employees provided by the company	not quantified
In-kind Giving	Gifts of product and equipment or use of company premises	554
Employee Matched Giving	Matching the cash gifts of employees to charities of their choosing	799
Employee Volunteering	Cash granted to support employees in community activities of their own choosing (GrandMet does not quantify 'time off')	17
Facilitating Giving	Companies using their relationships with customers and consumers to collect for good causes	53
Sub Total		**5,021**
2 Social Investment	**Sustained involvement in issues important to the company**	
Grants	Cash invested in programmes to achieve specific agreed goals	4,350
Secondments & Consultancy	The loaning of employees to community organisations on a full-time, long-term or part-time basis to achieve mutually agreed goals	335
In-kind Contributions	Gifts such as product and equipment that are central to the success of a focused programme	2,586
In-house Training	Work experience and training opportunities for young people or representatives from the public and non-profit sectors	not quantified
Supplier Development	Additional costs associated with creating jobs for disadvantaged groups as suppliers to the company	2
Sub Total		**7,273**
3 Management Costs		
Charity & Social Investment Costs	The salaries, benefits, overheads and operating budgets of the company's community support activities	582
4 Commercial Initiatives	**Partnerships to promote and protect commercial interests**	
Sponsorship	The amount of a sponsorship given to a charity or non-profit organisation	282
Cause-Related Marketing	The funds raised for a charity and other funds or assistance given	353
Strategic Contributions	Gifts to universities and trade related organisations whose activities support the success of the business, its employees and retirees	3,232
Staff Training	Community assignments as part of company's training plan	not quantified
Sub Total		3,687
Total		**16,743**

* This table is taken from the Grand Metropolitan Report on Corporate Citizenship and is also reproduced in its original context in Appendix 3.

The concept of the Licence to Operate was taken up and developed by the Tomorrow's Company Inquiry. In Chapter 6 it is described in more detail as part of the inclusive approach. Meanwhile leading businesses have been progressing to a sophisticated level of measurement of its impacts as the recent report from the London Benchmarking Group (LBG) illustrates. This has distinguished four levels of community involvement.

1. Philanthropic giving.
2. Long-term community involvement, for long-term benefit – for example, an education–business partnership.
3. Community involvement with a clear marketing benefit – for example, a programme to sponsor computers for schools.
4. Core business contribution – for example, jobs created directly or indirectly, local taxes paid and so on.

The LBG has also distinguished clearly between the mere reporting of spend-inputs – and the actual impact or outputs from the involvement.[11] This provides a clear framework for the measurement and reporting not simply of the financial or in-kind inputs made by a company, but also the outputs – the benefits enjoyed by the community.

In the most soft and imprecise of business relationships, the hard discipline of measurement and reporting is making rapid progress, as the example from Grand Metropolitan on page 63 shows.

All a company's relationships with human beings converge in the community relationship. Tomorrow's Company will only win in unforgiving markets if it combines the two surfaces of the 'Velcro' organisation. It needs a hard edge of focus on performance, measurement, and cost. It needs to be relentless in pursuing and overtaking the best in the world. And at the same time it needs the human edge of self-expression, understanding and loyalty to its own beliefs if it is to be an organisation worth relating to.

This is not the way we have been trained to think about community relationships. The businesses which are reaping the fullest advantage in their community relationships are those which have cleared their minds of 'either/or' thinking. But there remain some who are still stuck on the old arguments, and missing opportunities because their boards insist 'We have no right to spend the shareholders' money on the community.' This is the self-limiting language of those who think *firm* not *company* (see Chapter 2). The costs of such thinking will ultimately be borne by their shareholders.

CUSTOMERS IN TOMORROW'S COMPANY

There was a jigsaw puzzle of which our four-year-old son was very fond. Imagine his sorrow when he discovered a vital piece chewed by the dog. My wife wrote to the manufacturer (a company called Willis). Was it possible, she asked, to obtain a replacement for the missing piece which the dog had damaged? By return of post, we received not the missing piece, but an entire puzzle. And with it was supplied a bonio (a bone-shaped biscuit) for the dog to chew. That's what I call 'exceeding expectations'.

Customers in tomorrow's company will be more demanding and less forgiving. They will not have time to stand in queues. They do not want to be treated like a number on a list. They want to be treated like individuals. Technology makes its possible to treat them like individuals, and winning companies will find cost effective ways of doing so. One of the best ways of doing so is to ask them what they want, and then to work, not simply to fulfil but to exceed their expectations, as Birmingham Midshires Building Society (BMBS) have done.

Treating customers as individuals starts with understanding them as individuals. And that means breaking out beyond some of the standard categories into which we allocate them. For example, we must expect people buying consumer products to be more critical about where, how and at what wages they were produced. These concerns will be met alongside the steadily rising expectations of price, quality and value.

Empathy – putting yourself in the other person's shoes – has always been a sound principle for success in any relationships. It is surprising how rarely we put it into practice. Adams is a British retailer of children's clothing. They took the logical but unusual step of finding out what children wanted from shopping – and this is what they found, according to Chris Onslow, visual merchandising director.[12] 'They didn't want to go shopping for clothes at all. If they did go shopping, they certainly didn't want to try clothes on.'

Parents needed them to go, and try things on. So Adams designed a fitting room that looks like a playroom. And they started re-interviewing staff and recruiting others from outside to make sure they would 'live and breathe' the brand. The effect was an immediate 20 per cent increase in transactions.

In the 1980s, the big-spending 'DINKIES' (double-income no kids) were often characterised as the 'I want it now' generation. But new forms of retailing are enabling all customers to be far more choosy and efficient about how and when they buy things. Kevin Gavaghan, one of the brains behind the invention of First Direct, has called this the 'out-of-place/out-of-hours' society. You order your groceries and do not have to move from your arm chair until they are delivered. You read a review of a book in a Saturday paper in the early hours of Sunday morning and order it by e-mail or telephone.

There is another side to treating people as individuals. Have you ever noticed how some friendships can just drift along, and then be revived after a really good row? Loyalty is a spectrum. At one end of the spectrum is fidelity, a commitment 'for better or worse'. At the other end is inertia: you still have the customer's business, but it is more out of habit than any positive decision. Outstandingly successful companies have discovered an interesting paradox: the best way to earn a customer's lifelong loyalty seems to be to make a complete mess, and then do an outstanding job in recovering the situation. Perhaps it is the admission of error that makes you human, and the extra effort you put into recovering the situation that puts the individual first. British Airways reported that customers who never complain are far more

Textbox 5.1 Birmingham Midshires Building Society

Mike Jackson was appointed as chief executive of Birmingham Midshires Building Society (BMBS) in 1990. At that time BMBS was suffering dramatic turnover in customers and its strategy for turnaround was based upon the very simple recognition that it had not simply to meet but to exceed customer expectations. In 1990, says Mike Jackson:

> We weren't even meeting the expectations of most of our 860,000 customers, 2,200 of whom work for the society. We started with the basics – asking our members and customers what they wanted, and then developing a plan of action for everyone who could help us deliver that.

Developing and communicating the company's values was a critical part of the process. BMBS set out its values in a ten-point statement of values which it called the 'Pillars of Excellence'. BMBS then developed measures of success which reinforced those values, thus rewarding the type of behaviour that it wanted to see at every level in the organisation. All this was communicated through 17 road shows, three different booklets, newspapers, workshops, and other events.

But as BMBS mastered these objectives, and reflected on customer satisfaction scores, something interesting was noticed. While the number of customers satisfied had steadily grown from 88 per cent to 97 per cent in four years there was not an equivalent improvement in the number of customers delighted. And in-depth research told BMBS why. It wasn't enough to give people exactly what they were asking for. To exceed customers' expectations, the Society had to change its own behaviour. It was the manner of doing business as much as technical achievements which mattered. Hence a new initiative, entitled the 'Exceeding Customers' Expectations Programme'. The aim of the programme was 'to exceed our customers' expectations by always treating them better than they expect'.

In the course of this programme BMBS developed its seven service values programme, based upon an analysis of 8,500 customer comments. Research indicated that customers wanted BMBS to be helpful, friendly, willing, attentive, obliging, smiling, polite, professional and cheerful. Customers also wanted staff to provide an efficient, prompt service, always to keep customers informed, respond to individual needs, take ownership of problems and earn customers' trust. Or, to paraphrase the results of the survey, BMBS found that exceeding the expectations of its customers had everything to do with treating them as individuals rather than account numbers, and building lifetime relationships with them.

So the Society set out on a fresh programme of preparing and coaching its people to live up to customer expectations. The Society rewarded staff caught doing something right – giving thank-you cards and on the spot cash awards, and celebrating particularly impressive examples of unprompted helpfulness or imagination with nominations for their Magic Moments award, which recognises service excellence.

There is clear evidence that all this effort has paid off. Post-tax profits rose from £6.3m in 1991 to £45.2 million in 1996. In 1996 96 per cent of customers were satisfied or more than satisfied with the Society's service; the number stating that they were highly satisfied grew to 75 per cent (from 50 per cent in 1990) while the number saying that BMBS had 'exceeded expectations' increased from 15.5 per cent in 1994 (when the measure was introduced) to 17 per cent in 1996. According to MORI evidence 89 per cent of those working for BMBS now understand the Society's goals, 77 per cent would recommend it as a place to work, and 80 per cent were proud to work for it.

But this is a never-ending journey, as Mike Jackson admits. 'Expectations grow alongside our ability to anticipate and satisfy our customer demands. Once you start on the road, you can't stop or go back. Just as you think you've got it right it changes in front of your eyes.' To ensure BMBS keeps exceeding customer expectations, the home telephone numbers of the Society's chairman, chief executive and top management are published in the Annual Report and Mike Jackson has his home number on all customer satisfaction questionnaires that are sent out.

likely to be fickle than customers who do complain. BMBS found that customers who complain bitterly, but have their complaint resolved effectively, become among the most delighted. It appears that customers who are emotionally involved with the business – even when that means complaining – are more likely to stay loyal! Earlier evidence published under the title, 'The profitable art of service recovery' confirms this: the authors found a higher repurchase rate in the case of customers who had complained and had their complaints resolved.[13]

THE PEOPLE WHO WORK IN TOMORROW'S COMPANY

It is therefore too simple to say that tomorrow's companies will need to cultivate loyal customers, or loyal people. What tomorrow's companies will need will be living relationships with their customers and employees, the kind of relationships in which there is constant feedback. Through this feedback the organisation is intensely aware, like the different players in an orchestra listening to each other as they play. This in turn means that problems are identified early, and dealt with, more often than not by the person who identified them, who has the authority, know-how and the confidence to do so.

The same paradoxes will dominate the company's relationships with employees. In Tomorrow's Company, there is one sense in which everybody is a manager. A manager is a person who has discretion over a resource. Information is the key resource for the future, and every employee or associate who has contact with a customer, supplier or business partner is in touch with relevant information and needs to act on it. The cost-effective way to deal with that information is locally, and immediately, without reference to a manual. The most effectively organised companies are those whose people deeply understand how the business makes its money (hard) and what its values are (soft) so that they learn to assess the risks they may be taking in agreeing or not agreeing to a customer's request. In Chapter 2, Blue Circle was used as an illustration of the way business leaders use hard shareholder value tools to make the case for change right through their business. On the next page Peter Mutter, Blue Circle's Personnel Director describes the company's changing approach to people.

Already, many new systems, standards, and disciplines are available for companies which are determined to prepare for tomorrow. But there is a world of difference between the followers and the leaders. The followers are those who plod along doing business as usual: then, every so often, they hear of a new initiative which other people seem to have taken up. Eventually they are made to feel that this new initiative is something that they cannot do without: consultants are called in, project managers are appointed, and the new initiative is duly announced. It is greeted, all too often, with cynicism, suspicion and what has come to be known as 'initiative fatigue'.

Leaders behave very differently. They have a clear idea of the personality of the business. They have a gleam in their eye about the business they want to grow in the future. A new initiative or project is not an end in itself: they

Textbox 5.2   Blue Circle's inclusive approach to people

1. **PROVIDING A SENSE OF PURPOSE:** employees demand to know, more than ever before, what the company is trying to achieve and what role they can play.

2. **EQUIPPING EMPLOYEES WITH THE SKILLS THEY NEED:** many organisations have not conducted the necessary skills analysis and are frequently held back from multi-skilling by traditional demarcation restrictions.

3. **DEVELOPING AN ENVIRONMENT IN WHICH PEOPLE HAVE FREEDOM TO ACT:** often expressed as empowerment and equally often misunderstood. It is not an environment in which management give up their responsibility, but rather one in which employees have a clear understanding of their role and in which there is a mutual trust so that when the unexpected happens they feel confident to react and take the appropriate action. It is of course a major culture shift, one which requires managers to adapt from being controllers to being coaches, and to experience the satisfaction which can be derived from seeing people become more confident and taking responsibility for solving their own problems.

4. **DEVELOPING A PAYMENT SYSTEM WHICH REWARDS THE BEHAVIOUR WHICH WE SEEK:** many of our traditional systems, which include overtime and premium payments, do nothing more than encourage employees to extend their work to more 'profitable' hours. The challenge is to devise simple systems – e.g. for example 'Annualised hours ' – which meet the needs of the business.

5. **REMOVAL OF INSECURITY:** as companies have repeatedly downsized, the feeling that by helping to improve productivity and efficiency employees are cutting their own throats is beginning to emerge. We have to find ways to counteract these feelings through redeployment, retraining, and, where appropriate, through security agreements of the type recently pioneered by United Distillers and Blue Circle.[14]

clearly explain to all who work in the business how it fits into the realisation of their vision.

In the UK, 'Investors in People' is the standard that has been pioneered; increasingly, it is being used widely around the world. While some may be adopting it because they feel they have to, the best companies are using it as part of a wider plan to equip business for the changing world in which they expect to compete. This is how Peter Mutter describes the part that an initiative like Investors in People plays in helping Blue Circle to realise their vision of Tomorrow's Company.

The place of Investors in People in Blue Circle

To a certain extent the "Investors in People" standard has given the company recognition for policies and practices which have been in development for a number of years. However all of our businesses have found the standard an excellent framework against which to audit their activities and a public demonstration of the company's high standards.

Investors in People means setting and communicating business goals and developing people to meet these goals. It uses employee involvement to gain the commitment of people to improve business performance.

The award focuses on an organisation's business planning, staff appraisal, communications, training policies and induction procedures. Assessment for the award is based on what is actually happening in the workplace now, and the attitude of management and staff to their own development.

Many (in Blue Circle) commented that the journey to reaching the standard was as rewarding as achieving it . . . The business results of investing in people speak for themselves: improved efficiency, increased sales, reduction in lost-time accidents. Employees have also benefited: they are more skilled and flexible and know that there is a future commitment to continue to provide further opportunities for development.

As we moved into the 1990s it became clear that for some time we had been in a 'battening down the hatches' mode. While it was still important to improve the return on our existing businesses, it was obvious that if we were to continue to succeed we needed to move from a position of consolidation to one of moderate growth. Given the financial strength of the company it was doubtful that money would be the restraining issue. It was more likely to be the human resource aspect of our business which would hold us back.

The Blue Circle Way – our vision for senior management development – recognises that to secure our long-term future we continually have to develop new skills to remain competitive; insists that development be appropriate to the business needs; and demands that every effort be made to provide roles in which individuals feel challenged and rewarded.

Working with Ashridge, we talked to senior managers throughout the group to identify what managerial skills would be required over the next 5–10 years to enable us to grow the business as planned.

We agreed a series of competencies which included strategic thinking, commercial awareness, leadership, financial astuteness and decision making . . . surprisingly perhaps, one of the most successful aspects was the introduction of 360 degree feedback. Each manager was requested to provide their boss, peers, and subordinates with a questionnaire, to assess how they fared in each of the competencies. In earlier discussions it transpired that often it was the relationship with their boss that managers considered to be the most productive. What they discovered through "360 degree" was that they learnt so much more about themselves from their subordinates. Even though some of what our senior managers learnt may not have been to their credit . . . there was no defensiveness.

An indication of how the culture of Blue Circle has changed in recent years became evident when participants were asked to identify the characteristics of the 'old Blue Circle man' as opposed to the 'new Blue Circle man'.

'The old Blue Circle man' was described as inward looking and averse to risk; feeling powerless and afraid to rock the boat; shifting blame elsewhere; afraid of customers and technology and production focused . . . Our senior managers' ideal of the 'new Blue Circle man' included a manager who looks to the future, manages risk, and takes ownership of problems. Someone who feels involved and takes charge of their own development and that of the team, and is customer-, product- and service-focused.[15]

Changing people's attitudes from *firm* to *company* is often not easy. There is a lot of pain and contradiction to endure if you are trying to change old habits. Many people who read this account of the direction of change will say, 'It may be like that in a few companies. But for us nothing has really changed. We are still pawns in the game. We still feel manipulated as we always have. It's just that people have trendier words like "re-engineering" or "downsizing" to describe it all'.

A book by Alan Cave shows people are right to be cynical. In the 1980s and 1990s it did become easier – in the UK as in many countries – to fire people. Cave's research is summarised in two parallel trends. For example, there is more promotion on individual merit . . . and yet at the same time a tendency not to promote the 'awkward individual'. Local managers have more discretion, and sometimes they treat their people arbitrarily and badly because they do not have the skills or the values to make proper use of their new freedom. Many businesses have freed themselves of old union ties . . . and failed to fill the gap with more trusting relationships.[16]

The new 'managers'

In other words, many organisations have cleared some of the ground to create Tomorrow's Company, but they lack either the values, the understanding, or the skill to make the most of that opportunity. It will take time to develop enough of the 'coaches' to take over from the 'controllers'. One important characteristic for tomorrow's company is the ability to see the organisation as an adaptive organism, and not as a machine. Perhaps this is one of those areas where we can learn from Japan, as did the Association of Manufacturing Excellence, USA, in its quarterly magazine *Target*.

> Mayekawa was established in 1923 as a small, family-run, company in the Fukagawa district of Tokyo. It supplies heavy refrigeration systems to industry. In its early days it had no formal structure. It had skilled craftsmen: everyone played the part that was needed. In the 1960s it grew fast, and became bureaucratic. Its new President was fascinated by the idea of the company as a living organism, and tried to apply the idea to the company as it grappled with the familiar problem of how to be both large and flexible. In 1970 Mayekawa broke into a series of divisions and flattened the organisation. In 1983 it began separating operating divisions into autonomous and legally independent cells (*doppos*) – the smallest possible unit that could serve a customer. The smallest were 10 or 20 people. The largest – production units – were 100. Each industry it serves has different needs. The *doppos* study the industry and its needs, and those of its customers. Their approach requires total empathy with the customer.
>
> The essence of manufacturing quality results is to learn to think like a customer, and like a customer's customer, and then create or adapt a system that fully satisfies real needs, whether or not anyone can clearly articulate them. Just satisfying the first tier customer falls short of Mayekawa's ideal.[17]

Mayekawa's marketing principles are

1. Break big markets into small ones.
2. Transform old commodity markets into new, exciting ones.
3. Give specific solutions, not variants of general solutions.
4. Find creative solutions, not prosaic ones.

Each *doppo* sees itself as a 'mutation' of Mayekawa. It avoids the problems of isolation faced by smaller enterprises by associating with other *doppos* in forums called blocks which share technology development and other support services. These blocks link them to the *Zensha* – the overall company. The *Zensha* takes care of group public relations, and capital provision. But its main function is 'the care and feeding of the Mayekawa culture'. The common features of Mayekawa are a core technology (hard) and shared respect for the primary values (soft).[18]

A growing proportion of those who work inside Tomorrow's Company will see themselves as managers. Taking the UK as an example, we are told that approximately 630,000 new managers will be needed by 2001. Alongside them there will be a steady growth every year in the demand for professionals.[19] The skilled trades will reduce by 0.5 per cent every year. There is a curious paradox here around the meaning of the word 'manager'. For those jobs which have not been made obsolete by technology, the chances are that the job-holder will enjoy the kind of discretion traditionally associated with a manager. But it is unlikely that many will enjoy that title. Companies will only make it to tomorrow if they cut out many of the 'middle management' (control) jobs previously seen as managerial. The surviving leaders who have responsibility for the effectiveness of others, will be expected to achieve previously unthinkable results through the contribution of all the 'non-managers' around them. 'Manager' will no longer have an *exclusive* definition. A manager will cease to be someone who has the title on the office door and feels free to hide – behind both the title and the door! We can expect to see a new fluidity in the roles, and the space which we all occupy in organisations. Territory and title will decline in importance; life for more and more of us will seem like a succession of projects.

For reasons described in the previous chapter, there will be too many crises and adjustments for us to want uncomplaining and uncritical employees. Companies will want to work together throughout the supply chain to generate an atmosphere in which decisions are challenged. They will need people who ask 'Why?'. Unipart have actually taken the technique of the 'Five Whys' and made it part of their continuous improvement process. (See the Unipart case study on page 77.) In Tomorrow's Company the managing director creates an atmosphere where anyone can challenge a decision or publicly criticise the company at a meeting – provided that the person expressing the criticism is prepared to accept some responsibility for helping to put things right. In yesterday's company the criticisms only start when people reach the safety of the bar.

In Barings, we are told, many millions might have been saved if there had been an atmosphere in which people with unpopular messages were encouraged to come forward.

> The hole [in the balance sheet] was first discovered in April 1993, when it stood at £10m, by Tony Hawes, Treasurer of Baring Securities . . . Throughout 1994, Hawes became increasingly worried by the lack of detail given by Leeson when he made his daily claims for cash collateral . . . By September 1994 the gap in the balance sheet had reached £144m. Hawes was conscientious and hardworking, but he was neither self-confident nor assertive. He was worried about the lack of detail in Leeson's demands for cash, but he lacked the authority to insist on a halt to Leeson's trading until his queries were sorted out. Ron Baker, head of derivatives trading, had much more clout. If Hawes' worries proved groundless, he feared that Baker would be merciless.[20]

In Barings the man who had the best insight into the growing threat did not feel powerful enough to use it: he feared being humiliated by somebody worse-informed but more senior. In Tomorrow's Company it is unlikely to be the people with, traditionally, the most power who have the most important information. In all too many businesses, but particularly in the City of London and other financial centres, results are everything, and the temptation to cut corners can become too high. This need not be true. I remember talking years ago to a highly successful Asian banker operating in the USA whose bonus scheme balanced financial performance, with employee feedback, and customer and community impact. What Tomorrow's Company needs is an atmosphere in which results matter, but in which everyone is equal before the values of the business. In Tomorrow's Company results (hard) are only acceptable if they are produced the right way (soft). Anyone would feel able to identify and challenge those who were not practising what the business preached. Think of the company more like an organism, less like a machine. In an organism every cell matters, and the cells that determine whether the organism changes are those closest to the world outside.

Philip Condit, chief executive of Boeing, has said: 'In any company you can find some areas where amazing things are happening and other areas where they aren't. And invariably that traces back to the willingness of leaders to listen to people'. Condit, who sometimes employs a poet to stimulate his senior managers to be more alert and creative, emphasises the importance of diversity – another of the 'soft' qualities needed to achieve 'hard results'. 'I am a great believer in diversity in the broadest possible way – people with different experiences, different backgrounds, different training – because I think it makes the product better.'[21]

Condit's belief would be fully tested by the attempt to merge Boeing with Mcdonnell Douglas. A merger is one of those business activities which start with unemotional considerations like price, market share, and shareholder approval. But they ultimately stand or fall by the way leaders handle emotional issues. Most mergers burn large holes in the pockets of the acquiring company. That is hardly surprising when you start to think what it feels like to be acquired. One moment you are being told by your employer that you are one of its most prized assets. The next you hear that you are being taken over by your greatest rival. Tens of thousands of jobs are to go . . . many of those who remain will have to move to another part of the country. Even if you eventually keep your job there is uncertainty. The fact of the takeover must feel like a vote of no confidence in what you have just been doing.

The story of successful mergers is the story of managing the hard and soft surfaces of success. It means moving fast enough to eliminate unnecessary uncertainty, but slow enough to affirm the existing contribution of people. It means listening and learning from them even as you introduce new methods and disciplines. It means urgently bringing two cultures together while showing respect for both. It means creating a new organisation that people will believe in. Without sensitivity and respect, the promised payback will melt away, because it has to be delivered by people. Perhaps there should be more corporate poets brought in alongside the acquisition lawyers, the merchant bankers and PR experts!

The same is true of partnering and alliances, an increasingly important part of corporate life. By the mid-1990s the top 1,000 American firms drew nearly 6 per cent of their revenues from alliances, a four-fold increase since 1987.[22] This was only the beginning.

But the evidence was that most alliances were failing and the reasons for failure, according to a Conference Board Europe study, were in the implementation, not the planning. The issues were about leadership, cultural incompatibility and rapid changes in the business environment.[23] Or, as Rosabeth Moss Kanter put it, North American companies had a 'narrow opportunistic view of relationships, evaluating them strictly in financial terms or seeing them as barely tolerable alternatives to outright acquisition'.[24]

 Tomorrow's Company will be very demanding in its all its relationships. But its toughness will be a two-way toughness, the kind that equips you to receive tough messages as well as hand them out. It will be ruthless in its insistence on measurement, but at the same time sensitive to all forms of feedback, however received. It needs to know what its people are doing, but also insist that they supervise themselves and hold each other to its stated values. It needs to be highly combative in the marketplace while being highly collaborative with its business partners, suppliers and customers – some of whom will be the same people it is competing with!

It needs to manage its people costs, but it will be more successful where bold leaders find a 'win-win' basis for doing so. Consider this example from *Lean Thinking*, by Womack and Jones:

> When the new cell system was proposed, many of the production workers were baffled or dismayed. As Bob Underwood, one of the most skilled workers on the floor noted, 'We were used to a system in which each of us had a set of hard earned skills – welding, machining, and, in my case the ability to adjust nonconforming parts so they would fit. We were used to doing our own work at our own pace in our own department. As long as we met our daily production quota we were left alone.'

> When the conversion week was completed and the new cell was ready to go, it didn't work. All kinds of problems, long submerged in Lantech's massive

73

inventories and closely held work practice, suddenly emerged . . . The wide-spread feeling was that Ron Hicks was pushing a novel concept that would never work at Lantech.

At this point Jose Zabanah, the production manager, played the key role. 'I was so fed up with our failures and so taken with the logic of the new system that I threw my heart into it. I called a meeting of the workforce and announced that I would stay all night and all weekend to work hands-on on fixes to the problems we were encountering with the new cell, but that I would not spend one second discussing the possibility of going back to the old batch-and-queue system.'

The consequences for performance were truly staggering. Although Lantech's headcount stayed constant at three hundred the number of machines shipped doubled between 1991 and 1995 . . . To speed this remarkable transition, Pat Lanson made two promises to his workforce. First he promised no-one would be let go because of the lean conversion . . . A breakthrough team was created from freed up workers . . . to plan the improvement of other activities . . . After every improvement the best (not the worst) workers in the revamped process are transferred to the *kaizen* [continuous improvement] team, making clear this is a promotion, not a punishment. The steady growth in the output of the newly competitive Lantech has meant that within a short period these workers have been needed again for production work.

At the same time Lancaster reviewed Lantech's wage policy and adjusted the base wage upwards (by over 20 per cent). As Ron Hicks noted, 'We had been running unskilled workers through like McDonalds, with a sharp premium for our small core of skilled workers. It quickly became apparent that all workers in the new Lantech would be skilled workers, but with a very different type of skill. So we had to pay all of them a better wage. As a result turnover fell quickly to just about zero.' Note that because each machine was being made with about one half of the formerly needed hours of human effort, a 25 per cent wage increase is easily affordable.[25]

WHERE SUPPLIERS AND EMPLOYEES OVERLAP

In future it will become harder to tell where employees stop and suppliers begin. In 1995 Rank Xerox switched a significant portion of its production from Japan to its Mitcheldean, Gloucestershire factory in the UK.

Mr Jerry Lane, director of the Mitcheldean plant, said productivity had risen by about 40 per cent since 1990. 'We have done more with less, building quality into our culture,' he said '. . . All workers . . . share in a scheme that hands out bonuses – expected to total £500,000 this year.' But who are the workers and who are the suppliers?

A feature of the Mitcheldean factory is Rank Xerox's innovative contract with Manpower, the employment services group, under which it tops up its need for staff by using short-term contract production operators on Manpower's payroll. About a quarter of Mitcheldean's 2,000 workers are employed in this way - giving the company greater leeway in changing its workforce to fit shifts in demand.[26]

Here is a classic example of the end of compartments and the importance of overlap in tomorrow's company. Manpower train and motivate their own staff. To be loyal to Manpower they must be loyal to Rank Xerox. And to work alongside Rank Xerox employees they must show ultimate loyalty to the end-user of the desktop copiers which Mitcheldean is supplying to markets in Russia, Africa and the Middle East.

The transfer of loyalty can work the other way. The F.I. Group was started by Steve Shirley to enable women like her to work from home as computer programmers. It now undertakes major computing services work on behalf of large companies. A few years ago it took over the IT services department of Whitbread. Imagine what your feelings might be if a blue-chip employer like Whitbread told you that your job with them was finished, and you were now working for F.I. as a supplier to your old employer. F.I have a long tradition of employee share ownership. They made their new employees feel part of F.I. Within a year two thirds of them had decided to become employee shareholders.

Both employees and suppliers are contributing to the creation of value for the end-user. In the course of that value creation, no company is an island. And while loyalty to your company and its values is important, it cannot be allowed to become exclusive.

SUPPLIERS IN TOMORROW'S COMPANY

The British motor industry has undergone a lean revolution. Component suppliers are now accustomed to just-in-time deliveries, and learning first-hand from *kaizen* consultants flown in from Japan. Until cars leave the production line, the process is lean and fast. But then it enters a time warp. Finished vehicles can sit for three months before being moved to the dealer or final customer.

In Tomorrow's Company, no enterprise can afford to be an island. Efficiency will be measured right through the supply chain. In the cut-throat world of supermarkets, 85 per cent of the cost of a can of cola are outside of the retailer's control. To stay in business in the future it will not be enough to be a highly-organised company with highly-motivated people, if you depend upon an inferior supply chain. The boundaries will be redefined. 'Customer' will refer not to the immediate recipient of goods and services, but to the ultimate user whom the supply chain is serving. 'Orders' will be the end-user's orders known simultaneously to the whole supply chain through a shared information system, not a time-wasting paper chase repeated across every conventional business boundary. 'Competitiveness' will only be achieved through a collaborative search between business partners for lower costs and higher standards of service, exploiting electronically shared information throughout the supply chain.

A recent survey by A. T. Kearney showed that European companies expected their order cycle time to drop by an average 57 per cent to ten days.[27] AT&T's chip manufacturing outfit, Lucent, has committed itself to achieving a 48-hour delivery – worldwide – for its chips. It knows it can only do so by choosing a business partner which knows as much about distribution as it knows about manufacturing. AT&T knows it will fail unless DHL, its chosen partner, has comprehensive access to its management information. Currently less than 25 per cent of companies have EDI (Electronic Data Interchange). The next generation of business development is about breaking down walls and building up shared information (hard) and the shared commitment to the customer (soft) on which future effectiveness in the supply chain depends.

For significant further savings to be made in highly-competitive industries, barriers between supplier and customer have to be broken down, and businesses have to become closer in understanding as well as in the exchange of data. In a successful partnership, each partner has its own priorities. But it has learnt, like a mature adult, that you get the most out of a relationship only if you put a lot in, and that success starts with understanding the needs of the other partner. Reciprocity – always being alert to how you can help your partner – is a feature of the Velcro-like ability to combine toughness and empathy. It does not undermine the traditional hard-headedness required to focus on the company's self-interest. It reinforces it. It helps everyone focus on achieving better service at lower cost for the end-user – the one who keeps everyone else in business. Without a partnership mentality, people will not be able to obtain those benefits. Without a rigorous analysis of the value chain, the opportunities will not be found. *Both/and* rather than *either/or* thinking is required.

CONCLUSION: RELATIONSHIPS ARE NOT A COST

In the next chapter, the subject is the inclusive approach and how to begin to apply it to your business. Chapter 7 then deals directly with the vexed question of corporate governance, and Chapter 8 with the relationship with investors. Throughout the argument runs the consistent contention that companies will do better if they behave and think as living organisms which are made up of relationships, and not as machines processing bundles of contracts. Facing outward is a better foundation for success than looking inward. Sharpening your human sensitivity in all your relationships will be essential if you are to meet the hard tests of competition. Those organisations which learn to create generosity and trust in their relationships will add more value for shareholders than those which are stuck on narrow self-interest. The last chapter revisits these issues on a longer timescale, from the point of view, not of any one business, but of the business community as a whole.

Textbox 5.3   Unipart and Ten(d) to Zero

Unipart stepped out on its own in 1987 as part of a management buy-out. It hit the headlines when it offered 12 per cent of shareholding in the company to employees and it made the offer in a four hour theatrical presentation using dancers and musical numbers to explain the concept of shareholding to its new employees. It was ground-breaking stuff years before the government ever thought of telling Sid. The shareholding principle was an early step in the development of Unipart's big idea, that not only should employees be shareholders but they also should be recognised as *stakeholders*. Together with customers, investors, suppliers and the communities in which Unipart does business, they complete the ever-widening circle of people and organisations that have a long-term, shared destiny with Unipart.

What's stakeholding got to do with business? Neill outlines the scenario in his course. 'In the global markets of today and the even more fiercely global markets of tomorrow, Western industry now has to compete with the highly efficient, highly technological emerging companies of the tiger economies. In these new economics, people pay themselves between one tenth and one hundredth of what we earn in the West. Competition is about cost, and quality and service. We just can't compete on effort alone.'

Western economists, says Neill, gave us bad thinking. They said costs bottom out. For a customer to win, a supplier has to lose. But Neill takes a lesson out of the book of his Japanese customers. He says that costs come down forever through implementing continuous improvement and fast-paced, breakthrough learning from the best in the world. Motivating and involving employees and suppliers and customers to work together to bring costs down throughout the supply chain is a survival plan for the millennium.

The stakeholding notion grew from tough business decisions about changing the very way people think about their relationships in the supply chain. 'Ten years ago,' says Neill, 'we introduced a programme through which we could work with our suppliers to take out costs and waste, and deliver productivity improvements right down the supply chain. When our own people learned about the programme they said 'great, this is another stick we can beat the suppliers with'. That was the first place we had to start working. We needed to change our own thinking.'

Neill defines two business models, he calls them model A and model B. Model A is a short term, traditional, adversarial relationship; the once-a-year price negotiation, a knock down, drag out fight between supplier and customer. 'That model,' says Neill, 'ends up in a train smash.' Suppliers facing ever decreasing margins, cut corners, reduce quality and ultimately go out of business. It's the short termism driven by, in some cases, the city's desperation for short-term 'shareholder value'. Then there's model B, the long-term, shared destiny approach. It's the very core of stakeholding: the company's commitment to consider those people with a stake in the company's future, in all its decisions. The company takes a strategic view about these stakeholder relationships.

Long term, shared destiny, shared vision, these warm and fuzzy management terms are still very trendy. But they are not just trendy in Unipart, they underline every one of the company's actions and its consistent strategy for growth.

Neill says change doesn't take place in the boardroom, it takes place on the shop floor. A man who stands in front of a machine every day has a far more interesting and rewarding outlook on his job when he's trusted to be able to make improvements and changes that reduce cost, increase productivity and improve customer satisfaction. That's the business strategy for stakeholding. 'It's a win-win scenario,' says Neill, 'and it's not about cosy relationships.'

In Unipart, cosy relationships are replaced by the Ten(d) to Zero (TTZ) supplier relationship programme. It is a programme in which teams from Unipart and teams from suppliers work on improvement projects for mutual benefits. People in TTZ take a quick step out of their comfort zone. Cross-company teams are formed to make improvements that ultimately take costs out of the relationship. They study the ten key elements of the relationship between customer and supplier.

Textbox 5.3   Unipart and Ten(d) to Zero (continued)

'Non-value added activity accounts for a staggering 60 per cent of human endeavour,' says Neill. 'A further 35 per cent is defined as necessary but non-value added. If we can work on taking out even a small proportion of that waste, we can reduce costs, increase value and retain profitability.' The Ten(d) to Zero scoring system is universal and takes the politics out of supplier assessment. It motivates suppliers to learn from each other. At Unipart, they say that for every one point advancement in the TTZ measurement scale, Unipart saves £0.5 million.

The mathematics are simple, the work's a lot harder. Implementing high value, waste cutting technology like EDI – Electronic Data Interchange – between customer and supplier is a complex project. But the big hurdle isn't the technology or the process management, it's the trust. Trust doesn't come naturally in business.

Ten(d) to Zero delivers a common framework, a common measurement, a common language, and a common understanding of the problem for both companies taking part in the programme. They work together across a wide range of business problems and issues focusing very carefully on those to which they can make improvements. Then the team from the supplier and the team from the customer become one team and the barriers drop. The secrets are no longer secrets, and the business problems that seemed unsolvable are unravelled with painstaking care and solid business thinking.

Far from being a cosy relationship, Ten(d) to Zero requires tough business thinking and hard decision-making, but the benefits have been seen time and time again. Take the story Neill tells of one supplier who came to Unipart with a 25 per cent price increase. 'The increase,' says Neill, was unacceptable, 'it meant we would never be competitive in supplying product to our customer.' The supplier had a fair business case because the raw materials simply went up in price. Unipart teams worked with the supplier sharing know-how and helping to make large productivity gains. The ultimate conclusion was a 4 per cent price reduction on the original price. The benefits to the supplier were new techniques for improving productivity, cutting out cost in the process, and achieving a sustainable margin. Those benefits were not just passed on to Unipart, but to all the supplier's other customers as well. The stakeholding relationship in this and hundreds of other stories brought direct benefit to the bottom line: and there is nothing warm and cosy about that.

(Reproduced by kind permission of the Unipart Group of Companies.)

6 THE INCLUSIVE APPROACH

Business, as the last chapter made clear, is about relationships with people. The qualities that make companies successful in their relationships are little different from the qualities that make individuals successful in theirs.

Listen carefully to the people you know. Some are anxious to fit in and be accepted by the crowd. Some prefer to be themselves. Some are trustworthy and utterly consistent; others will vary their tune and their tone to suit the person they are speaking to. Some are rigid and routine-bound – others thrive on the unexpected and are always willing to learn.

The same is true of companies. Some are proud of their character and their individuality. Others want to be part of the crowd. Some change their message to suit the tastes of their audience. Others know what they stand for and stick to it in front of any audience. Some can adapt fast; some cannot. Some inspire loyalty, others indifference.

DEFINING THE INCLUSIVE APPROACH

The inclusive approach is quite simple. It is an outlook which helps people in a company or any organisation to define what it stands for, what its goals are, who and what could help or hinder the achievement of those goals. That, in turn, enables the people managing the organisation to judge what to encourage and what to measure, in order to achieve the best results.

This inclusive approach, then, requires clear leadership and ever-improving measurement in all relationships. It is demanding: each company has to work out for itself what it has to do to succeed and what needs to be measured. This means taking the trouble to understand the needs of each business partner and then meeting these needs in a balanced way.

There are five essential stages in the inclusive approach:

1. Define purpose and values.
2. Review key relationships.
3. Define success.
4. Measure and communicate performance.
5. Reward and reinforce.

It sounds obvious. Yet, as the research for the *Tomorrow's Company* Inquiry clearly established, most companies miss getting the obvious things right, assuming that everyone knows what they stand for and what their goals are. They assume, too, that they know where they should be spending their time and that what they have always measured is the key to future success. They think they are being 'focused' and 'disciplined' in concentrating on the bottom line when, in fact, by this excessive reliance on inherited success measures, they are missing opportunities and increasing risk. Indeed, what many would regard as 'keeping your eye on the ball' of financial measurement, turns out to be dangerously near 'taking your eye off the ball'. Of the 11 companies who topped the profitability league tables between 1979 and 1989, four had collapsed before the end of 1990! [1]

Table 6.1 Britain's Top Companies				
YEAR	COMPANY[1]	MARKET VALUE (£)	RETURN ON INVESTMENT (ROI)[2]	SUBSEQUENT PERFORMANCE
1979	MFI	57	50	Collapsed
1980	Lasmo	134	97	Still profitable
1981	Bejam	79	34	Acquired
1982	Racal	940	36	Still profitable
1983	Polly Peck	128	79	Collapsed
1984	Atlantic Computers	151	36	Collapsed
1985	BSR	197	32	Still profitable
1986	Jaguar	819	60	Acquired
1987	Amstrad	987	89	Still profitable
1988	Body Shop	225	89	Still profitable
1989	Blue Arrow	653	135	Collapsed
	[1] Where a company has been top for more than one year, the next best company has been chosen in the subsequent year, e.g. Polly Peck was rated top in 1983, 84 and 85			
	[2] Pre-tax profit as a percent of invested capital			
Source: Peter Doyle				

DEFINE PURPOSE AND VALUES

The inclusive approach was developed by the 25 companies who participated in the *Tomorrow's Company* Inquiry. The Inquiry started with purpose and values, for several commonsense reasons.

First, the Inquiry team members were all business leaders who were convinced that leadership was crucial. You cannot have effective leadership without a clear purpose and a clear sense of values. You cannot inspire people to go the extra mile without clear goals and clear sense that this is a business worth committing to.

Second, they came to the conclusion that no company could be trusted and therefore effective in an age of instant communications unless it was consistent in the messages which it communicated through all its relationships. Since you cannot know whether a particular audience contains shareholders and suppliers as well as employees, it is foolish as well as dishonest to develop different messages. The most familiar example is that of those chief executives who tell investors about the labour 'costs' they have cut, while they continue to tell their staff that 'You are our greatest asset'. Such double standards are responsible for the cynicism that so many employees feel about the companies they work for.

Thirdly, they could see the way that power had moved. They recognised that organisations could not be likened to machines, where those 'in charge' press buttons and pull levers. The company is an organism. Every cell in that organism has a life of its own, and is affected by the world around it. What matters is the central nervous system that connects all the cells, without undermining their freedom. 'Your priority is to give us managers a decent policy manual', was how one of the site's most experienced managers welcomed me to my personnel job in GEC in the mid-1970s. He wouldn't be saying that today. In tomorrow's company, information and intelligence are vital resources which everyone contributes. The reputation of most businesses depends on the thousands of judgements which all those people make.

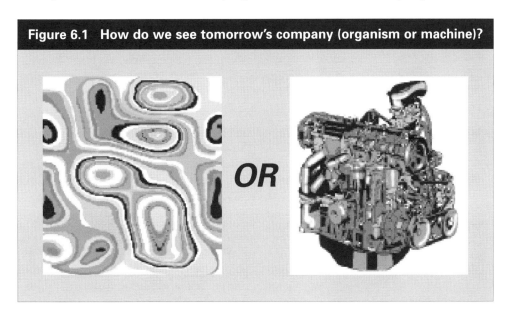

Figure 6.1 How do we see tomorrow's company (organism or machine)?

The most successful companies may have a manual and they do have clear policies. But they know that the real test will come from challenges that no manual could anticipate – like the celebrated receptionist in the Amsterdam Marriott Hotel advertisements, who drove the customer to the airport in her own car when the taxi failed to arrive. The consumer businesses that are famous for exceptional service such as in this example have instilled some general principles, and reinforced them by continuous example, practice, and feedback. Outstanding customer service cannot be learned by rote: people have to aspire to give that service and be equipped with a framework of trust and guidance that enables them to do so in their own way. It's the same with bringing up your own children – in the end they are more influenced by your behaviour than your lectures!

In a fast-moving business everyone has to be trusted to take some risks. The way to manage the risk which this devolution brings is to use influence first and control as a back-stop. The best defence against major fraud or mis-judgement is to have a clear set of values which people are asked to follow, and to lead by example in rewarding adherence to those values and penalising deviation from them. If everyone is aware of the values governing how the business should be conducted, then it is less likely that one rogue trader will go undetected when the rules and formal controls get broken. If, on the other hand, everyone is made to feel that it is only results which count, people will hesitate before challenging the methods by which results are being obtained. With control by manual, you are at the mercy of the foresight of the author and the oversight of the supervisor. With an organisation-wide sense of purpose and values, to which all employees have a genuine commitment, every single employee has the potential to help defend the organisation against the rogue trader. Just as 'good house-keeping' in a factory is a stronger guarantor of health and safety than any list of do's and don'ts, however exhaustive, so a clear ethical tradition is the best guarantor against fraud and corporate disaster.

In Chapter 3 the conclusions of the Collins and Porras study, *Built to Last* were summarised (see page 36). This study of the USA's most visionary enduring companies is particularly instructive on the subject of purpose and values: out of the 18 companies which Porras and Collins singled out for their visionary qualities and their enduring financial performance, 17 were distinguished from their comparator companies by having a 'core ideology' – the authors' shorthand for statements that embody values and purpose. Values are defined as the organisations's essential and enduring tenets. Purpose is defined as the organisation's fundamental

---

Textbox 6.1 Defining and communicating purpose and values

TOMORROW'S COMPANY is clear about its distinctive purpose and values.

YESTERDAY'S COMPANIES do not see the need to have a distinctive purpose or values, and often confuse purpose with measures of success (for example upper quartile earnings per share) or are content to leave the definition of their purpose to habit or to others.

TOMORROW'S COMPANY defines its purpose in a way that inspires whole-hearted commitment to achieving goals which are shared by all those who are important to the company's success.

YESTERDAY'S COMPANIES define their purpose in a way that excludes some of the people who are important to their success.

TOMORROW'S COMPANY communicates its purpose and values in a consistent manner and acts in a manner consistent with its statements, enabling it to give a clear lead in all relationships.

YESTERDAY'S COMPANIES have different messages for different audiences (for example to providers of capital, employees are labour costs to be cut, while to the employees 'you are our greatest asset').

Textbox 6.2   The organisational values of Hewlett-Packard

HP's values are a set of deeply held beliefs that govern and guide our behaviour in meeting our objectives and in dealing with each other, our customers, shareholders and others.

We have trust and respect for individuals. We approach each situation with the belief that people want to do a good job and will do so, given the proper tools and support. We attract highly capable, diverse, innovative people and recognize their efforts and contributions to the company. HP people contribute enthusiastically and share in the success that they make possible.

We focus on a high level of achievement and contribution. Our customers expect HP products and services to be of the highest quality and to provide lasting value. To achieve this, all HP people – but especially managers – must be leaders who generate enthusiasm and respond with extra effort to meet customer needs. Techniques and management practices which are effective today may be outdated in the future. For us to remain at the forefront in all our activities, people should always be looking for new and better ways to do their work.

We conduct our business with uncompromising integrity. We expect HP people to be open and honest in their dealings to earn the trust and loyalty of others. People at every level are expected to adhere to the highest standards of business ethics and must understand that anything less is totally unacceptable. As a practical matter, ethical conduct cannot be assured by written HP policies and codes; it must be an integral part of the organization, a deeply ingrained tradition that is passed from one generation of employees to another.

We achieve our common objectives through teamwork. We recognize that it is only through effective cooperation within and among organizations that we can achieve our goals. Our commitment is to work as a worldwide team to fulfil the expectations of our customers, shareholders and others who depend upon us. The benefits and obligations of doing business are shared among all HP people.

We encourage flexibility and innovation. We create an inclusive work environment which supports the diversity of our people and stimulates innovation. We strive for overall objectives which are clearly stated and agreed upon, and allow people flexibility in working toward goals in ways that they help determine are best for the organization. HP people should personally accept responsibility and be encouraged to upgrade their skills and capabilities through ongoing training and development. This is especially important in a technical business where the rate of progress is rapid and where people are expected to adapt to change.

'HP's objectives and values have guided us very well for more than half a century. We believe they are what will give us firm footing in this rapidly changing environment.' Lew Platt, 1994

reason for existence beyond just making money . . . not to be confused with specific goals or business strategies.

Like the fundamental ideals of a great nation church, school, or any other enduring institution, core ideology in a visionary company is a set of basic precepts that plant a fixed stake in the ground: 'This is who we are; this is what we stand for; this is what we're all about' . . . Core ideology is so fundamental to the institution that it changes seldom, if ever.[2]

There are two messages from the *Built to Last* findings. First, the importance of having something that you stand for; second, the superior performance of companies which stand for more than mere financial returns. Collins and Porras, again:

> Contrary to business school doctrine, we did not find 'maximising shareholder wealth' or 'profit maximisation' as the dominant driving force or primary objective through the history of most of the visionary companies. They have tended to pursue a cluster of objectives, of which making money is only one,

---

Textbox 6.3   The corporate objectives of Hewlett-Packard

HP's corporate objectives are guiding principles for all decision-making by HP people.

Profit. To achieve sufficient profit to finance our company growth and to provide the resources we need to achieve our other corporate objectives.

Customers. To provide products and services of the highest quality and the greatest possible value to our customers, thereby gaining and holding their respect and loyalty.

Fields of interest. To participate in those fields of interest that build upon our technology and customer base, that offer opportunities for continuing growth, and that enable us to make a needed and profitable contribution.

Growth. To let our growth be limited only by our profits and our ability to develop and produce innovative products that satisfy real customer needs.

Our people. To help HP people share in the company's success which they make possible; to provide employment security based on performance; to ensure them a safe and pleasant work environment; to recognize their individual achievements; to value their diversity; and to help them gain a sense of satisfaction and accomplishment from their work.

Management. To foster initiative and creativity by allowing the individual freedom of action in attaining well-defined objectives.

Citizenship. To honor our obligations to society by being an economic, intellectual and social asset to each nation and each community in which we operate.

'Improvement is accomplished by better methods, better techniques, better machinery and equipment and by people continually finding better ways to do their jobs and to work together as a team. I will never see the day when there is not yet room for improvement.' Dave Packard, 1957

and not necessarily the primary one . . . Indeed for many of the visionary companies, business has historically been more than an economic activity, more than just a way to make money. Through the history of most of the visionary companies we saw a core ideology that transcended purely economic considerations and – this is the key point – they have had core ideology to a greater degree than the comparison companies in our study.[3]

A detailed pair-by-pair analysis in the study showed that the visionary companies have generally been more ideologically driven and less purely profit-driven than the comparison companies in 17 out of 18 pairs. Profit maximisation does not rule, but the visionary companies pursue their aims profitably. They do both. The key point, then, is for companies who want to be successful to decide what they stand for and what they want to achieve. At one extreme, the answer may in practice be that what they stand for is making their owner or their directors rich. Provided that they are quite willing to advertise that objective to customers, employees and government alike, that is a perfectly legitimate objective, albeit one that is likely in practice to be self-defeating. At the other, like the successful American company Servicemaster, the goal may be to 'honor God in all we do'. For most companies the choice will fall somewhere between these extremes!

What the Inquiry team found remarkable is how few companies still realised that they had a choice. If we put together a group of leading business people and chief executives to discuss our findings several would start by saying, 'There's some good stuff here but then you go and spoil it by introducing all this stakeholder stuff. Why can't you make it clear that the purpose of every business has to be to maximise value for its owners?'

Behind their comments one can sense a real fear: they feel answerable to the shareholders, particularly the large institutions; they know that they are judged on their effectiveness in delivering a result. Failure to live up to investor expectations can result in their removal from office within a year to 18 months. How can they risk taking their eye off the ball of shareholder value?

I was reminded of a Latin teacher under whom I suffered for five years. We pupils were so frightened of him – all of us – that we could never manage to say anything useful when he asked us to stand up and translate our set text. The answer, I realise now, is that a state of fear is not the foundation to build anything of lasting value. And, at one of our consultations a chief executive who, minutes before had been criticising the report for straying from the true path of shareholder value, suddenly added the comment 'Mind you, whatever I may think about shareholder value, I find it's not a very effective tool for motivating my managers or my people'.

And so, he made it clear, he talked one purpose for his board and his fund managers, and quite another for his people. You could call it the 'multiple choice' approach to purpose and values. Normally the phrase 'multiple choice' refers to exam questions. Many UK business people have developed the habit of giving multiple choice answers to questions of business purpose. The director of one UK public company, whom I asked 'What is your company for?' answered revealingly: 'If you were a journalist or a politician, I would say that the purpose of this business is to provide goods and service that improve the quality of life of our customers. But, as I know you, I would say that in fact our real objective is to enrich our shareholders!'

The multiple choice answer is the coward's way out of a dilemma that the authors of *Built to Last* describe as the 'Tyranny of the or'. Too many people believe that you cannot simultaneously make money and make a social contribution – that purpose has to be about one or the other. But they are wrong. A company does not have to choose between saying 'We're here to make our shareholders rich', and saying, 'We're here to produce high quality goods', and even, 'We're here to have fun'. The most successful companies, Porras and Collins noted, are quite prepared to describe their purpose and values in terms that mix up the achievement of wider ideals with the achievement of narrower economic goals. But, having got the mix clear, they then stick to it and instil it in all their people. They do not vary their answer according to the audience.

It is interesting to reflect on the pressures that have driven intelligent and decent chief executives into a corner from which double talk is the only way out. In Chapter 2 we looked at the gap between real human behaviour and the caricature used by economists. It was suggested that in Western business we have allowed ourselves to be seduced into an over-simplification about human motivation. The error is quite simply to assume that in business money talks and nothing else counts, and to forget about the qualities of empathy, imagination and leadership that are essential to the creation of wealth. Modern companies are built on the belief that business is about three-dimensional man, with a richer range of motivations and desires than rational economic man.

> In 1950 George Merck II expressed Merck's 'core ideology' in 'both...and' terms.

> 'I want to express the principles which we in our company have endeavoured to live up to... here is how it sums up: we try to remember that medicine is for the patient. We try never to forget that medicine is for the people. It is not for the profits. The profits follow, and if we have remembered that, they have never failed to appear. The better we have remembered it, the larger they have been.'

> The contrast with Pfizer is stark. This is John McKeen, President of Pfizer during the same period:

> 'So far as is humanly possible, we aim to get profit out of everything we do. ...Idle money (is) ..a sinfully non-productive asset....I would rather make 5% on $10m of sales than 1% on $300m (in ethical drugs).'[4]

To achieve anything practical it is necessary to keep things simple. 'Business is about making money' is an over-simplification that contains an important truth: the making of a profit is indeed a necessary condition for the continuance of business. But it does not tell us all we need to know. Even if we accept that business is about making money, and not products, or wealth, or livelihoods, we still have to remember that business is an activity which involves human beings in working together. It has to take account of the whole mixture of motivations that drive human beings – what Maslow calls our 'hierarchy of needs'.

Textbox 6.4   Guiding principles at Toyota

1. BE A COMPANY OF THE WORLD
2. SERVE THE GREATER GOOD OF PEOPLE EVERYWHERE BY DEVOTING ATTENTION TO SAFETY AND THE ENVIRONMENT
3. ASSERT LEADERSHIP IN TECHNOLOGY AND CUSTOMER SATISFACTION
4. BECOME A CONTRIBUTING MEMBER OF THE COMMUNITY IN EVERY NATION
5. FOSTER A CORPORATE CULTURE THAT HONOURS INDIVIDUALITY WHILE PROMOTING TEAMWORK
6. PURSUE CONTINUING GROWTH THROUGH EFFICIENT GLOBAL MANAGEMENT
7. BUILD LASTING RELATIONSHIPS WITH BUSINESS PARTNERS AROUND THE WORLD

People who allow others to tell them what they think are not usually respected. Companies are no different. A company's statement of its purpose should be a reflection of its personality. It should have character and uniqueness. It should not be drafted with a view to avoiding any upset to shareholders: the evidence from Chapter 3 shows that shareholders are far more likely to benefit from a company which states a purpose that goes beyond the 'counting of coins'. You, the people who form the company, should make up your own minds, and not be ashamed of including some romance and adventure in your statement of purpose. That is a task of leadership. It will be a more powerful and lasting statement if it wins the assent of the many people you work with – for reasons explained in the next section. But the first stage is the act of invention and leadership, to capture people's imaginations and to make the whole process exciting.

Starting as you mean to go on

When I present *Tomorrow's Company*, I often ask my audience, 'Hands up if you really believe in your company's mission statement'. I find the percentage of directors and senior managers who can say, 'Yes' is rarely more than half. People have become cynical about mission statements. Too often, the fine words they contain are rendered hollow by the manner in which they are prepared and introduced. Inclusive intentions often founder as a result of exclusive execution. The top people go away to a country house hotel and have great fun developing a new mission statement. They come back full of enthusiasm. Yet the people upon whom the statement is then launched do not share the enthusiasm: they do not feel involved. There has been a failure of leadership in that most critical area of matching what is practised with what is preached.

It is better not to start down the road of a new statement of purpose unless

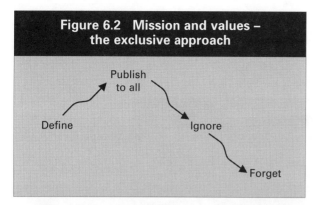

Figure 6.2   Mission and values – the exclusive approach

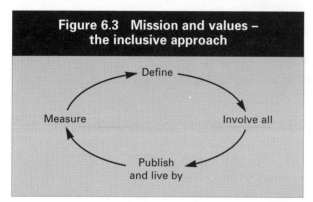

Figure 6.3   Mission and values – the inclusive approach

you intend deeds to match words. The test will come early. It might be a matter of applying your own code of values to the way you compete for new business. It might be the challenge to be as open and transparent about pay and benefits as your statement of values suggests. In many organisations people have been let down before: they want to know if you mean what you say.

One of the best ways of signalling seriousness of intention is to ensure that the company goes about formulating its mission and values in an inclusive way.

In his book *Practical Business Re-engineering* my colleague Nick Obolensky describes the remarkable transformation of the head office of Oticon, a privately owned manufacturer of hearing aids. In his first two years as chief executive Lars Kolind reduced costs by 20 per cent and restored profitability but it was clear to Kolind that in the long term the company had no sustainable advantage. Kolind concluded that the head office

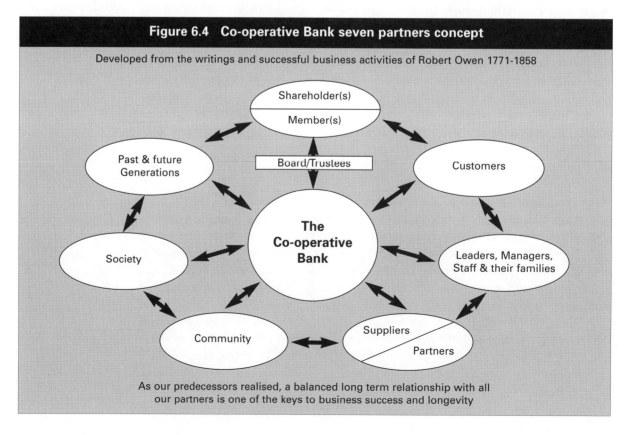

Figure 6.4   Co-operative Bank seven partners concept

Developed from the writings and successful business activities of Robert Owen 1771-1858

As our predecessors realised, a balanced long term relationship with all our partners is one of the keys to business success and longevity

needed radical change. It employed 150 people and represented 30 per cent of overhead costs, but more than that it set the corporate culture, and the result was an organisation that was slow-moving and unresponsive.

What is interesting is the way he went about changing it. He wrote a radical four-page document entitled 'Think the Unthinkable'. In it he described his vision of a 'seamless borderless head office without internal walls or partitions'. The head office vision had no titles, grades or departments, no job descriptions. He described as a metaphor a large room with 1,000 birch trees on castors which would move to form groups when needed before moving to form new groups . . .

. . . In the first three months after he devised the plan, he discussed it with sceptical senior colleagues. Then he brought together the entire 150 head office employees and described it to them. Of those present 95 per cent were against the change: but he had credibility from two effective years as chief executive. He worked steadily to stir the head office into action. He stimulated informal groups to work on aspects of the plan. Within three months about 50 people – few of them managers – were involved in some aspect of the change plan whose goal was a 30 per cent improvement in efficiency in three years. There was just one person employed full-time on the tasks.

His techniques included:

- late afternoon seminars, with outside speakers describing a knowledge-based learning organisation
- a 'dialogue shop' where the management team presented as a team and then submitted themselves individually to detailed questioning by a middle management group
- the chief executive himself buying 17 per cent of the equity from the private foundation which previously owned 100 per cent then offering the opportunity for employees to buy shares, thus extending the stakeholding.
- a computer Christmas: state of the art PCs were bought by Oticon, and for a nominal price any employee was able to rent one at home. Delivery was arranged just before Christmas: people took them home, became computer literate and – an unexpected by-product – started to work at home.
- individual counselling sessions to those resisting change
- a values conference for all staff held at the stage when the design for the new office was nearing completion – with most of the old systems and controls being thrown away. This involved all staff in discussing and agreeing the values of trust and teamwork on which they would be asked to operate.

Implementation took place on a specified day. Initially there was chaos and morale was affected by the need for redundancy. But over a three-year period revenue was increased by 45 per cent and return on equity increased from 6.7 per cent to 36.9 per cent.

This was a company that ensured that the manner of its formulation of change fitted the intended end result. Too often companies defeat themselves by using exclusive methods to formulate inclusive plans.[5]

Textbox 6.5 Placing a positive value on relationships

TOMORROW'S COMPANY values reciprocal relationships. It thinks win-win, understanding that by focusing on all those who contribute to the business it should improve returns to shareholders without in any way diminishing the company's accountability or focus on returns.

YESTERDAY'S COMPANIES are locked in adversarial relationships. They think in terms of zero-sum, imagining that if they were to make customers, employees, suppliers or the community more important, the shareholders would be the losers.

TOMORROW'S COMPANY is managed by people who can hold collaboration and competition in their heads at the same time, and see the company's identity as including all stakeholders.

YESTERDAY'S COMPANIES are managed by people who see only themselves and their immediate colleagues as us, and everyone else as them.

TOMORROW'S COMPANY aims to learn from all its relationships. It thinks of itself as an adaptive organism. It sees every relationship as a nerve end, connecting it with new intelligence about the marketplace and the opportunities or threats it contains.

YESTERDAY'S COMPANIES think of themselves as machines in which decisions are made and 'driven down' by those at the top. Because they refuse to see key relationships as learning opportunities, they quickly get out of touch. They deny themselves opportunities to reduce costs and to enhance the performance of their products, and become uncompetitive.

TOMORROW'S COMPANY maintains a global perspective and is ready to work with others whose cultures are different from its own.

YESTERDAY'S COMPANIES assume that everyone else will learn their culture and language.

It will be obvious from this example that the five stages of the inclusive approach can never happen in a tidy sequence. The way you formulate your purpose is, in practice, as important as the words you choose. The next two elements are equally interlinked. Once an organisation is clear what it exists to achieve, and what it stands for, it then has to deal with the next two 'stages' in parallel. It cannot define success unless it is clear about its key relationships. Equally it cannot define its key relationships unless it is clear about success.

REVIEW KEY RELATIONSHIPS

There are at least two elements to the process of reviewing relationships. Many mis-understandings and fruitless disagreements arise if the two are not distinguished. Someone will say, 'Ah yes, but how can we be inclusive unless we pay equal attention to all our stakeholders?'. Someone else will retort that business is about priorities and choices and you cannot possibly give equal attention to all.

Scan the horizon

The truth is that they are both right, but they are talking about two different stages in the process of reviewing relationships. In the first stage you are scanning the horizon, and working out your map of possible relationships. At this stage it is essential to include all the relationships. Otherwise you will miss opportunities and expose the organisation to risks. (A useful checklist for this review process was provided in Chapter 2.)

Identify key relationships

Having reviewed the map of possible relationships, any organisation then has to make some choices. It has to answer questions like:

'What does success look like, next month, next year, and five years from now?'

'Who is 'us'?' For example 'Does "us" encompass:
the owner or owners of shares
the bankers
the managers
all employees
some or all suppliers
some or all customers
the communities in which the company operates
the country or countries in which the company operates?'

'What do we regard as sources of intelligence for the improvement of our business? (Every business would expect its managers to be sources of intelligence. Most businesses would recognise that customers and employees should be a source of intelligence.) But suppliers? The local community? The general public?'

As was shown in the Community section of Chapter 5, the harder a company thinks about the sources of success, the more important it becomes to regard all these relationships not simply as necessary evils, but as potential sources of value. A few years ago the RSA's Environmental Management Awards were won by B&Q, a 'Do it Yourself' subsidiary of Kingfisher, a retail group based in the UK. In making their presentation the B&Q team described how they started by reviewing their buying policy for hardwoods. They began to feel that they should do something to satisfy themselves that they were buying timber from renewable sources. At first this felt like a matter of public conscience, at a price to the bottom line and to shareholders. Several years into the programme the attitude had changed. Virtually all the directors could see benefits in their own areas of responsibility. What started as, apparently, a costly community obligation began to look like good business sense measured in old-fashioned financial terms. In that case it paid to be responsive to social pressures: but the company would never have discovered the payback if it had not started by following its social instincts.

Look through the other end of the telescope

At the end of this process the organisation has a sketch-map of its key relationships, and the part each of those relationships play in the success of the whole venture. (See, for example, the way the Co-operative Bank used the inclusive approach to define their seven partners, Figure 6.4, page 88.)

This in turn lead to a second, and more detailed, drawing of the relationships map. And this time, the organisation starts to consider not simply what it is looking for from the relationships, but also what success looks like from the other end of the telescope – from the point of view of actual or potential customers, for example. (For an example of how to pull this together into a framework of success, see Appendix 2, pages 158–159.)

The company wants its customers to buy its products but in order to do so, it has first to understand those customers in all the complexity of their feelings, their values and their requirements. It increases the value it gets out of the relationship by increasing the value it puts into it. The company wants to buy products and services from its suppliers. The more closely the company can align its definition of success with that of those suppliers, the more momentum there is behind the success of the company. The ideal is that each of a company's relationships are what John Neill has called a 'shared destiny relationship': the commonality of interest is strengthened and the conflict of interest is minimised.

The benefits of this way of thinking are evident in some of the examples of Unipart's co-operation with its suppliers. (See the Unipart case study, Chapter 5, page 77.)

The inclusive approach prompts you to consider the underdeveloped potential of each relationship. In defining where success will come from and the relationships on which such success will depend, the company is forced to ask itself difficult issues, like that of motivation.

'Why should the people whom a company employs want to give their very best? If the company exists purely to make shareholders rich, and if it is not able to offer any guarantees of employment security, why should its managers imagine that its people will fall over themselves to work for it?'
'What is this company's personality and character?'
'How do people feel about working here?'
'How do we want people to feel about:
   buying our products
   working here
   supplying us
   having us as neighbours
   investing in us?'
'Are the feelings we want to encourage likely to be reinforced or weakened by our current:
- statements of purpose, and values
- the success model
- behaviour
- reward and recognition system?'

Define your licence to operate

There is a shadow side to the definition of your key relationships. It is the question, 'Who can stop you doing business?'

Many entrepreneurs bridle at the bureaucratic ring of the 'licence to operate'. Why, they ask, do they need anyone's permission to set up in business? It's a free country, isn't it?

For some businesses in all countries, and for all businesses in some countries, there is indeed a formal permission, granted by the government. And, indeed, the absence of excessive curbs on entrepreneurial activity is an important condition for the success of the free-market economy. But behind this formal permission, as one UK chief executive put it: 'We all manage with the implicit permission of our people'.

Such humility is not an abdication but rather an underpinning of leadership. The licence to operate may be seen as space within which the company can move. Surrounding the company are all those who by their combined reactions can either give the company more or less room for manoeuvre.

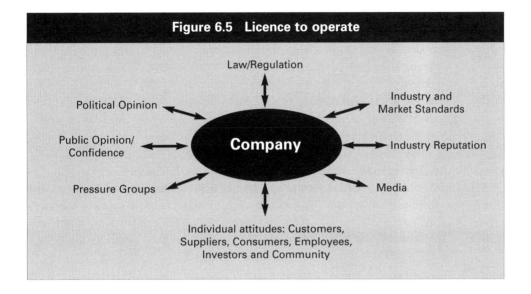

Figure 6.5   Licence to operate

The licence to operate is, then, the aggregate of all these different reactions to the company – and is itself a living changing licence. For example, bad customer experiences can feed public perceptions which in turn increase the pressure for government to act. Or, media publicity about one piece of irresponsible behaviour by a competitor may increase the scrutiny of all the other companies in the industry by the media, pressure groups and government.

When Shell spent over one million pounds to establish that the sea was the safest place to dump a redundant oil platform – and got the agreement of the UK's Department of Trade and Industry (DTI) – it thought that it had all the permission it needed. It was wrong, as its president has been honest enough to admit.   Whatever the factual merits of their case, and the inaccuracy of 'some' of the statements made by Greenpeace, public perception – not just of Shell, not even perhaps of the oil industry, but of industry generally – was so unfavourable that it overwhelmed Shell's scientific efforts to assess environmental impact. Although Shell had convinced the UK government, there were other governments who, under pressure from their own public, media and pressure groups, were less convinced. There was a storm of emotion, quite out of proportion to the individual case, which forced Shell UK to retreat and left the DTI feeling bewildered and let down. It is not enough for one company to look at its own behaviour and its own relationships. Its licence to operate may depend on the attitudes of a faraway public whose judgements may be influenced by the behaviour of its competitors. That is one reason why Tomorrow's Company cannot behave as an isolated unit, but has to recognise the impact which it and its fellow-producers are having.

Many boards and business managers spend their lives attempting to make tiny percentage improvements in production efficiency or cost reduction, and measure every dimension of the task rigorously. Yet they may have no measures of success that tell them about the health of the licence to operate. This is irresponsible. If they forfeit the licence to operate they can destroy overnight more value than their incremental efforts may have achieved in a decade. In the UK in the last few years it has happened to some privatised utilities – most notably British Gas – and it happened to the beef industry. With the benefit of hindsight, decision makers for the beef industry would have managed their risk very differently. They would not have allowed narrow cost considerations to deflect them from a ruthless and early crackdown on any contamination or corruption of the food chain: they would have insisted on prompt and precise public communication of the facts and, by doing so, they would have saved the livelihoods of many thousands of people employed in the industry. Mismanagement of the licence to operate has been valued in billions of pounds, and the damage has spread across much of Europe.

To take a more parochial example: one of the companies studied in the *Tomorrow's Company* Inquiry was a brewer and operator of pubs – literally, licensed premises. The more this company thought about its licence to operate, the more attention it started to pay to its relationships with the police and the magistrates. At an industry-wide level, similar concerns have led the drinks industry in the UK to form and finance the Portman Group, a charity concerned with preventing the misuses of alcohol. (The importance of the company's long-term relationship with the community is considered in more detail in Chapter 9.) The wisdom of this approach became evident in the UK during 1997, as the industry faced a public backlash against 'alcopops', a range of alcoholic drinks which it was claimed were designed to attract young drinkers.

DEFINE SUCCESS

Many companies still suffer from a machine-age view of measurement. They assume that the accounts tell them all they need to know about success and failure. They are pressing buttons and pulling levers at the top of the machine: the results of all their efforts are factually recorded in the management and the financial accounts.

Even when companies start to recognise

Textbox 6.6 Maintaining a strong licence to operate

TOMORROW'S COMPANY expects its relationships to overlap and seeks to reinforce the commonality of interest between them. It recognises that its long-term future is enhanced by a supportive operating environment and acts, with others where necessary, to strengthen its licence to operate.

YESTERDAY'S COMPANIES think of stakeholders in terms of either separate transactions or conflicting priorities. They are reluctant to acknowledge the concept of a licence to operate, often clinging to the notion that the law adequately describes the public acceptability of business conduct.

TOMORROW'S COMPANY recognises the critical importance of achieving environmental sustainability in the interests of all stakeholders and accepts the challenge this poses.

YESTERDAY'S COMPANIES view environmental concerns as peripheral and react defensively when issues arise.

that it may be unbalanced to rely solely on backward looking financial measures, this machine-age view can still get in the way. Many of those who attend performance measurement conferences seem to be looking for a new measurement machine which they can install, ready-made to meet the new measurement needs of their business.

In the last few years all sorts of tools and techniques have been developed to help people with measurement. Some of them, such as the balanced business scorecard, the European Business Excellence Model and its transatlantic cousin, the Baldrige Award, have been invaluable in helping businesses to measure what really counts, instead of measuring what they have always been in the habit of counting. As the examples used later in the chapter show, these tools can provoke thinking. They can be a useful framework for comparison and benchmarking. They can provide a common language for discussing what you are trying to achieve. But they are no substitute for original thought. And it is original thought that you need if you are to build a business that is unique in what it offers and how it gets there.

A success model is like a recipe. It describes how an organisation puts together all the ingredients that result, reliably and systematically, in a successful business outcome. What is it that uniquely equips your business to add value? What combination of people, place, organisation, price, technology, reputation, market knowledge, product or service design do you intend to deploy to achieve the return which you desire?

These are obvious questions, but it may be that many businesses have not thought about them. 'Who would like to tell me their company's success model?' I asked a seminar full of IT directors, after explaining what was meant by a success model. There was a reticence which I felt was not wholly explained by considerations of commercial confidentiality. I persisted, homing in on a friendly face which I knew worked for a household name services company.

'I'm not sure that we have one,' said the owner of the face. I explained in more detail what I meant. He still wasn't sure. Eventually he said he thought it was 'something to do with customers'. I've tried the question several times since, with other groups of senior managers. It is not often that more than half can describe the particular mix of skills and opportunities that make their company unique in its approach to success. Even senior people end up saying things like, 'It's obvious, isn't it? We're here to make a profit?' They don't appear to have thought of the many different routes by which their company might choose to arrive at that profit.

MEASURE AND COMMUNICATE PERFORMANCE

The real significance of the success model, and the inclusive definition of key relationships is found in the clues which they offer as to how managers should be spending their time and what they should be measuring.

Managers are not used to being asked what they think they should measure. They are much more comfortable managing against a prevailing system of measurement. It is easier to play an established sport, where you know clearly what constitutes winning and losing, than to be asked to participate in devising a new sport which best reflects your particular strengths. And so, in many companies, we go merrily on, retrieving the wrong balls because our accounting systems keep throwing them for us, and taking our eye off the ball marked 'sustainable success' which is to be found with much greater difficulty, at the end of determining our success model.

My own brief and unfulfilling time as a sales director in a printing company, involved lavishing much time, towards the end of an accounting period, on trying to boost my figures for invoiced sales. This meant persuading everyone else in the supply chain to organise work in the order which suited my monthly sales figures rather than in the order which suited efficiency or quality. This practice was supposed to improve cash flow, but what would really have increased cash flow in the longer term would have been a focus upon exceeding customer expectations and not meeting artificial internal deadlines. Instead of focusing on the appropriate success model for the printing business, I was allowing the existing measurement system to distort my behaviour.

The European Business Excellence Model which forms the basis for the European Quality Award has proved to be a remarkably successful common language for companies which are serious about mapping out their own route to success. The Model starts by distinguishing between the how and the how much, the enablers and results as it calls them. It builds on an indisputable logic from the enablers (starting with Leadership, and moving through People Management, Policy and Strategy, and Resources) through the business

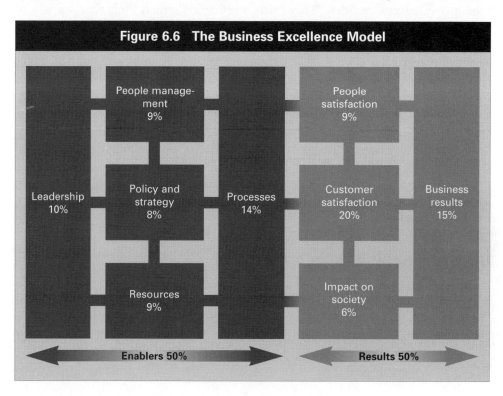

Figure 6.6 The Business Excellence Model

People management 9%		People satisfaction 9%
Leadership 10%	Policy and strategy 8%	Processes 14%	Customer satisfaction 20%	Business results 15%
Resources 9%		Impact on society 6%

Enablers 50%   Results 50%

processes towards the results (Customer Satisfaction, People Satisfaction, Impact on Society) and through the combination of these to business results. It provides a common language by which people in different departments of a company, or different subsidiaries of a group, or entirely different businesses can assess themselves and compare their performance.

The Balanced Business Scorecard applies a different but complementary logic. It supplements traditional financial performance with criteria that measure performance from three additional perspectives – those of customers, internal business processes (how effective the organisation is in achieving its objectives) and learning and growth. The Scorecard can be used simply to measure what the business has done, or to help re-design what the businesses should do. Ideally, its use should ensure that the fine words in the mission statement about creativity, innovation, customer commitment and employee development are not brushed aside by a planning and budgeting process that exclusively focuses on immediate financial goals. Companies which take the Balanced Business Scorecard seriously develop it into something which covers strategy planning and performance measurement. Any strategy is a hypothesis. It is based on assumptions about the underlying linkages – for example, the assumption that 'if we increase customer satisfaction we will increase loyalty, and if we increase loyalty, we will increase profitability.' The scorecard should be designed to show these linkages at work and so test them. It should, in particular, link the leading indicators (like loyalty) to the lagging indicators (like profitability). Financial goals are accompanied by people goals: short-term targets are balanced by milestones towards long-term development.[6]

It isn't enough to have caught measurement measles. A confused or unbalanced strategy is not made good by a rash of additional performance measurements. There has to be a simplicity at the heart of the business. People have to have a clear and simple idea of the company's recipe for success.

People often ask what is the proper relationship between the *Tomorrow's Company* framework, the Business Excellence Model, and the Balanced Business Scorecard. The first answer is that it depends what they want to achieve and what they find helpful. Several of the founder members of the Centre for Tomorrow's Company use all three. The second answer is that the use of *Tomorrow's Company* is particularly helpful in enabling a company to embark on creating a measurement framework. It helps it to decide what relationships and what measures should go in the Scorecard and – in the language of the Business Excellence Model – it offers a way of challenging the company to fill in what should be in the 'Leadership' box.

In one sense, the *Tomorrow's Company* framework is more prescriptive: it insists that a company looks first at purpose, values and relationships, and it steers the company towards identifying what makes it unique. That leaves each company with the challenge of identifying all the links in the chain leading to sustainable success. This is where organisations may find it helpful either to draw on the ready-made structure of the Business Excellence Model, or to accept the challenge offered by the concept of the Balanced Business Scorecard, which forces you to link all your measurement logically together in a way that helps you shape and test your strategy.

While each company will make its own choice, the evidence is already suggesting that, for organisations facing change, the use of a broader measurement framework will be essential. A study of 23 big companies undergoing change concluded that there was a correlation between companies that had changed successfully and the use of broad based measurement systems. About 80 per cent of the more successful companies, compared with 40 per cent of the rest used broad 'transformation scorecards' which tended to be loosely based either on *Tomorrow's Company*, or on the Business Excellence Model, or on Balanced Scorecards.

And the authors, Keith Ruddle and David Feeny, commented that: 'All participants expressed the opinion that, with hindsight, a broader measurement focus earlier might have influenced the success or pace of change'.

They quoted one manager from a consumer products company, '[We] could have done it in six years rather than 15, given what I know now – do more things at once and start with the customer'.

Another said, 'The whole behaviour and values problem is something I should have paid attention to earlier!'[7]

Textbox 6.7 The principles of an effective measurement system

- *manages complexity to create clarity* – it should encompass a coherent set of carefully selected key measures

- *matches the success model* – for example, General Electric's model is expressed in terms of customers, employees and cash, and the key measures are customer loyalty, employee morale and cash flow

- *includes one leading indicator from each relationship* – for example, Unipart's supplier relationship programme *Ten(d) to Zero* enables a supplier's progress to be assessed, by the supplier and company alike, using a universal ten-point scale on which progress towards zero reflects progress towards the company's strategic goals of cost reduction and continuous improvement achieved through long-term relationships

- *includes measures of the strategic health of the business* – for example, the rate of introduction of new products, the extent to which the stated values are shared by all employees, or progress towards agreed learning targets

- *enables benchmarking against the performance of world-class companies* – benchmarking is the continuous process of measuring products, services and practices against the toughest competitors or those recognised as world leaders

- *balances immediate results with future capabilities* – in other words, balances current *performance* with the development of *prospects*

- *includes measures which assist the board in risk assessment and management* – for example, with regard to the environmental impact of the company's operations.

The Centre for Tomorrow's Company is itself reviewing the research which others have done into the use of broader performance measurement frameworks.[8] The evidence from the United States is that financial measures now account for a minority of participants' measurement criteria, and that most organisations can now show how success as measured in one key relationship or category of measurement links to success in other areas. However some of the UK evidence reviewed by the Centre shows a continuing gap between what managers believe to be important for the success of their companies (their success model) and the measures actually used.

In Chapter 7 the relationship with investors is considered in greater depth, but if there is one single question a fund manager or a non-executive director has time to ask of the chief executive at their first meeting, it should be 'What is your success model?'

Whether asked of the group of companies, or at the level of an individual business, this question stimulates an answer which tells you if the company's brain is active or on auto-pilot. Assuming the company has thought out what its formula for success is, the answer tells you more. It begins to map out what it is the company needs to be measuring to assess its progress towards success. It eliminates all the alibis about inappropriate, externally-imposed yardsticks. It doesn't reduce everything to one, inevitably incomplete, measure such as profit before tax, or cash flow or earnings per share. It acknowledges the uniqueness of each business, and gives that business' management full scope to design its own framework of measurement. It sorts out the leaders from the followers, the thinkers from the sleep-walkers.

At the end of the process implied by the inclusive approach, the annual report should

---

Textbox 6.8 Developing and applying a unique success model

TOMORROW'S COMPANY develops a clear success model of its own.

Both for the company as a whole, and for each of its business activities, it is able to define unique advantages and show how these will be exploited to achieve sustainable success. The model includes an explanation of the importance of each relationship to the company's success – in other words, it identifies not only what, but also who, will give the company the capability to succeed.

YESTERDAY'S COMPANIES take it for granted that 'everyone knows' what success is, and allow existing systems of measurement to define it for them.

TOMORROW'S COMPANY matches performance measurement to its purpose and success model, so that it can assess areas of risk, the health of relationships and the degree of renewal, and can anticipate fully its opportunities.

YESTERDAY'S COMPANIES are content to measure returns. Because they have no, or inadequate, measures of the value embedded in their relationships, they have to take hard decisions in the dark. They risk destroying value rather than creating it.

TOMORROW'S COMPANY measures what matters most for future success. It accepts that competitiveness will be driven by change and will constantly be redefined for the company through an iterative process between itself and its key stakeholders.

YESTERDAY'S COMPANIES measure what they have always measured in the past.

99

be barely recognisable. To yesterday's company, the annual report is simply a means of communicating with shareholders. There are some statutory nods in other directions – the required statement on training, equal opportunity, or the environment. But the report is a machine-age document, limited to statements about what has been produced and what cash flow and profit may have generated, and what balance sheet that leaves.

To Tomorrow's Company the annual report is an inclusive statement. It sets out the organisation's purpose and values. It states the success model – the recipe by which shareholder value will be generated. It shows the part that people in all the key relationships play in generating the financial returns which it reports: it captures measurements of the health of all these relationships. It educates and informs all those who have a relationship with the business, how their contribution is linked to that of others. In Tomorrow's Company the shareholders are interested to know about the health of the licence to operate – just as the community is interested to understand how effectively the business is creating value for shareholders.

REWARD AND REINFORCE

Matching deeds to words, it has already been recognised, is a crucial task of leadership in Tomorrow's Company. Leaders show their true colours in the way they pay themselves and those around them.

This requires a radical departure in thinking. Whatever choices the company makes about pay, it has to bear in mind that it will reap whatever it sows. In a crisis, the chief executive needs to be able to say 'We're all in this together'. At Unipart, 70 per cent of the workforce are employee shareholders. At Pertemps, over 30 per cent of the capital value of the company has been given to the workforce in the form of shares.

At AEA Technology, Sir Anthony Cleaver and his board horrified the institutions advising them on flotation by choosing to commit future profits to give shares to all employees, rather than seeking share options that would have made them millionaires in the event of a successful outcome to the flotation. At John Lewis Partnership, all the employees enjoy a profit share – worth 20 per cent of salary in 1996-97. At Birmingham Midshires Building Society, managers are empowered to give cash rewards for 'magic moments' when staff are observed going beyond the call of duty to treat their customers well. One retailer – the same one who told me 'We all manage with the implicit permission of our people' – organises 'town meetings' where subordinates' judgements on their senior managers are posted publicly for everyone to see.

FEDERAL EXPRESS: THE INCLUSIVE APPROACH AT WORK

Federal Express use a 'leadership index'. At one level, the success model at Federal Express is about logistics – distributing packages fast all over the USA using a single central hub. But beneath that there is a sophisticated set of measurements to enable people to see for themselves whether they are achieving the targets they need to achieve, and beneath that, in turn, there is a belief that customer service really begins with employee satisfaction, embodied in the three word statement 'People–Service–Profit'.

The people first philosophy at FedEx leads to rigorous screening and profiling to ensure that all those in contact with the customer have the personalities that are suited to the task. It leads to an annual, 29-question, upward appraisal survey which yields for each individual manager, and for management as a whole, a score against the leadership index.

Then there is the guaranteed fair treatment policy by which grievances can go all the way to the top of the organisation and be resolved in 21 days.

It is easy for companies to set ambitious goals in their success models. Without measurement, they cannot know if they are achieving them. The founder of FedEx, Fred Smith, laid down 100 per cent customer satisfaction as the objective. But he also insisted that the company devised systems that enabled them to measure their success. Supertracker is a bar-code based system that enables the company to identify exactly where any package is in its system. It also makes possible a daily measure of customer service called SQI (Service Quality Indicator). Every late delivery, every damaged item, every invoice adjustment, every lost item is recorded and scored. At the end of the working day the total is calculated and made known to every employee. In 1994 the typical total score was 130,000. Within the next five years the company's aim is to cut the score to one tenth of that total, without allowing for increases in volume.[9]

Notice, also, that in FedEx there are two kinds of measurement going on. One is to measure to ensure FedEx is better than its competitors at what it did against commonly recognised criteria such as service quality. The other is a measurement that tests FedEx against goals and parameters that are uniquely its own – like the leadership index.

In Tomorrow's Company, as in a game of golf, you measure yourself both against your competitors and against your expectations of yourself.

That is the inclusive approach at work. A clear set of purpose and values, reflected in the success model, and in the measurement system. The details of organisation are in line with its purpose and values. As a result of this attention to detail, fair treatment for employees not only reflects a deeply held value: the company has a means of making sure it happens.

CONCLUSION – PERSONALITY PAYS

Appendix One contains the Agenda for action developed by the *Tomorrow's Company* Inquiry. This has been used by many boards in the UK as the basis of a fundamental review of their progress. This may, in turn, lead them to develop their own framework for success, an example of which is shown in Appendix 2 (see page 158). It has proved to be a powerful way of helping businesses to strengthen their individual identity. Too many companies describe their purpose and their values and their success model in terms that make them sound alike – 'Our aim is to deliver above average returns to our shareholders over the medium term', and so on.

Why do companies have to worry about being different? It is true that there are still likely to remain pockets of business which are unaffected by global competition. A generation from now, perhaps, a barber's shop will still be a barber's shop in spite of the attractions of the robotically pro-grammed haircut delivered in your own home! A bed and breakfast in the Scottish Highlands will, it may be hoped, retain its attractions. But even in those two cases, the prospects of untainted survival may have much to do with the fact that these are small businesses where the personality of the proprietor shines through. The businesses at greatest risk from increased competition, changing aspirations, and new technology are businesses which lack personality.

There are many forces which push companies towards being the same. For example, as competition in the world of retail intensifies, the competitors strive not only to match each other on cost and value for money. They try to make shopping in their stores different, more pleasant, even fun, as in the Adams example quoted in Chapter 5 (see page 65).

The same logic will prevail in those areas where there is a shortage of the skills a company needs. Of course, companies will compete with each other on pay; and those companies failing to keep up with market rates will find recruitment and retention of scarce people difficult. The winners in the competition to attract and keep the best people will be companies with personality – preferably an attractive personality – although being a likeable rogue of a company will probably do far more for you than having no personality.

Once you have recruited people, personality – yours and theirs – is equally vital to performance in any except the crudest commodity business. It is the personality of your business that determines how they really feel about coming to work. Since the UK adopted a National Lottery, businesses have been given a simple test of their personality. If a syndicate of your employees had won the Lottery on Saturday night would they still be in to work on Monday morning? And if you overheard people from your company in the pub, telling someone else about the company and what it was like, what would they say? Would they say they were lucky to work for such a good company? As competition intensifies, it is only through the people who work for a company, the creativity and commitment they display, that any company will be able to stand out from the crowd.

For people, and companies, the age of conformity is over. Success – as well as happiness – can only come from being true to yourself, and unafraid to say what you stand

---

Textbox 6.9 The *inclusive* approach differentiating Tomorrow's Company from yesterday's companies

Tomorrow's Company:

- clearly defines its purpose and values, and communicates them in a consistent manner to all those important to the company's success

- uses its stated purpose and values, and its understanding of the importance of each relationship, to develop its own success model from which it can generate a meaningful framework for performance measurement

- values reciprocal relationships, understanding that by focusing on and learning from all those who contribute to the business, it will best be able to improve returns to shareholders

- works actively to build reciprocal relationships with customers, suppliers and other key stakeholders, through a partnership approach

- expects its relationships to overlap and acts, with others where necessary, to maintain a strong *licence to operate*.

for. That is what the inclusive approach is about – companies taking charge of their lives. Tomorrow's Company starts with purpose and values: it goes on to success model, and key relationships, and it concludes with licence to operate. If your company has never searched its soul and consciously determined what it stands for, who matters to it, and where it is going, the chances are that it doesn't have a very bright future. It certainly won't be fulfilling its potential because it won't be aware what that potential is.

This means that investors, bankers, pension trustees, and anyone else interested in achieving a sustainable return on their investment will have to become used to a very different way of measuring success in the future. That is the subject of Chapter 8. Before leaving the entrepreneur or manager's view of the problem, however, there is an important question to ask. It is the question that was asked constantly by business leaders throughout the Inquiry. The inclusive approach seems so obvious. So what is stopping people acting inclusively?

The short answer, according to the Inquiry, was two thought processes, which combined together into a powerful narcotic from which business people found it hard to shake themselves free. One was a heavy dependence on financial measures as the only recognised language of success. The other was a widespread misconception about the duties owed by directors.

The next chapter describes how these two flaws stop corporate governance working as it should.

7   CORPORATE GOVERNANCE

Businesses are started by entrepreneurs   They put in their own money, their time, their concentration, and all their know-how. The entrepreneur is at one and the same time, manager, owner and steward for the well-being of the enterprise.

The limited company is designed to protect the entrepreneur and the initial backers from being personally liable for all the debts of, or claims on, the company. (This protection is, in most cases, diminished by the personal guarantees required by the bank!) As the business grows, it needs more capital than the entrepreneur can provide. Other backers are brought in. Most companies combine debt (usually from the bank) and equity. With the first, the lender's risk is reduced: interest is payable at an agreed level, and there is some security in the form of charge on the assets. With equity, the investor takes a greater risk of losing the entire investment but with a matching potential for success.

As the business continues to grow, it may decide to go public. This means that equity (shares) in the business become tradable on a recognised stock market. The investor has the ability to move more easily in and out of shares. The company gains the ability to obtain larger sums of equity capital.

Again, the company makes a trade-off: it subjects itself to more exacting external controls and regulations, in exchange for creating a market in its equity, which allows it to spread risk across a wide range of shareholders.

From the formation of the public company, leadership is formally in the hands of a board of directors, who in turn appoint the chief executive. Their formal task is to secure the long-term prosperity of the business, not by managing it themselves, but by ensuring that the business is being soundly managed in the long-term interests of the shareholders, while conforming with company law and accounting and stock exchange regulations.

What determines the long-term prosperity of a business? Among other things the quality of its leadership, its products, the efficiency of its processes (the way it works), the skill, creativity and commitment of its employees and its suppliers, the strength of its balance sheet, the health of the external environment in which it is operating, and its overall reputation. It is the chief executive and the managers appointed by him or her, who lead the business and who are fully involved in judging and balancing all these factors. It may happen to be a public company. Yet, its success still depends not only on the investments of its shareholders but the strength of relationships with customers, employees, suppliers, and the community. Here is where corporate governance becomes an issue. To whom should the entrepreneur and the managers be accountable for the health of these relationships and for the stewardship of all the company's assets? And how to strike the right balance between accountability and enterprise? A maturing business continues to need the entrepreneurial qualities that led to its creation. It still needs to be led by one or several entrepreneurs, inventive, restless, often defying convention in the search for competitive advantage. But the large public company needs what many entrepreneurs might regard as a contradiction in terms – accountable entrepreneurs, people with individual flair combined with a dedication to the company and all that it stands for, and not simply to themselves.

THREE DEADLY SINS

As the enterprise grows up, and becomes a public company, it needs to guard against the three deadly sins which undermine enterprise and accountability. The first is *sloth* – loss of entrepreneurial flair. Enterprise can give way to administration. Managers may lose their hunger and their drive for constant renewal. The symbols of this are complacency, unthinking routines, internal politics, and dead man's shoes. The second is *greed* – for power or wealth. Managers may remain highly enterprising, but dedicate their enterprise to their own comfort and their careers, rather than to the long-term prosperity of the corporation. The symbols of this are lucrative rolling contracts, over-cosy share-option packages, and, in the most extreme example reported about one celebrated businessman in the eighties, using the company jet to convey your pet poodle from one company home to another.

And the third sin is *fear* and subservience – the 'frightened rabbit' syndrome. There was a time in the UK when many decisions were dominated by fear of the unions. Today, it is more likely that fearful, subservient directors see themselves as the hirelings of the investors. Some boards forget that their task is to secure the long-term health of the business, and not simply to keep the investors off their backs. Appeasing commentators and analysts, or looking for enough immediate 'goodies' to keep the shareholders happy may look like accountability. If it is, it is the accountability of a *firm*, not of a *company*. The symbol of this is the chief executive who always has his eye on the screen which tracks today's share price. It is not to be confused with leadership.

CORPORATE GOVERNANCE – THE THEORY

The theory is that companies can be kept on track by market signals and financial incentives. The managers themselves can be encouraged to act like 'owners', by having a significant capital stake – share options or share-price related payment systems.

Analysts, researchers, and investment experts closely monitor the performance of companies and if a company's prospects diminish, its price suffers. Management take the action necessary to restore the business, or in due course, one of two things happen: either the representatives of the shareholders replace them, or there is a take-over bid by a new 'owner' claiming to be able to do a better job with the shareholder's assets. If that does not work there is always the possibility that a new 'owner' can bid to take over the ailing company. In this way the company can be induced to retain its focus on 'shareholder value' or 'owner value'.

Many company directors and managers live their lives by this theory. But does it work? Does it protect companies from the three deadly sins of sloth, greed and fear? There are two particular concepts that have to be sound if companies are to work in accordance with this textbook theory. First, the theory talks about owners and managers. Second, it talks about performance, performance monitoring, and accountability.

OWNERS AND MANAGERS

It doesn't take long to detect *sloth* – the decline of enterprise – in the way our corporate governance works. It is there in the words we use – and the ones we avoid!

A business is started by an entrepreneur. But 'the entrepreneur' rarely figures in discussions of corporate governance. It is the chief executive, or the managers, who are to be made accountable to the owners. There is, apparently, no longer an entrepreneur.

Secondly, notice the use of the phrase 'owners'. When an entrepreneur starts a company he or she is seen as the effective owner, even if there are other financial backers, just as the householder is seen as the owner of the house, even if 90 per cent of the capital has been lent by a building society. Yet in the discussion of a public company, and its governance, the entrepreneur has been tamed, and replaced by the managing director or chief executive. Meanwhile, the shareholders wear the mantle of owners. But something has been lost in the translation. This is a very different kind of ownership.

The family farm is a traditional example of ownership at work. Whoever manages that farm – whether a member of the family or a hired manager – has a very clear sense of accountability to the owners. There is the need to produce a regular flow of income: but this is balanced by the need to safeguard the assets for future generations. Success is judged as a balance between immediate performance and future prospects and this yardstick can continue to be applied even where the people managing the farm may be distinct from those who own the farm.

There are many family businesses embodying the same values. Ownership implies stewardship. The board have a point of reference beyond immediate financial performance: they see themselves as stewards for a company with a life and character of its own and a continuing capacity to create wealth.

The owners of the family farm identify the continuance of the farm with the continuance of the family. In the same way the (family) owners of shares in a long-established family business identify the continuance of the business with the future well-being of the family. In the family farm, the owners are also trustees for all the relationships of that business. Because the farm is intended to be there for generations, there is a reason to take care of the environment. Because the farm depends on the co-operation and goodwill of the surrounding community, there is an incentive to treat its neighbours well. Because the farm hopes to have dealings with the same customers and suppliers for generations there is good reason to treat each fairly.

The same cannot be said of a quoted business, the majority of whose shares are owned by institutions. The conduct of the business is in the hands of the board and the managers. Managers are the only trustees of the continuity of relationships with suppliers, employees or customers, and it is not ownership of shares that conveys this sense of stewardship to them. The less confident they feel about their own ability to stay in post the less attention will they pay to these long-term relationships.

In the large public company of today there has been a double separation. It is not simply that the managers are distinct from the owners. It is that the owners are now widely dispersed. A minority of shares are in the hands of individual shareholders. In practice, it is impossible for the company to have a meaningful dialogue with the individual shareholders about their wishes for its stewardship.

The majority of shares are held by intermediaries like insurance companies or pension funds who act at second or third hand on behalf of individual investors. For example, the beneficiaries of pension funds are a widely dispersed group of individuals, whose interests have to be interpreted first by the pension trustees who represent them, and then in turn by the fund managers appointed by those pension trustees. The trustees appoint the fund managers, and it is their responsibility to give the fund managers a clear brief. This brief can specify what balance of investments to make, what kind of companies to invest in or avoid, the timescales for achieving investment returns and the approach to risk. Too often the trustees do not recognise the power they have to determine how fund managers approach their task. Several senior people admitted to the Inquiry that when acting as pension trustees they had set crude performance targets which contributed to precisely the kind of short term investor behaviour which they found so unhelpful to their own companies! The fund managers in their turn have limited time and limited information on which to exercise judgement across their widely diversified portfolios. They also tend to be measured by the pension funds whom they serve on the basis of periods as short as one or two years. (The relationship between fund managers and companies is explored further in the next chapter.)

This is where the traditional textbook theory of corporate governance as accountability to owners starts to break down. Ownership of the farm implies trusteeship for the future. Ownership of tradable shares in a public company implies a much weaker sense of obligation for the future of that company. And, the fund manager, unlike the owner of the family farm, cannot be a trustee for the long-term prosperity of the farm. The fund manager is a trustee for the pension fund. For years the management textbooks have recognised a separation between ownership and control. Now there is often a second separation within ownership itself.

The stewardship of the company cannot lie with the owners of the shares: the fund managers who represent them already have a stewardship responsibility and that is to all the beneficiaries they represent. This changes everything. If it is to have some stability and direction, a business needs someone to perform the role of steward. And if the owners of the shares are unable to perform this role, the stewardship role traditionally performed by an owner has to be performed by the board. Unless and until a different structure is devised, stewardship of the assets, the relationships, and the prosperity of the company has to lie with the board, with all the risks implied by that concentration of power.

This puts the executive directors in a difficult position, which only the most courageous and entrepreneurial survive. The textbook talk is all of their accountability to owners. The corporate governance movement is busy trying to impose additional restraints on the managers to protect the company from the corrupting effects of the second of our three deadly sins – excessive concentration of power. But in its emphasis on protecting companies from the greed of their managers for power or wealth, the movement is using methods which encourage the other two deadly sins which beset the mature business – the erosion of enterprise and the encouragement of subservience. There is a danger that the task of sustaining the enterprise is left in the hands of hireling managers who have one eye on the share price and the other on the governance and remuneration codes which rule their lives.

In reality, ownership is now separate from stewardship. And that imposes a strain. It is the executive directors who carry the key burdens of the continuing enterprise, the responsibility for continuous renewal that comes from the true entrepreneur, the responsibility for stewardship of the purpose and values of the company, and the health of the relationships of the company. Yet the corporate governance textbooks expect the executive directors to talk and behave as if somebody else were the owner! Ownership and stewardship are not that easy to prise apart!

As Dow Votaw puts it in his 1965 book *Modern Corporations*:

> Property consists of a bundle of rights which the owner of property possesses with regards to some thing – rights to possess, use, dispose of, exclude others, and manage and control. The corporate concept divides this bundle of rights into several pieces. The stockholder gets the right to receive some of the fruits of the use of property, a fractional residual right in corporate property, and a very limited right of control. The rights to possess, use, and control the property go to the managers of the corporation.[1]

This is the paradox facing the board of a public company. Directors are the real stewards of the company's future. They may not be called the owners.

The people who are called the owners cannot be the stewards of the company's future – they can only be investors. The conventional rhetoric of Anglo-Saxon corporate governance is a recipe for impotence. You cannot expect to create wealth on the foundations of an impotent ownership. Businesses need stewarding.

From time to time the corporate governance experts turn to the fund managers and urge them to exercise their full ownership responsibilities. But, in practice, UK fund managers make it quite clear that they do not see themselves as stewards for the company. When I made the case for patient investment at a corporate governance conference in London, a representative of one of the leading pension fund managers commented during the panel session that she liked the sound of what I was saying. But, she added, in practice her clients (who were the trustees of pension funds and their advisors) did not give her a sufficiently patient timescale to make such questions as company stewardship relevant!

So, who will take up the responsibilities of stewardship? UK company law allows boards to assume them. Too few boards understand what the duties of a director are.

MISCONCEPTIONS OF COMPANY LAW

The successful companies are those which defy the traditional textbooks. The entrepreneurs stay entrepreneurs, retain their sense of stewardship of the business and treat their major investors as just that – investors, not owners. That does not diminish their accountability: it clarifies that accountability into something achievable and desirable for the creation of long-term shareholder value.

The RSA *Tomorrow's Company* Inquiry research identified a frustrating gap between rhetoric and reality. Directors overwhelmingly recognised the importance of long-term co-operative relationships; yet they appeared to have made few moves to act on that recognition. This puzzled the Inquiry team. What was stopping the people who ran companies doing what was so obviously in the long-term interests of those companies? The answer, it seemed, was a powerful brew of habit, over-simplification about the bottom line, and a misunderstanding about their duties as directors.

One of the most surprising findings of the Inquiry was that many directors misunderstood their duties under UK law. Two fallacies have developed: in practice, they threaten to undermine the robustness of the public company as a wealth-creating vehicle. The first is the belief that the board are simply accountable to the shareholders. The second is the view that it is only the present shareholders who matter.

For the idea of the public company to work as intended the board can only serve the shareholders by serving the company. The moment the board allow themselves to start seeing the property rights of shareholders as distinct from, and more important than, the total value of the company as an enduring concern is rather like the moment when water is allowed to seep into the cargo deck of a ro-ro ferry: it creates a fatal instability.[2]

The second, closely related, fallacy is the belief that the board has an immediate accountability to shareholders. Since it takes years for the most important corporate decisions to take effect, and since the paper ownership of shares is changing constantly, it is common sense as well as simple company law that directors are not deemed to be accountable to whoever happens to be on the share register at a point in time, but must have regard to the interests of the general body of shareholders from time to time. The commonsense test should be: have we acted in a way of which the general body of shareholders will approve once the decision has had time to work through?

Textbox 7.1   A legal memorandum on directors' duties

1. Directors' duties are owed to their company, and not to any third party. This is true even of the statutory duty to have regard to the interests of employees. But they are bound, as fiduciaries, to have regard to the interests of shareholders, and also, in the case of an insolvency situation, to the interests of creditors.

2. Their obligation to have regard to the interests of shareholders is not related to the actual shareholders at a particular time (subject to the obligation, as a matter of regulatory compliance and perhaps also of fiduciary duty, to make recommendations in relation to a take-over bid). Rather it is related to the general body of shareholders from time to time. This is demonstrated by the fact that, if the directors act ultra vires (in the sense of beyond their delegated authority rather than beyond the powers of the company), their action may be ratified by the body of shareholders at the time such ratification is sought rather than at the time of the act in question.

3. There is nothing in law to prevent the directors having regard to other interests if they *bona fide* and reasonably judge that to do so is conducive to the welfare of the company; as *Gower* says (*Modern Principles of Company Law*, p 555), 'dissatisfied customers and an aggrieved public or Government department are not conducive to the future prosperity of the company!'

4. It is the duty of directors, in having regard to the interests of shareholders, to arrive at a balanced judgment. This does not exclude a reasonable financial return for members in the form of dividends; as Lord Evershed MR said (in relation to voting in general meeting, but the same principle applies), 'the phrase "the company as a whole" does not mean the company as a commercial entity as distinct from the corporators'. But nor does it compel directors towards a short-term view of maximising returns for the present body of shareholders; because their duty is owed to the company, it is better expressed as taking a longer-term view of maximising its value on a sustainable basis.

10 May 1995   Philip Goldenberg, Partner   S J Berwin & Co

The publication of the Inquiry report led to some controversy about this interpretation of legal duties, but there has been no challenge to the position set out by the Inquiry and its legal adviser, Philip Goldenberg of S. J. Berwin & Co. And, since publication, the Centre for Tomorrow's Company has confirmed the Inquiry findings that many directors of UK-based companies do not understand to whom their duties are owed. Many chief executives and boards appear to believe that it is their duty in law to concentrate their attention on satisfying current shareholders. Of course they are accountable to shareholders, present and future, but they are accountable for the company.[3]

This misunderstanding gets in the way of wealth creation. It diverts newly-floated companies from their true long-term stewardship. It confuses institutional investors into believing that they should take on an ownership role for which they are rarely equipped. It gives comfort to the cynics who portray business as moneymaking, not wealth creation. It feeds public cynicism about business.

In time, there will be change, in the UK and elsewhere in the capitalist world. Societies will become intolerant of the business community where it appears to put too large a gap between the creation of shareholder value and the creation of social value. Businesses themselves will experiment with structures that allow them to have personality, flexibility and humanity. If boards of directors persist in their misunderstanding of the legal position, it may be felt necessary to redefine company law to remove this misunderstanding, although it is to be hoped, that this will be done in an enabling rather than a prescriptive way. But the most powerful obstacle to success will continue to be our own habits of thought. Many managers have been trained at business school to believe in an exclusively profit-maximising view of man. They have come into companies where the talk is all about accountability to the shareholders. Most analysts have been trained to look at company success purely in terms of mathematical ratios. The public has observed the extravagant pay packages of a minority of business people, particularly those running privatised utilities, and has drawn the understandable but mistaken conclusion that whoever goes into business is solely in it for the money. The truth is much more mixed. Achievement, power, ideas, money, fun, glory, ego, desperation and a point to prove all play their part in stimulating people to be in business, and a successful business sector will have room for all these motivations. It is only an immature business that believes that success has to come from greed.

PERFORMANCE MONITORING

The second concept on which the effectiveness of the public company depends is that of performance monitoring. 'Managers' are giving an account to 'owners' of their performance.

In order to be accountable to shareholders for the success of your enterprise, you first have to communicate that success. In order to be accountable to them for your stewardship of the assets of the company, you have to communicate how well you have discharged your responsibilities. In order to communicate you need a common language which reflects agreed assumptions about what it is that you are trying to achieve. The common language by which companies communicate with their investors is financial; the performance upon which they are assessed tends to be immediate past financial performance, and there is no equivalent common language by which companies may communicate with investors or with anyone else about the health of their relationships or skill with which they have been stewarding their assets. In the textbook view, the manager is accountable to shareholders through the audited accounts. In addition, investment analysts follow the industry and the companies within an industry, and the chairman or chief executive meets with serious institutional investors twice a year.

But experience has undermined the traditional view. Financial accounts are open to manipulation; acquisitions have been used to convey a false glow of growth and dynamism. Exceptional items have been used to disguise embarrassments.

Even when they are not subject to manipulation, the accounts give a retrospective view. They rarely describe the quality of relationships a company enjoys, or the company's capacity to create wealth in the future. In the UK the weakness of accounting practice has been the object of a concentrated and highly effective onslaught of reform by the Accounting Standards Board, under the leadership of chairman Sir David Tweedie.

In the traditional version of corporate accountability for performance there is also one telling omission. There is little talk about stewardship, or relationships, or about holding managers to account for what the company stands for. Accountability is usually described purely in terms of the immediate financial value that the managers have delivered. There is little focus on ways in which managers might be judged on their stewardship of all the company's relationships. What the published accounts and the reported conversations with fund managers dwell on is outcomes, not the inputs. The reader can only guess at what is going on in the 'real economy' that underlies the figures – the health of customer relationships, the capacity for innovation, the level of employee motivation, the company's reputation or relationship with regulators in its key markets all over the world.

But if you don't check whether the company is remaining true to what it stands for, and if you don't monitor the health of the key relationships of the business, you are putting at risk the long-term return to shareholders. Few companies appear to recognise the importance of the inclusive approach in the accounting and reporting process.

A telling illustration of the way values are sidelined came in the consultation on the *Tomorrow's Company* Inquiry, when I met a public affairs director who was explaining the process which led to the preparation of the annual report. I asked him what the report said about the company's purpose and values. 'Oh, we had that in last year,' he replied. 'But a number of shareholders complained last year that there wasn't an index, so this year we will be putting the index in and leaving out the statement of values.'!

The published report and accounts are the tip of the performance measurement iceberg. The advantage of financial measurement is that it is a common language and one which concentrates the mind. For example, if a papermaking foreman sees a daily sheet which tells him that his energy consumption is 200 units of electricity over budget, that may not have the same impact as being told that this item is costing the company £30,000 a week.

The danger is that examples such as the one above give financial measurement a spurious authority, allowing users of the accounts to forget that many assumptions and judgements have to be made in determining a profit. Traditional accounts are not objective reality. They interpret in financial language what has been achieved: they do not describe the capacity of the company to achieve future results. It is much harder to turn information about the strength of relationships, or the level of risk or the strength of shared values into a financial value, but that does not make any of these pieces of information less important. Tomorrow's Company will need to develop a new success language through which it becomes possible, natural and habitual for companies to communicate in an inclusive way. The financial results would be set in the context of the company's purpose and values, the success model, and the key measures that were implied by that success model. The report as a whole would acknowledge what were the key relationships for the company, and offer clear indicators of the health of each of the company's key relationships, and of its licence to operate. It would, in other words, be an embodiment by the management of their stewardship of the company's assets. It would serve as an effective guide to investors (see Chapter 8) of the current health of the company. It could, at the same time, be an account of the shareholder value and the social value that the company had added.

TAKEOVERS AND THE INCLUSIVE APPROACH

The winners and losers of take-over battles can bear witness to the importance of these principles. The inclusive approach to the stewardship of a business will help make a success of a take-over. Failure to adopt the inclusive approach in communicating to investors will leave key assets undervalued and make a take-over more likely.

It is hardly surprising that the majority of contested take-overs end in tears, particularly for the shareholders of the acquiring company. The 'market for corporate control' sounds an impressive mechanism for waking up the management of sleepy companies. But, to put it in the language of the *firm*, the success of a take-over depends upon paying the right price for the assets, and being able to extract the full value from those assets once they are yours. Increasingly, the full value lies in territory which nobody can own – the creativity of teams, their belief in what they are doing, and sometimes the extraordinary skills of talented individuals. The acquiring company which sticks to conventional measurement of the value of those assets is putting its own shareholders at risk. The right price of the business can only be known once you understand the context in which past earnings have been achieved, and the legacy of decisions which you will inherit when you acquire a company – the history, the values, the health of relationships, the licence to operate. And making the most of your investment in the future will depend, above all, on the reactions of people. If the acquiring business treats people solely as if they are assets to be sweated, the best of them may melt away. This is confirmed in research conducted by the University of Warwick.[4] Researchers found that in unsuccessful take-overs managers gave their attention to the integration of systems and procedures and offices, and not to the integration of the people or cultures. When Glaxo Wellcome was created out of the merger of Glaxo and Wellcome Trust, the company made a conscious effort to involve people from both sides in the building of a new culture. They started, naturally, with an intensive exercise designed to generate a new statement of mission values to which all employees of the combined company could commit. And that statement of mission and values was framed in terms of the challenge of curing disease – with the creation of value for shareholders being seen as a by-product.

Not all take-overs are bad. Ironically, many businesses deserve to be taken over precisely because they have never valued people and relationships properly, or, even if they have, they have never communicated that value to the investors who will decide the outcome of the take-over. In a take-over battle the investors have to decide whether the price being offered by the acquiring company is a true reflection of the present and future value of the company. One director of a major UK company explained a few months after it had lost a fierce take-over battle that, during the conflict, his company was convinced that it had been undervalued by the stock market. The company tried to explain to investors how much additional value there was in the relationships and the quality of the people, value that a conventional financial assessment would miss. But it was too late. Before the crisis, the company had not made the same effort to communicate in this new success language. Investors were cynical about the apparent deathbed conversion. The battle had been lost in the years before.

It is an interesting paradox. You don't create long-term value by treating the present shareholders as your masters. You have to think as much about the future shareholders. Yet the take-over is the one situation where your future is decided by the present owners of the shares. And it is the company's thoroughness in the past at using the new success language that may tip the balance.

In avoiding the third deadly sin – fear – the board must not veer towards complacency in their relationships with shareholders. Accountability without subservience; stewardship with due reference to the future as well as the present, and reporting that covers the health of relationships as well as results . . . these are the keys to good governance.

For the new owners, while many changes may have to be made dramatically and immediately, the long-term task is to ensure that the managers they 'acquire' retain this accountability and stewardship without fear or subservience. There is such a thing as an inclusive take-over. I also remember talking to a sales director of another company that had been taken over. It was a year after the battle. He had kept his job. He spoke highly of the new owners:

> We realise that we have gained much more than we have lost in this take-over. We respect our new owners. They respected us. They did not run our flag down the flagpole the minute they arrived. They showed us that they understood what we stood for, but encouraged us to take advantage of the combined strength of the new group. Now, a year later, we are losing our old identity and we don't mind, because we like being part of the new set-up and can see it as progress.

THE FLAWED LOGIC OF CORPORATE GOVERNANCE

Neither of the two concepts on which the conventional theory of company effectiveness depends turns out to be sound.

First, the theory talks about owners and managers. But it takes entrepreneurship for granted, and it over-simplifies ownership. It neglects those aspects of ownership that have to do with stewardship. The theory may be fine for *firms*, concerned only with transactions and not with long-term prosperity – but for *companies* it neglects the very activities that are essential for their lasting success: relationships, values, the capacity to inspire people to constant renewal and improvement.

Tomorrow's governance will only work if it encourages entrepreneurial managers who insist on retaining their roles as stewards of the long-term prosperity of the company – that element of ownership which the owners of a diversified portfolio of shares cannot display.

Second, the traditional textbook method depends upon the effectiveness with which managers give an account to owners. For tomorrow's governance to work it needs a process of communication between managers and long-term investors which focuses both on current results and future capacities to form a judgement about the company. It requires a success language which enables the company to communicate what it is trying to achieve, how it thinks it is going to achieve it, and what it thinks it should be measured on. It requires investors who review results both against the company's own success criteria, and on the more objective measures, against its competitors. They do not despise mere numbers, but they look at them in context. They place considerable weight on the qualities of leadership and entrepreneurship.

But who are those investors, and what is their proper function? Clearly, it is misleading to see them as owners. In the next chapter we will see who they are and how best they might contribute to sustainable wealth creation.

8 INVESTORS

Investment is a form of recycling. What it means to the individual investor is the deployment of financial assets to achieve a return which may take the form of income or capital growth, or some combination of the two. The investor is balancing two other benefits with the return: first, security – the balancing of risk against reward – and, second, the usefulness, or what an economist would call utility: the value which the investor places on the need that is being satisfied.

Although it is often said that investors are only interested in how much money they can make, there are investors who put a strong emphasis on the desirability of the assets or the activity invested in, even if that increases risk or reduces returns. Few people invest in a struggling football club or a provincial theatre for monetary gain alone – they are at one extreme of the spectrum. At the other end there may be some people who do not care where their money is invested and would not even be concerned if they were making their money from the sale of instruments of torture. The vast majority of us are somewhere in the middle. We do not know a great deal about the process that leads to our dividend or pension: but the more we find out about the process, the more choice we might want to exercise.

When you or I make a direct investment, we are not obliged to explain to anyone what we want from it. It is simply a matter of personal preference, but investors should be able to guide their decisions in a similar way to the early bankers who relied heavily on their judgement and their knowledge of individuals. My great-grandfather started a bank in Newcastle in the nineteenth century. One of the new companies to which he lent was Hawthorns, which had been created by Sir Benjamin Browne to build marine and locomotive engines. Browne's description of his relationship with his banker suggests that the banker's judgement of the worthwhileness of the project and the individual entrepreneur was at the heart of all his commercial calculations.

> Both he and his partners treated us with the most extraordinary kindness and confidence: not only were they always ready to give their advice and assistance, but they behaved with the most extraordinary liberality in the matter of financial accommodation and overdrafts. We could not possibly have got on if they had not allowed us the most liberal accommodation for long periods – and that for many years after we had begun. In those days bankers used to trust much

more the individuals who were borrowing the money, and much less to mere security, and the old bankers considered that in that way they made far fewer losses and larger profits. I can only say that for myself, like two or three other large manufacturers on Tyneside, I was entirely made by the bank.[1]

THE INVESTMENT CHAIN

Investment, like banking, has come a long way since then. Capital markets are now international, and are gradually becoming integrated. UK-based investment institutions are more likely to be part of a worldwide organisation: they have access to know-how and technology which enables them to invest funds anywhere in the world. Investors are developing international portfolios, which allow them to achieve a better balance of risk. Restrictions on the movement of capital have been removed. A global capital market is available to channel the excess funds from Japanese savers towards the capital-hungry United States.[2] Cross–border transactions in bonds and equities amounted to 3 per cent of America's GDP in 1970 – and had risen to 136 per cent by 1995. All this is made possible by the technological change described in Chapter 4, and reinforced by deregulation, and the development of derivatives and securitisation of lending – in other words, methods which package and sell a thousand and one ways of lending, borrowing, and managing your currency risk and, if you want, speculating on it. In a recent ten-year period world financial assets more than tripled. They increased at more than three times the rate of economic growth, and this pattern is expected to continue. An additional $12 trillion dollars is expected to become available for investment over the next few years as older generations enjoy higher incomes. Younger people will need to invest more to fund pensions and to meet the costs of care in their old age that might in previous generations have been met by their extended family. On the demand side emerging markets will absorb much of this capital, but there will also be competition from governments forced to borrow to pay for their welfare costs.[3]

Imagine what my great-grandfather would have made of the investment decisions in government bonds now being made by means of artificial intelligence, on software designed by G. M. Hughes Electronics, a giant defence group. The head of research at the firm of fund managers involved commented on the parallels between war and investing. 'Both have lots of data and a poor signal-to-noise ratio; both require quick decisions based on robust models of what's going on; and both punish wrong decisions with loss.'[4]

And yet, in spite of these changes in the number and complexity of intermediaries, and of financial instruments, in spite of the enhanced ability for people to spread risk, make speculative trades and balance their portfolios across continents, technologies and market sectors, there are some fundamentals of investment that have not changed. The overall prosperity of the world's savers will depend on the overall profitability over decades of the companies in which they invest. The chain of investment may be longer, but at the end of that chain will lie investment decisions based on an investor's judgement about the prospects and the performance of individual companies.

Wherever there are markets with imperfect information, people will speculate. There is no point in condemning speculation. Indeed it may be argued that all investment is speculation, although some types of speculation are more destructive than others. Every market has its share of those who attempt to use their knowledge of what is happening to market sentiment to turn a quick profit. The important thing is not to confuse the oil that lubricates the engine from the engine itself.

The engine itself is the real world of investment in wealth creation – the process by which individuals or organisations who want to save are linked to businesses which need investment or loans. What has changed since my great-grandfather's day is not the underlying nature of investment, but the links and complexity in the chain that connects savers with their ultimate investment.

The chain of accountability is a long one. Again, consider the example of a company pension scheme (see diagram above).

Even this is an over-simplified account of the chain of accountability. For example, the investee company may itself be an investment trust which itself invests funds in other companies.

Textbox 8.1 Chain of accountability – the pension scheme

Pension scheme member (saver)

(Independent financial adviser)

Pension scheme trustee

Consulting actuary

Fund manager (Investor)

Fund manager's researcher/investment analyst

Market–maker/stockbroker

Investee company

119

A LOGICAL INVESTMENT WORLD

At the risk of incurring the wrath of all the experts in this chain, consider for a moment what a logical investment process for our pensions might look like. It would be one that used market methods to offer individual savers an array of choice in how best to balance risk, gain, and utility to meet their individual priorities. And, because all markets depend on information, it would provide a comprehensive flow of information through which those people to whom savers entrusted their savings could give an account of their stewardship of the assets. The savers – whether acting in concert as members of an occupational pension fund, or for that matter individually through a personal pension – would be offered a range of investment policies from which to pick and mix according to their needs and values and their particular blend of preferences.

Where the saver acted as an individual, this blend would be defined very precisely, and acted upon with the help of an independent financial adviser. Some savers might choose a highly speculative investment policy, risking the transaction costs associated with active trading of stocks or even the capital risks involved in exposure to derivative trading or currency speculation. At the other extreme, others might look for 'patient capital' vehicles which enabled them to invest in new or growing enterprises.

Modern communication and information systems make it easier than ever for investment portfolios to be tailored to individual preferences. Very few people would be 100 per cent speculators or 100 per cent business angels. But even the more cautious might wish to reflect in, say, 10 per cent of their portfolio a commitment to environmentally-friendly investment or investment in a 'patient' investment fund that would support the future of their own country's manufacturing base.

Pension trustees would follow the same thought processes. Some might agree a uniform investment policy: others might wish to incur the additional expense of offering individual choice to investors while staying within the risk parameters set down by the consulting actuary.

As in any marketplace, investment and fund management companies would offer a range of products to help individuals and groups to fit their investment most closely to their preferences. Investee companies would for their part seek out those fund managers whose investment philosophies were most suited to their approach to business – their own unique purpose, values and success model.

The process of informing investors about the progress of the company would therefore become richer and more complex. Companies would know that without delivering the kind of financial returns which they promised they would be jeopardising their credibility with capital markets, and their ability to raise capital in the future. This would remain the overriding concern of their investors. At the same time they would know that they were dealing with investors who expected to see some account given of the company's performance and prospects in terms of the particular priorities of the investment funds involved. A company which wanted to modify its commitment to, say, retaining a strong manufacturing and knowledge base in the UK, or developing environmentally sustainable technologies might have some explaining to do to an investment fund which had declared a special preference for such particular investment applications. But if the board had decided that that was the right decision for the business, then it would be logical to go ahead with the change of strategy, and find a different investment fund more suited to its new direction.

Those fund managers whose policy was one of stable investments and not speculation would take an inclusive approach. They would want to understand the critical success factors for the business, and want to be reassured that the company had a clear success model. For example, a company claiming an important part in its success model for its skill in managing supplier relationships would be expected to produce regular evidence in measurable form that there was improvement in performance in that relationship.

Just as every investment manager would be concerned about financial results, each would also want to study risk closely. Spectacular cases of fraud or misjudgement are often analysed in terms of the need for 'better internal controls'. But, as we saw in Chapters 3 and 4, increased flexibility and discretion and trust are essential if the company is to be fast enough on its feet. What few companies have yet realised is that the key to risk management in an extended, expert-dependent business is the assessment of people and their values, not the traditional stable-door controls on behaviour. Ironically, some of those in the City of London whose business is risk seem to have more to learn than many of the 'risks' in which they are invested. At Barings, Jardine Fleming, and Morgan Grenfell the individuals whose deviant behaviour destroyed so many hundreds of millions of pounds of shareholder value were all apparently producing impressive results. In a results-dominated culture you do not challenge people who are 'delivering the goods'. There appeared to be no effective mechanism for routinely checking the values of some of those in the front line of their business against the stated ethics of the business. Yet, in a logical investment world, any investor anxious to minimise risks on the health of the investment would ask tough questions of the investee about the methods by which the organisation assesses the values of its people – unless you know the key people in the business so well that you do not need to ask.

INVESTMENT RESEARCH

Analysts provide investment managers and market-makers with research. The most respected analysts know in great depth what is going on at the company – not just from published information but from their own detective work. I was told some of the tricks of the trade by an experienced analyst. For example, if she wanted to check a company's current sales levels in the absence of any recent information from the company, she would make a few calls to the manufacturer of the cardboard boxes used for packaging the product.

But analysts depend on available information. The more sophisticated companies become in measuring their performance in each of their relationships, the more opportunity analysts will have for comparing them. In a logical investment world, the chairman of the company would go into an analysts' meeting expecting to face questions about customer loyalty, employee morale and development and innovation rates, as well as the more predictable questions about activity levels and operating profits. In a well-researched investment system, analysts would want to get behind the numbers to the health of the underlying performance that made them achievable. They would also be developing new tools, and refining the existing ones, for comparing the progress of different companies in the same industry on quality management and business excellence, customer loyalty, investment in people, the effectiveness of the supply chain, and the motivation level.

The company's published accounts would also reflect this balance between the financial outputs and the human and physical inputs that made them possible. There would be numbers and there would be narrative. Numbers without narrative would not be enough, because they are so easy to manipulate. Narrative without numbers would not be enough because the ultimate vindication of the credibility of forward-looking information is to turn it into bankable profits. If the company painted a rosy future based upon information about employee loyalty or product innovation, the investors would gain confidence in this forward-looking information only if in due course they saw the progress reflected in financial results. If the numbers do not bear out the narrative, something is wrong, either with the company's success model or with its management. The UK has seen progress towards this with the introduction by the Accounting Standards Board of the Operating and Financial Review: this does put numbers and words together to provide a more meaningful report of the company's progress.

This would be a rational operation of the investment process. The reality is altogether less logical, even if each actor in the drama feels that he or she is being perfectly logical in the role he or she is performing.

THE IRRATIONAL 'REAL WORLD' OF INVESTMENT

Take pensions as an example. At one end of the investment chain sits the saver. The timespan for the investment starts by being measured in decades. The saver is setting aside sums now to create a fund which can pay an annuity up to 40 years hence. As the saver grows older, the time span gradually shortens. If the age profile of the pension fund as a whole is skewed towards those near to retirement, the fund needs more income to meet its commitments. That is one pressure upon the trustees and the actuary and the investment manager.

There is a second pressure. The trustees are held accountable for the long-term ability of the fund to deliver the results. The only measurement they have of the success of the investment managers is to look at the recent financial performance of the fund or, as one investment manager put it to the *Tomorrow's Company* Inquiry, 'The long-term consists of a series of short terms'.

Too often the trustees have failed to set a clear policy. Too often fund managers do not appear to have a clear success model to help them to analyse what is really going on in a company and to predict future performance from an inclusive range of indicators, or if they have the model, they seem to lack the success language through which to communicate that understanding and win confidence. They do not have a yardstick or language by which to defend themselves. In a year when, judged on the current value of the portfolio other funds may appear to be performing more impressively they need to be able to say: 'In spite of poor dividends this year, we have fundamentally sound investments. The customer relationships in our portfolio are stronger than they have ever been, the development work is on target, the investment in new plant and processes in our investee companies is strong; therefore we should not panic.'

In the absence of a clear success language, the fund managers are therefore measured on the past performance of the funds under their management over two or three years, with the measurements updated every quarter. There is intense competition between them. There is the fear of losing business to the competition, and the uncertainty of demonstrating over two years that an investment philosophy geared to ten or even more years is paying off.

That fear and uncertainty has in the past been exacerbated in countries like the UK by the experience of high inflation. The higher the inflation the higher the hurdle rates – the return on capital required before an investment will be considered by any investor, whether a fund manager or a company investing in plant and equipment. While the era of high inflation may be passed, the behaviours that became habitual during that time still remain. The journalist Will Hutton chaired a discussion between the chairman of Laird Group, a UK-based international engineering group, and the chairman of Boss Group Limited, a German-based international engineering group. Hutton asked each of them about their hurdle rates. The chairman of Boss Group Limited quoted a figure of 8 per cent. The chairman of Laird quoted a figure of 20 per cent, with an expected payback within five to seven years. Interestingly, Laird expected just as high a return in Germany, where the inflation had been less, but admitted that the actual return is often more like 8–10 per cent. The Boss chairman, Bob Bischof later explained to me that there is another disincentive to investment in the UK: because wages are higher in Germany, the time taken to pay back the new investment is shorter. And he observed that the problem is compounded inside UK companies by the boosting of profits through inadequate depreciation.

THE THREE FAILURES OF INVESTMENT

As we follow the chain of accountability linking the saver to the company where his or her savings are being invested, we can see three failures. These are choice, timescale, and yardsticks. Let us look at each of them in turn.

Choice

The first failure is neglecting to reflect the full complexity of an investor's wishes in the investment policies of the fund or the fund manager. Few investors would define success in terms that take account of income and risk, but ignore utility – the practical value being achieved by the chosen investment. Given the opportunity, most small investors, like most big investors, would prefer to invest in activities and in entrepreneurs they believe in. So far, the investment industry has largely left investor preference in the box marked 'too difficult'.

The ethical investment movement has arisen as a crude attempt to redress this balance. It started by offering investors a limited choice: screening out obviously undesirable activities investors do not approve of, such as tobacco production. But after the initial screening this, by itself, has no influence on the behaviour of companies in the mainstream. It does not change the timescale over which ethical fund managers are judging the performance of companies, nor does it encourage those fund managers to challenge companies on their overall attitude to doing business. A banker like my great-grandfather would expect to know where capital was being invested; he would expect to make choices and put money into areas which produced a satisfactory return through what he considered valuable activity. There was until recently one clearing bank in the UK which made it a matter of policy to have leading decisions made by people who were not specialists in the industry!

By contrast, a modern investor relying on numerous intermediaries has no such opportunity. And this in spite of the huge increase in investor sophistication, in spite of economies of scale and in spite of the intense competition among pension providers to come up with new and attractive products. The marketing people in financial services have been very slow to wake up to the changing values described in Chapter 3! The quantity of offers has increased much more than their variety. If the the financial services sector were selling bread, its shelves would be packed with 200 varieties of white-sliced! Even those seeking a personal pension seem to have the investors equivalent of choosing between thin, medium and thick-sliced: they are usually offered low risk, medium risk, or high-risk/high-growth investments.

This absence of choice allows, by default, a distorted pressure through the investment process upon companies. Instead of policies reflecting the whole kaleidoscope of investor wishes, one of the three dimensions has been given supremacy – financial return.

This was vividly illustrated for me when I went to meet the fund manager of a company which provides one of the best known environmental screening services. It became clear that, to him, ethical investment had nothing to do with making different investment decisions. He simply screened out a few arms manufacturers and polluters, and then proceeded to manage his portfolio in the usual speculative manner. He did not see his job in terms of selecting high-quality companies and sticking with them. His aim was to guess changes in stock values, and to get in when they were undervalued and get out before they 'peaked'.

This is offering a choice, but a very limited choice, to investors. And it does not put the companies whose behaviour is offensive to investors under much pressure to change! Indeed it could be argued that the ethical investor who wants to make a difference should deliberately invest in the less ethical company because that is where a difference can be made!

The investment industry is missing an opportunity to be different and to offer choice. It has ignored the three dimensions on which its customers' preferences may vary: risk, return and usefulness. We now live in a high-technology age where retailers talk about treating every customer as an individual, and where even supermarkets are building up profiles of the preferences of individual customers. The investment industry is capable of offering investors choices on all three dimensions but, with some honourable exceptions, it hasn't begun to think hard enough about the issue.

There is no iron law of investment which says that fund managers should only be interested in financial returns without regard to how they are earned any more than there is an iron law which says they should only be interested in income and not growth. The task of the institution is to know its market and to offer choice. When providers of investment opportunities realise how few of the possibilities for consumer choice they have exploited, there is room for the kind of explosion of products that became possible when TV went from two channels to hundreds.

Timescale

The second failure is compression of the timescale over which investors want a return. There appears, on the face of it, to be a mismatch between the timescale which matters to the ultimate investor, and the timescale applied by the fund manager. From the moment I make a start on saving for my pension my timescale is thirty to forty years: yet the people employed to look after my money are being judged on its growth over two or three.

There is at least one understandable reason for the mismatch. The value of many pensions depends on the stock market price of those assets on the day of retirement. So, for many individuals, it is the snapshot at the end and not the whole video film of the forty years which matters.

There are other less understandable or admirable reasons. It is often forgotten that most UK companies have a very direct influence on the behaviour of investors. They set the terms of reference for their own pension funds. If the pension funds produce exceptional yields, there is even the possibility that the company may be able to enjoy a pension 'holiday', thus reducing costs and enhancing profits. If there is a pressure for short-termism which comes from the investment community, it is certainly being fuelled by companies themselves in their capacity as influential pension trustees with a residual responsibility for contributing to the fund. One fund manager has described to me his experience of participating, along with his competitors, in a 'beauty parade' presenting to a group of local authority pension trustees. He pointed out to them that the rate of return which they were asking him to deliver over five years was a rate of return which had only been achieved by half of one per cent of all fund managers over the previous five years. It is this kind of unreal expectation-setting, he told me, which leads fund managers away from prudent policies and into the temptation to speculate in the hope of achieving the target.

Yardsticks

The third failure, closely linked in its causes to the timescale failure and the lack of choice of investment vehicles, is the narrowness of the yardsticks of success and the language used to communicate success.

The behaviour of people at each link in the chain is dependent on the measures of success applied to them. The fund manager sees his or her fund being compared with competitors for the business of the pension funds. There are quarterly league tables produced by the actuaries which compare the performance of different funds. Within the risk profile dictated by the consulting actuary for a particular pension scheme the fund manager feels under considerable pressure to turn in a sparkling investment performance. The fund manager must outperform his or her competitors, year by year, if not quarter by quarter, for growth in the capital value of the funds managed. The only results available in this over-simplified measurement system are financial results and, unless the fund manager is armed with an impressive long-term track record, recent financial results at that. A fund manager would be less than human not to transmit that pressure to the investee companies even though doing so might damage the ability of investee companies to deliver long-term returns.

It is still possible for companies to thrive under that pressure: UK and US companies learn to demonstrate great ingenuity in combining immediate improvements with a longer haul. And, if the company has been pursuing its long haul for some years, and it is doing it well, the results should be there to show for it. But it takes leadership and conviction to stick to a long-term strategy when you are under short-term pressure. It helps fund managers if they and the researchers on whom they rely have the new measures of success by which to show their customers that the financial results from the long haul should be worth waiting for. The question for the investment community is whether the pressure for performance which it currently imposes is really calculated to give its ultimate customers the sustained improvements in performance that we want. You don't improve a child's education by moving schools every time the league table is published. You don't improve the health of a tree by digging it up and moving it several times a year.

THE DIALOGUE OF THE DEAF

It would be misleading to give the impression that companies are like tiny corks, bobbing along on a shifting turbulent ocean of impersonal ownership. It costs money to buy and sell shares. If you are a large institution holding 5 per cent of a company's shares, you cannot sell more than a sliver of your holding without depressing the price and so shooting yourself in the foot. If you are an indexed fund you are, by definition, committed to hold on to your stake. There is every reason to want to improve the quality of your portfolio through 'voice' rather than 'exit'. The average length of time that a share is held in the UK is, on the latest research, at least six years.[5]

The issue for those fund managers who find themselves, unwittingly, as the critical ligament between the investment decisions of millions of individuals and the capital needs of companies is how to exercise influence in a way which enhances entrepreneurial behaviour by companies. At one extreme, they can start to behave like old-fashioned proprietors, concentrating their holdings and becoming heavily involved in the running of those companies. At the other, they can decide to keep their distance and spread their risk. What is likely to emerge is a market in which different managers seek to differentiate their offering by different philosophies. But wherever they choose to stand along the spectrum between anonymous trading and relationship investing, their effectiveness will be determined by the tools that are available to help busy investors to discriminate between what is, for them, a bad investment and a good one. Investors will have different definitions of a good investment, according to their own particular success criteria. Each individual will put different weightings upon present financial results and indications of future growth. To some, the use to which investment funds are being put will be irrelevant. To others, the approach to business taken by the investee company is important.

The *Tomorrow's Company* Inquiry concluded that it was the absence of a clear statement of investment policy, compounded by shortage of the right tools for measuring and communicating sustainable success that creates the present, irrational climate, in which the consumer is not offered these choices, and investee companies are not encouraged to differentiate themselves. The problem is compounded by the mutual misunderstanding that appears to cloud the conversation between fund managers and chief executives of public companies.

After the publication of the Inquiry's interim report one fund manager was heard frequently complaining. 'They keep talking as if fund managers are not interested in customers, suppliers and employees. Do they imagine we never talk to companies about these things?'

In conversation with chairmen and chief executives I would draw this comment to their attention. 'Oh, that's interesting', said one blue-chip chairman in what turned out to be a fairly typical response. 'That fund manager comes here twice a year. He was here last week and I can never remember him asking me a single question about customers, suppliers or employees'.

The major fund managers, when asked, say that they would like companies to tell them what their success model is, and give a full account of their performance and health in all their key relationships. The problem is, they say, that the companies do not seem that interested. All they produce is financial information. The chief executives, on the other hand, say that they regard this information as important, but they don't produce it because the investors are only interested in immediate financial information.

It is what the Inquiry called 'the dialogue of the deaf'. Each is allowing their picture of the other to be shaped by the least constructive aspects of the other's behaviour. It is companies who can most easily break the deadlock.

HOW COMPANIES CAN IMPROVE THE DIALOGUE

It is only through adopting the new success language that boards of companies will begin to give themselves the room for manoeuvre that they need to become inclusive, and thereby sustainably competitive. And both in the UK, with the Myners Report, and in the USA, there is now a serious effort being made to encourage companies and investors to improve the quality of their dialogue.[6] Also, they will find over a period of time that they can change the behaviour of the analysts and fund managers. For example, one company involved in the Inquiry's case studies began publishing information about its customer relationships. At first, the analysts ignored this information. But after several quarters, one of the industry's leading analysts got the point, and issued a strongly positive report on the company, pointing out the encouraging implications of these figures.

The inclusive approach is the basis for business success because it means taking a comprehensive view of all the factors in all of the company's relationships which will contribute to the company's success. It is equally essential for any investor who is interested in sustainable success.

HOW INVESTORS CAN IMPROVE THE DIALOGUE

There is, of course, a difference between the self-interest of the individual fund manager and that of the investment community as a whole. As one fund manager pointed out to me, his ideal would be for him to have the information and his competitors to stay in the dark: he was therefore not very excited by my pleas for more transparency all round. It was the greater ignorance of others that gave him room to stay ahead! But that is merely to take the immediate, trading view of competitive advantage.

For investors, as for company managers, the inclusive approach is needed if there is to be an informed dialogue which helps fund managers identify and back companies with the greatest potential for sustainable success. In addition to the existing array of data, investors need to start by understanding the company's idea of what it is trying to achieve and how it hopes to be successful – its success model – as the basis for their questioning and measurement.

This in turn leads to other questions, about the company's progress in its relationships, about its licence to operate, and, of course, about its purpose and values.

Investment remains a world where many of us are bemused. Investment choices influence how companies behave, how they are led, and how they treat their people. Shareholders are often treated as dark figures whose insatiable appetites distort the operation of business, at least in the Anglo-Saxon world. And yet those shareholders are ordinary insurance policy-holders and savers for pensions – people whose values are gradually changing and who are enjoying fresh opportunities to make choices in all the ways described in Chapter 4. The future value of their pension and life policies will be determined by the success of the companies in which they are invested – and that success will, as was argued in Chapter 6, more than ever be determined by how companies are led, and how sound their values are. In investment, as in every business, tomorrow's customers will not be content with a 'black box' view. They cannot know how much they will get in thirty years time. They will want to know how it is being earned, and what the risks are. It is time to open up the black box. Alongside an account of how much has been earned in the last year, investors will be expected to show how they will continue to build value for the coming decades. Tomorrow's customers want results, but they do not want them blind. While those who manage companies can set the agenda through the way they communicate, analysts, fund managers and pension trustees also have a contribution to make in developing a success language based on the inclusive approach.

Each member of the investment chain has a contribution to make if we are to move towards a more logical investment world, which better meets the needs of the human beings whose pensions and life insurance policies it is ultimately intended to serve. In 1996 the Centre for Tomorrow's Company took its own initiative, working together with Greenly's and Kleinwort Benson Investment Management to develop a new class of growth fund based upon Tomorrow's Company principles.

Meanwhile it is *investment managers* who can:

- offer a wider and more clearly differentiated range of products;
- state quite clearly what their investment policy is – if their policy is to churn shares consistently, potential savers can be told that this is the use to which their funds are being applied;
- improve the depth and quality of their dialogue with companies, using a wider range of success measures;
- challenge companies to state how they will achieve success (their success model) and to demonstrate through appropriate measurement the progress they are making.

It is *pension trustees* who can:

- take an inclusive approach to their investment policy, offering individual members of defined contribution schemes the opportunity to make choices;
- obtain a clear mandate from members of defined benefit schemes; and set out clearly what kind of influence they would like to see fund managers bring to bear on companies;
- guard against being seduced by unrealistic claims made by investment managers, and set them terms of reference which emphasise a sustainable return achieved through an approach to investment selection which meets the needs of their beneficiaries.

It is *investment managers and researchers* who can:

- insist on understanding a company's unique approach to success; challenge companies to state how they will achieve success (their success model);
- strengthen their ability to assess and measure leadership, values, relationships, and the licence to operate;
- thereby develop a wider range of ratios by which to judge the present and likely future value of companies.

It is *actuaries and professional advisers* who can:

- help the trustees of pension funds or the holders of personal pensions to understand the range of choices available to them and the significance of their own influence over the investment management approach of fund managers;
- guide trustees and individual policy-holders on the importance of setting out a clear specification of the investment policy which they would like to see followed, including criteria covering the investee's values and business approach as well as financial criteria;
- stimulate fund managers to offer new products to meet the full range of investment preferences stated by trustees and individual investors.

9 WORK, WEALTH AND WORTH

I often talk to students about Tomorrow's Company. They like what they hear. They want to believe that business is about something more worthwhile than the impersonal pursuit of 'shareholder value'. Some find it strangely appealing to be told that business leadership can be about inspiring people to meet human needs. But there are always some cynical chuckles, usually prompted by examples where the result of people's ingenuity comes in the form of less people needed to do a particular task.

THE CAUSES OF CYNICISM

Many people find it impossible to believe that business can be ethical or worthy of their serious commitment when all the time it talks with an apparent sense of satisfaction about getting rid of jobs. Trade union representatives of bank employees or textile or steel workers find themselves staring incredulously at employers predicting the removal of tens of thousands of jobs. A study in Boston at the end of the 1980s found that over two-thirds of young men believed they could make more money 'on the street' than in jobs. The figure had doubled since 1980.[1] The American cartoonist Scott Adams, creator of Dilbert, has testified to similar cynicism among managers in the USA. He described in a radio interview the one phrase calculated to reduce an audience of American managers to a state of helpless laughter: 'Our people are our greatest asset'.

An Oxford University tutor described to me the choices that her students felt they faced in their last year. 'They feel they have to make this choice between going into business or doing something of value, between making money, or staying a lot poorer but keeping a conscience.'

Although business has given them a lot to be cynical about, the cynics are wrong. Wealth creation deserves to be celebrated. Businesses don't prosper over the long run unless they are founded on lasting values. At the same time competition is hard: it does force businesses to make decisions that hurt people's lives, and yet these can still be the right decisions, decisions which save the business and so protect many more jobs. There is, ultimately, no protection against the 'creative gales of destruction' described by the economist Joseph Schumpeter.

What those cynical chuckles tell us is that business is not getting the benefit of the doubt from the people on whose lives it has impact. Anglo-Saxon business leaders may say that a major redundancy is one of the hardest decisions they ever had to take. But the overall impression people have is of a business community more anxious to increase its own pay than that of its people, and prepared to do anything to please shareholders and secure annual bonuses.

And there is a cost that goes with such a reputation. In countries where attitudes like this harden, the result is inevitably more regulation, and restriction, and less recruitment into business of the best and the brightest.

Where people see a business sector that they deem, however unfairly, to be ruthless and uncaring, that gives business a problem whenever it needs the support of the wider community. It makes it more likely, for example, that government will increase the tax burden. It makes it less likely that a manufacturing plant will win a planning application. The community may well ask why they should make it easier for businesses to make their shareholders richer while providing less and less employment.

This problem becomes even more complicated in a global economy. Different countries and communities are now engaged in their own form of global competition, vying with one another to secure billion pound investments by the world's leading manufacturers. There is increasing force to the warning of those business leaders who say 'This country had better show itself welcoming to businesses here or they will go elsewhere'.

At the other extreme, there are a few regimes so determined to avoid the cultural defacement that comes from being part of the global economy that they even try to ban the use of alien Americanisms like 'fab' or 'video'.

THREE SCENARIOS FOR 2015

A German working in the USA told me his story about globalisation. A Japanese businessman takes his young daughter to Los Angeles on a business trip. On their way from the airport, she points out of the window. 'Oh, look, Dad, they've got McDonalds here too!'

What sort of world will we end up with? Will it be one where some countries pull up the drawbridge and stay poor but full of character, while the richer countries lose their individuality and their soul on a merry-go-round of intensified competition, all driven harder and unhappier by the relentless demands of big shareholders?

The Royal Institute of International Affairs, better known as Chatham House, has offered three possible scenarios for twenty years.[2] The first scenario, *faster faster*, sees a giddying pace of integration, commoditisation, and competitive downsizing. In other words, we will all be falling over each other to hang on to our jobs making the same things cheaper and faster. This is an efficient, accelerating and unappetising future in which winners outpace losers and few human beings feel that they have won. Unemployment and job insecurity increase. Poor districts and poor regions get poorer; there is a growing gulf between business and the community where it operates.

Meanwhile as its authors put it in a memorable phrase, 'Over all of this markets sit, scrutinizing events with lidless eyes'.[3]

The second scenario, *the post-industrial revolution*, is a world in which it is impossible to be a continuing winner without building lasting relationships. While there are a few truly global industries, different pockets of the world economy continue to have their own character within global competition. Each region develops special clusters of expertise: the whole world does not end up looking like Singapore! Flexible networks emerge. People with a common problem are able to co-operate across all the boundaries to produce their own solutions. In this future we will find that winning is about being different through better relationships with long-term suppliers, and a deeper commitment by our core staff, and through offering unexpected and imaginative new solutions to customers. To stay ahead of competitors, in this world, you do have to do more than follow their formula cheaper and faster.

The third scenario, *rough neighbours*, sees the failure of the industrialised countries to contain the tensions created by 15 per cent unemployment. There is a populist backlash in politics and a blame culture in society. People turn to fundamentalist religion and other purveyors of seductive certainty. The industrialised countries squabble among themselves and lose their influence as Asian and other economic blocs become more powerful. Poverty and environmental degradation are the chaotic result.

BEING CLEAR ABOUT IMPACT

None of us know which of these versions of the future will prevail, and where. Few can have decisive influence on them. But, if anyone can make a difference, it is the leaders and decision makers of business – not just the large companies, but the new companies, the ones who choose to compete by doing things differently. This is not to suggest that business people make business decisions by social criteria. Of course, business leaders will judge their actions by their long-term impact on shareholder value. Some may even be pressured into judging success by their short-term impact on shareholder value, misguided as that may seem to long-term shareholders. But you can be modest and realistic about the influence you have without being indifferent. People feel cynical about business because they believe businesses – and therefore business people – to be totally indifferent. They see business leaders thinking, 'Why should we worry which way the world is going, as long as there is still the opportunity for us to make money for our shareholders and land ourselves large bonuses?'

The truth is that business people are like any other group. They have to concentrate on their prime task, which is the creation of wealth, but most of them are also parents, neighbours and citizens. They have friends who have lost their jobs: they have children who are members of Greenpeace. They have half an eye on the quality of life in which they will be retiring, and more than half an eye on the sustainability of the pension they will be earning.

Business people feel undervalued by the rest of society, while at the same time many parts of society feel discarded by business. In the UK, for example, committed business leaders find it incredible that the achievements of the best of the country's businesses should be so little celebrated. In troubled inner cities, where young people are routinely without work four years after leaving school, society feels ignored or trampled on by business and unable to believe that business might have a social conscience.

There is now more connection than ever before between the worlds of business and education. Nevertheless, the two remain largely separate worlds despite the fact that a successful economy is one in which the different worlds respect each other's contribution.

So, what in practice can business people do to square the circle?

They are right to accept the imperatives of business performance. They are right to strive to deliver lasting value to shareholders. They are right to be relentless in the pursuit of lower costs, even when that means eliminating jobs. But if they want to be believed – not laughed at – when they say to their people 'You are our greatest asset', there has to be more. The real test of our commitment is always our deeds, not simply our words. In anything that affects shareholders, a business will have clear objectives and rigorous measurement. In anything that has become accepted as part and parcel of good business - health and safety, for example – businesses are, well, businesslike in the way they set out clear policies, clear responsibilities, clear objectives and clear measurement. If businesses are to be believed in what they have to say about their social concerns, it is important that they be as systematic.

Business people and their businesses are not expected to solve the problems of society. But the best of them do take business decisions with a wider sense of the impacts they would prefer to make, as well as the side effects they strive to avoid. It is reasonable to expect all business leaders to have some coherent idea about the place their business occupies in society, the part they play in its survival, and the impact which they would hope to have as a by-product of their main activity. It is no defence to claim that the side effects had not been thought about in advance, or that they were someone else's concern – unless, of course, you run one of those unusual businesses which are prepared to declare openly, 'We're here to make money for our shareholders without any regard for the effect on anyone else', and to take the consequences. These consequences can include attacks from politicians and pressure groups, unwelcome media attention, demoralised employees, bureaucratic interference and tougher regulation. Few companies could survive the backlash which they would create from such a glaring statement of contempt for their stakeholders. Many more stumble in the twilight. They mouth social concern but do not get as far as doing anything practical about it. People quickly notice the gap between action and words, and quietly lower their own commitment and loyalty.

In Tomorrow's Company, leaders will have a view about the sort of impact they would like to have on the world around them and will attempt to steer their behaviour to match that view. Then, as in any other area, they will do what they reasonably can to measure their impact, and to enhance the positive impacts, and reduce the negative ones. They will strive to increase the areas of mutual benefit – areas where doing the best by shareholders is also making a positive impact on the community – which, as we have seen, consists of the whole mix of shareholders, customers, and neighbours.

For example, Robert Shapiro, the chief executive of Monsanto, has set out to refashion the whole business around environmental sustainability. His predecessor had set aggressive targets and deadlines for limiting the company's negative impacts – including the reduction of toxic air emissions by 90 per cent in six years.

> But, even if Monsanto reached its goal of zero impact next Tuesday, that wouldn't solve the world's problem. Several years ago, I sensed that there was something more required of us than doing no harm, but I couldn't articulate what that was. So I did what you always do. I got some smart people together . . . and sent them off to think about it . . . My request to this group was: 'Go off, think about what's happening to the world, and come back with some recommendations for what it means for Monsanto. Do we have a role to play? If so, what is it? . . . People came away emotionally fired up. It wasn't just a matter of 'Okay, you threw me an interesting business problem, I have done the analysis, here is the answer, and now can I go back to work?' People came away saying, 'Damn it, we've got to get going on this. This is important'. When some of your best people care intensely, their excitement is contagious.

> There was a flurry of e-mail around the world, and in a matter of four months a group of about 80 coalesced. Some were chosen, many others just heard about the project and volunteered . . . They decided to organise into seven teams, three focused on developing tools to help us make better decisions, three focusing externally on meeting world needs, and one focused on education and communication.[4]

The result for Monsanto is a series of initiatives aimed both at creating new business opportunities for the company and at tackling problems of real human need – for example, projects concerned with genetic alteration of crops to avoid the need for pesticides, and projects to protect soil from salination.

And, reflecting on the significance of what has been achieved for the motivation of Monsanto people, Shapiro adds powerful support for the inclusive view that business is about meeting the needs of human beings, needs which cannot in the end be compartmentalised.

> People in large numbers won't give their all for protracted periods of time – with a cost in their overall lives – for an abstraction called a corporation or an idea called profit. People can only give to people. They can give to their co-workers if they believe that they're engaged together in an enterprise of some importance. They can give to society, which is just another way of saying they can give to their children. They can give if they believe that their work is in some way integrated into a whole life. Historically, there has been a bifurcation between who we are and what we do, as if who we are is outside our work. That's unhealthy, and most people yearn to integrate their two sides.[5]

Far from distracting people from the creation of shareholder value, such social concern can actually galvanise the organisation.

SETTING OUT WHAT YOU STAND FOR

This kind of thinking may have its roots in idealism and social conscience. But it makes business sense. As the Monsanto case demonstrates, it motivates people. It also helps a business face the more critical scrutiny which it must now expect to undergo from customers, employees, pressure groups, investigative journalists, regulators, and government in the course of earning their licence to operate. Larger and international businesses already expect to face challenges in all these areas. Corporate environment reports are now expected of major companies. It is only a matter of time before governments somewhere in the world start to require that these are externally verified, and perhaps even extended to ethical and social auditing.

The expectations of society will not go away, and it takes planning and forethought to meet them. Many of these lessons have already been learned in the area of environmental impact. Alan Knight, the Quality and Environment Controller at the UK Do-It-Yourself Chain B&Q (whose environmental initiatives were described in Chapter 5) says, 'We have learned one important thing about environmental issues: they take a long time to solve and you need to be at least on the way to a solution by the time questions are raised'.[6]

Businesses which speak in ambitious terms about their responsibilities to build a more sustainable world must expect particularly careful scrutiny. In the mid-1990s the much admired multinational ABB took on the £3bn contract to build the Bakun dam in Sarawak, Malaysia. A collection of 40 Malaysian non-governmental organisations described the project as 'socially destructive, environmentally disastrous, and economically misconceived'. The project had also been condemned by Greenpeace, Friends of the Earth, and the Worldwide Fund for Nature (WWF). ABB had been one of the leading companies to make a public commitment to sustainable development, and to call on other businesses to take a lead in making similar commitments. Not surprisingly, ABB faced heavy criticism for taking on a contract which would cause profound ecological damage and lead to the relocation away from their traditional existence of 10,000 villagers. ABB argued that Malaysia was a sovereign state, and was the customer, and must make its own decisions about environmental impact. Furthermore, the company pointed out, if ABB did not build the dam, its competitors would happily take on the contract.[7]

The critics argued that there were better options for generating the additional energy which Malaysia required. ABB found itself torn between its understandable loyalty to its customer, and its previous strong statements urging business to take a lead in 'solving environmental problems and promoting sustainable development' and 'communicating openly with interested parties in the communities and countries where ABB operates'.

At least ABB had had the leadership to set itself a high standard against which it would be judged: perhaps the company had not thought deeply about the practicalities of implementing the impressive-sounding principles. It might have avoided some of the pain and embarrassment if, before publishing high-flown statements of policy, it had followed Monsanto's example. This would mean bringing together some bright people and asking them to work through what dilemmas the draft policy posed in the securing of new business, relationships with governments, the signing of contracts, the choice of technology, the measurement of environmental impact and all the other ways in which the company's actions affect global sustainable development.

Similar challenges are on their way in the examination of a company's supplier relationships. For example, major retailers have come to expect critical media investigations into the possible abuse of child labour.

The lessons of experience in the environmental area are well known. The best businesses do not wait to be picked off selectively by their critics. They set out their own stall. They say what they stand for, and what impact they expect to have on others. They do not claim that everything is perfect: they educate, and they give their stakeholders realistic expectations. They are receptive to criticism and they encourage dialogue. They publish targets and encourage those outside the business to tell them when they fall short of these standards. They communicate their success model, and describe how progress in social and environmental areas is connected to the creation of shareholder value in achieving it. They take every opportunity to match together business opportunity and public benefit. I was recently asked to join the independent panel convened by the New Economics Foundation and Body Shop International, the cosmetics retailer. Our task was to review the process by which the Body Shop's values report had been prepared and verified. We spent a day reviewing that company's standards of measurement and method of reporting its impact on each stakeholder group. Where the company set out a socially ambitious policy – for example on increasing the share of its turnover accounted for by fair trade contracts – there were measures to judge actions against words.

Because good environmental practice means good stewardship of resources, there are plenty of opportunities for win/win. Imaginative businesses find new business opportunities around good environmental practice. They also recognise that if they want the community and society to give them the benefit of the doubt in areas where they do not meet outside expectations, they will need to have made large deposits in the bank of goodwill.

MEETING SOCIETY'S UNEASE

The same lessons now need to be applied in those areas which reflect the deepest unease society feels about its future. Parents, politicians, pupils, and many others are worried about work. They want to be able to see worthwhile opportunities opening up for the next generation. They want to be reassured that the vigorous pursuit of profit in a global market economy does result in opportunities for the next generation to prove itself. They want to believe that going into business is not the twenty first-century equivalent of selling your soul. The real challenge for businesses is to focus on sustainable wealth creation *and*, at the same time, strengthen and communicate the links between long-term shareholder value and long-term community value.

In the years ahead, work, wealth and worth in the social and community area are headings under which any business will need to make progress in describing its aspirations and measuring its impacts.[8]

What follows here is my own vision of how UK businesses can accentuate the positive in their impact. The challenge for each company is to work out its own impact, example by example, community by community, and country by country. That will give all its stakeholders something of the company's own purpose and values to judge it by. Much better than waiting for the single issue pressure groups to draw up their own list of desired behaviours, and face condemnation for failing to achieve objectives the company may not recognise!

Work

As we saw in Chapter 3, in a few years work has gone from being mostly manual, permanent, full-time, geographically rigid and predominantly for men, to being mostly knowledge-based, technical, part-time, geographically less rigid and increasingly open to women. More by accident than design, companies have been the agents of that change.

Wealth

During the 1980s and 1990s, the business community gradually learned to recognise the part it had to play to ensure that there was, physically, a sustainable environment left in which to create future wealth. As was shown earlier in this chapter, companies must now be accustomed to face severe criticism. So far business has made more progress in demonstrating that it is operating in an environmentally friendly way. The next challenge is described by Steven Robinson of the (UK) Environment Council: 'Companies seeking to create a sustainable business must not just examine *what* the organisation is doing but whether it should be doing it in the first place . . . Just because an activity is feasible, it doesn't mean it's desirable'.[9] Over the next two or three decades, the contribution of business to a sustainable physical and social environment will be subjected to a steady broadening and deepening of public scrutiny of the social value they are creating alongside the shareholder value.

A sustainable social environment is one where everyone feels needed: all have a contribution to make. In some places, and at some times, the sheer youth and dynamism of an economy, combined with the quality of education and training available ensures that everyone feels needed through the quantity of paid work available and the shortage of paid people to do it. This was certainly true of economies like Malaysia in the early 1990s.

In other countries, such as the more mature Western European economies, it has taken enterprise of a different kind to fill the gap. For example, there has been a remarkable growth of private sector/public sector partnerships in

138

Textbox 9.1   Work

Tomorrow's company will help itself and those contemplating working for it by charting its vision of the future of work. For example, one UK-based company with international operations might say:

'There are no guarantees of lifetime employment with Tomorrow's Company plc. Our only prediction is that the next ten years will be even more international, and even more unpredictable than the last, in which we have seen three redundancy programmes, one of them compulsory, and reduced our total numbers employed from 17,000 to 3,800, while increasing our sales in real terms by 85 per cent. However we offer all our co-workers a clear framework for learning: every person who works here knows what qualifications we would like them to be studying for next, and receives regular mentoring as well as financial help and time off to achieve these results.

It is a fact that

20% of those who joined us as graduates 15 years ago are still with us.

35% of our associates have a link that has lasted more than 3 years.

32% of all our UK-based employees have gained at least two NVQ level 3 qualifications

during the last two years with us.

and we continue to expect that the core of this company will be formed of full-time people with at least 7 years experience in the business, drawn from all the different communities and ethnic groups with which we deal. We regularly review the qualifications gained by our people. We also measure the value we add in terms of people's earning capacity. On average, people leaving us after five years have gained 40 per cent in their earning power.

An analysis of those people who have made the most progress (measured in terms of total remuneration) shows that 90 per cent have had a personal development plan in place for the last 5 years, and 60 per cent speak at least two European languages.

We as a company are working, in all the places where we offer employment, to contribute to a highly educated and highly motivated future workforce which will strengthen the prospects of the whole local economy. In particular we offer

Extensive work experience for secondary pupils and visits/projects for primary pupils

Support for Young Enterprise and other schemes designed to give young people the chance to experience running their own businesses

Financial and professional help to the Princes Youth Business Trust and other initiatives which help young people to start businesses

Time off for our people to be school governors

Work placements for teachers

Support and business opportunities to our own people who wish to set up their own businesses

We have clear objectives and clear measures of success in all of these areas. We report on our progress in these areas to everyone who is concerned. We tell our shareholders, because it affects our ability to create shareholder value. We tell the wider public, and communities in which we operate, because we want them to know what to expect of us. We tell our suppliers, because we hope it will encourage them to take similar steps to secure an honest and solid basis for their relationships with their people. We tell our customers, because they meet our people all the time, and we want them to understand the sort of business we are and the sort of relationships we have.

We therefore encourage all those who want to have a long-term relationship with us to

have a personal development plan

be able to demonstrate to us how their skills and outlook matches our own.

show evidence in their CV and record of achievement that they are intelligent, enterprising, adaptable and outward looking as well as academically able.'

cities like Newcastle, Bristol, and in West London. These partnerships have cut across the usual red tape enabling them to tackle the social problems which stood in the way of making communities healthy, lively contributors to the economy, rather than depressed breeding grounds for crime and prostitution.

Although conventional economists have not caught up with this innovation yet, this is wealth creation. It takes entrepreneurs with high skill to mobilise a depressed and downtrodden community, to build on its unique strengths, to deal with its legacy of obsolete plant or outdated skills or poor education or crime-ridden city centres. It takes the foresight of a real business visionary to understand that strengthening the community today is laying the foundations for effective business tomorrow. It takes foresight and leadership to go to the next stage, as Bill Castell of Amersham International does, and to make a point of telling fund managers, at his regular meetings with them, of the investment that he and his company make in the future health of the community.

One of the more irritating fallacies is the smug belief by some business people that, 'We create the wealth' and that social workers or housing departments and schools 'just spend it'. Teachers are wealth creators. Housing officers are wealth creators. Think of the wealth created by an effective social work team which prevents a family from fragmenting and saves its children from care or custody.

What's more, the family that stays together, the housing estate that is a good place to live, and the school that is helping to develop bright and adaptable adults are all directly contributing to the kind of environment in which business will flourish.

Measuring and reporting social impact as the basis for dialogue

Not all wealth creation is measured in traditional financial terms. Business has many positive impacts on the community around it that are not shown in its normal measurement and reporting. Just imagine the annual report of Tomorrow's Company. Alongside the detailed description of the value created for shareholders, the value created for employees and associates, the value created in the supply chain, and the value created for customers, is the description of the value created for the community. The summary report – what the Centre for Tomorrow's Company has called the core document – shows how all these different relationships come together to create value for shareholders. Reporting on community impact is not presented as a tokenist afterthought: it embodies the company's stated values and belongs as part of its success model. The summary report would be supported by more detailed reporting of impact on community, employees, suppliers, customers and shareholders in its description of its community impacts.

As time goes on, the supporting community report would become more precise. A business with three major manufacturing plants in different countries, and 70 distribution outlets would give an account of its total impact on each. If it had to close an outlet it would describe in its report the adverse effect on the economic and social wealth of the community of this withdrawal. If it had to make people redundant it would quantify the loss of experience and skills represented by the people going. If it was involved in offering work experience it would describe the effect of the work experience on the progress of pupils. Leading companies are already bringing this inclusive form of reporting to life: an example is provided in Appendix 3.

As in every other area of business, the effect of measurement would be to make people inside and outside business think harder about the total value of what they were doing. The result of that hard thought would be that, in time, the business would do it better. It would ask questions such as: 'How can we double the positive impact on the lives of the individuals involved in work experience for the same outlay?', and 'How can we minimise the adverse impact which we have on the local traffic problem?'

The relevant parts of the annual report would also be the subject of a public discussion with the community involved. This would help move the emphasis of community involvement, just as the emphasis has shifted in the world of health and safety, from crisis management to proactive management. If there were a crisis brewing as a result of lorries being loaded and blocking the residential streets into the early hours, it would be the subject of constructive dialogue long before protestors got out banners and alerted local radio and TV. The interdependence of sustainable business activity and a sustainable community would be clear for all to see. The business would regard it as natural to tell shareholders about the steps it was taking to build a more sustainable community as it would to tell the local community about the steps which it was taking to improve total shareholder return. And in areas where, previously, the business found itself under attack from single issue pressure groups for failing to live up to standards of performance which the business had never agreed were realistic, there would be intelligent and continuing dialogue about what was realistic and what was acceptable. For example, as the business reported regularly to the community on the value it had created for shareholders, the community might be encouraged to renew its efforts to provide, so as to help a supportive operating environment. Through imaginative outreach and communication the business could come to be regarded less as a parasite and more as a partner. Record profits would be seen outside as well as inside the business, more as a shared achievement to be proud of, and less as an obscenity.

For the smaller business, none of this need be complicated, as the Happy Computers statement (page 142) demonstrates. For example, a small local engineering business with 30 employees, might build its community report around four or five key measures of impact, publish it once a year as a supplement in the local newspaper, and then update it more regularly on the company's web site. Or, the relevant trade association might create simple common formats which could be used by all its member companies and so enable the industry as a whole to give an overall account of its impact. In the case of a billion pound retailer with multiple outlets and complex sourcing arrangements, the company's own reports might be independently verified by an independent assessor.

Textbox 9.2   Happy Computers' social statement

Happy Computers has, like all companies, a wide range of stakeholders, including staff, clients, investors and suppliers. And we have a statement of principles about how we treat people. When we were offered the chance to carry out a social audit, leading to the production of this Social Statement, we realised this was a chance to find out if we are putting these principles into practice. At one level it is simply a very comprehensive organisational review that enabled us to examine every part of our business. At another level, by working from the point of view of the stakeholder, it shows exactly how we affect those we come into contact with.

It also fulfils our belief in transparency. All information, particularly the detailed financial results, is shared throughout the company. In choosing to publish this Social Statement we are laying open how we perform as a company and exactly what our stakeholders think of us, including any criticisms.

When I founded Happy Computers I was told a lot of things by people with more business experience than me: I was told that business was a serious thing, that we couldn't succeed with such a silly company name, that work couldn't be fun, that you had to put profit first and that you had to keep careful control of your staff or they would take advantage.

This social audit confirms to me that this advice was wrong. The fun, positive approach of the company is one of its key advantages: It attracts freelance trainers (often earning less than elsewhere), motivates the staff, is seen as vitally important by clients and, most important, makes it easier to learn about computers (our core job). The wider principles are just as crucial. A key conclusion I draw from the audit is that people want to do business with and work for organisations they can feel good about.

One remarkable finding was that 54 per cent of clients responding stated that simply taking part in the social audit had made them more likely to book with Happy Computers. It is impossible to measure the precise benefit of this but growth has been substantial in the year since the audit. Bookings in January and February 1996 were respectively 66 per cent and 80 per cent above the 1995 levels and Happy Computers has doubled in staff during this period.

Happy Computers is a commercial company. We aim to grow and expand and we aim to make substantial profit in the future. The key lesson of this audit is that having clear principles and looking after the interests of all the stakeholders, even above short-term profit, is not only a nice thing to do but presents a competitive advantage in today's market.

Happy Computers is not unique in its approach and there are many companies that we learn from. We are seeking to be, in the words of one of our shareholders, a '21st century company'. We believe those companies that will succeed in the next decade will be those, whether large or small, who serve the interests of all those they work with.

We have learnt a lot from this audit and have implemented a wide range of changes, detailed in this report. We have already received a lot of positive feedback but I look forward to the next social audit, where we will find more exactly to what extent these changes have met the needs of our stakeholders.

We will continue to seek to make our work and our service as fun as possible. We will continue to reach for the skies in what we can achieve in terms of empowerment and fulfilling people's potential. We will continue to seek to live by clear principles. We believe that, like other companies that are following the same route, Happy Computers will grow and prosper as a result.

Henry Stewart,
Founder of Happy Computers

The key, in all cases, is: a willingness to be accountable for the wealth you have created for the community alongside what you have done for shareholders; the breadth to recognise that not all wealth is measured in monetary terms or created by salaried people; the self-discipline to set out the impacts which you wish to have, and to measure your progress against them; and the openness needed to have dialogue with all those who are affected. There is no need for any company to be lonely in its struggle to make its measurement and reporting more inclusive. The Institute for Social and Ethical Accountability has been established to provide independent auditing and advice, and has become the focal point for thinking about the concept of the social audit. Meanwhile Business in the Community (in the UK) and the Prince of Wales Business Leaders Forum continue as the business-led authorities on corporate community involvement.

Worth

A wider definition of wealth, and a more inclusive dialogue about the contribution business makes to its creation, will certainly reduce the cynicism and the hostility which many people feel towards business. But there are some hard facts which it will not alter. In all three of the descriptions of 2015 offered above, it is likely that there will be less people working full-time for businesses. What comfort is all this to a depressed inner city area where there appears to be little hope of economic reward within the law?

The people who keep such communities going are frequently the informal leaders, undervalued by the society that leans so heavily upon them. The real wealth-creators are people like the unpaid chairman of the tenants association, with a network of contacts and influences that any sales director would envy.

It seems illogical that people like this, who receive no wage or salary, and survive on state benefits, should be regarded as burdens on society. For sound economic reasons, developed societies will need to recognise that a person's worth is not determined by their wage, but by their contribution. People who are dependent on state benefits but contribute vital unpaid work which holds a community together deserve society's respect and acknowledgement. They should not be lumped together with people who are content to rely on state benefit but have no intention of doing anything in return.

Business belongs to the formal, paid, economy. But the formal economy depends for its survival on the informal economy. For example, in the UK there is the economy of nearly 7 million adult carers looking after old or chronically sick dependents. Nearly 1.5 million of these carers spend 20 hours a week at this work, which is not a job. It is in the interest of business to acknowledge this debt, by helping, and by showing how much it respects and relies on the unpaid wealth-creators.

This is an issue on which businesses can take a lead. They will show an intelligent awareness of the social risks that could bring their business down, and of the business opportunities that could be found if they tackled that risk.

The formation by Grand Metropolitan of an independent trust is a good example. Businesses are responsible for salaried work. Businesses which celebrate and acknowledge the unsalaried wealth-creators will send new messages of hope to society. For example, more businesses could examine ways in which they could provide some support and relief – or even just a cooked meal – to the millions of unsalaried carers who keep the economy going. They might encourage the formation within the organisation of small self-help teams who would cover the absence of one of their number who faced a chronic care problem with a child or a chronically sick household member. By allowing the team to provide for themselves they could reduce the likelihood of the time off being abused by any individual: it is much harder to stay at home on false pretences when you know that it is your immediate colleagues, and not the whole organisation, you are cheating.

Textbox 9.3   GrandMet report on corporate citizenship

For 15 years GrandMet Trust has helped over 150,000 young and unemployed individuals get jobs when employment has seemed a distant prospect. Now independent of GrandMet, with the company's continuing support, the Trust, a national charity, has changed its name to Tomorrow's People.

The Trust was established to address acute social issues potentially damaging to the UK business environment. Its origins date back to 1981, when young unemployed people went on the rampage. At a board meeting following that summer of discontent in the inner cities, GrandMet directors decided the company should try to do something about the problem.

GrandMet Trust was set up to offer unemployed people careers guidance, advice and training. It has since become a leading national charity dedicated to helping unemployed young people achieve self-sufficiency in partnership with a succession of public sector agencies and over 50,000 employers.

The Trust's work has been financed by our £15m core funding, a further £15m contributed by other companies and government agency contracts of over £100m. The management support provided by GrandMet has ensured high standards in charity finance reporting, human resource management, quality control and research and development.

Following extensive research and consultation with partners, government agencies and other firms, the trustees decided GrandMet Trust was ready to operate on a more independent basis and that this change in status should be reflected by a change of name to Tomorrow's People Trust.

The objective is to develop Tomorrow's People as the recognised national charity for the unemployed, addressing an issue of vital importance to businesses that is ready made for small, medium-sized or regional companies which lack the resources to run community involvement programmes of their own.

Tomorrow's People supporters groups are being formed in all the areas where the Trust operates and the GrandMet Foundation has committed itself to continue to provide core funding and support and remain involved on the Board of Trustees.

A full float-off of Tomorrow's People Trust as an independent charity for the unemployed is planned when the shadow trustees are confident it has achieved sufficient national momentum.

Michael Guthrie
Chairman of Tomorrow's People Trust

Anglo-Saxon businesses which pride themselves on their independence from regulation would have some reason to be horrified if such ideas were imposed on them. Too often they allow their resistance to imposed change to blind them to the benefits of embracing that change for themselves. The company is a human community. The chief executive who breaks new ground in reinforcing that sense of community is laying the foundations for durable value to be created – shareholders value *and* social value.

There are examples which show what can be achieved when business acts in partnership with the community and local government. In the UK, there is the work of the Prince's Youth Business Trust, and the Prince's Volunteers. There are outstanding stories of communities working closely with business to build a triumphant new existence out of the ruins of an industry, such as Penrhys, a village dependent on coal mining, which saw 2,000 jobs destroyed in 1985 with the closure of the local pit. Strongly supported by companies like Whitbread and Amersham International, the village rallied under the leadership of a remarkable Methodist minister, the Reverend John Morgans, and built a new community centre, rich in artistic performances, and developed a new community-based approach to tackle the traditional vicious circle of delinquent behaviour from nursery education onwards.

One of the most corrosive and limiting attitudes in the mature economies has been the view that equates resources with money. All kinds of desirable objectives in education are, we are told, beyond us because there isn't the money. This is an unnecessary limitation on progress. As soon as we recognise that wealth resides in human beings, businesses and their partner organisations can create opportunities for people to contribute to the improvement of their own surroundings, without money being seen as the key to all progress.

One of the by-products of businesses reporting on the community value which they have created would be to stop communities imitating the outdated habit of measuring purely in financial terms. If businesses gave a lead in measuring their total impact on the community, this should encourage the community both to take a wider view of all the resources available and to think harder about how it, in partnership with businesses, not-for-profit organisations and government might mobilise the talents of many more of its own citizens without necessarily paying them a salary. This could lead in turn to the development by countries, and regions, of their own version of the balanced scorecard.

The old indicators of progress, such as Gross Domestic Product (GDP), show an increase in wealth when the number of car accidents increase. In future, to judge their progress in creating work, wealth and worth, communities will need to balance GDP and productivity measures alongside a wider array of indicators of social progress and human development. Just imagine an annual report of a future government in which it gives an account of its stewardship against this scorecard!

To this might be added a balance sheet of human capital – for communities as well as businesses – showing just how much investment in knowledge and talent is being made, and also perhaps a 'social exclusion index' showing just how much of that talent is, at any time, not being occupied or fully rewarded. We need communities to become as imaginative and rigorous in the measurement of their progress as a company like FedEx, in its development of the leadership index (see Chapter 6, page 100).

(see Chapter 6, page 100)

Textbox 9.4   Work, wealth and worth: individuals

(drawn from Mark Goyder's lecture to the Institution of Engineers and Shipbuilders in Scotland, 1997) published in RSA Journal 1997.

Individuals

As individuals we need an inclusive approach as much as companies do if we are to manage the risk of living in these uncertain times. It starts with a clear sense of direction.

- every young person in school in this country to have a personal mentor – neither a parent nor a teacher. Business and other employers would provide half of these mentors, with retired and unemployed citizens providing the rest
- every young person at school to be challenged to update their personal learning plan at least annually. Financial support for further education to be linked to maintenance of these plans.
- Time given in every sixteen-year-old's life somewhere to the exercise of writing one's own obituary. It forces people to use their imaginations and think about what is important to them and how they would like to be remembered.
- First hand experience of being a leader or entrepreneur; for example expeditions, or Young Enterprise schemes where groups of students form and run their own businesses become a recognised part of the curriculum.
- Tax or benefit advantages for any young person who continues with community service and/or learning after they leave school.
- The European Union to develop schemes through which every young person spends at least a term of their secondary education in a school in a country other than their own.

Many businesses give practical support in the form of secondments. The huge numbers of people who by their fifties are found to be surplus to requirements by their business employers are often the backbone of such work.

In mature economies, like that of the UK, the case for a form of national citizens' service scheme has become overwhelming and appears to be close to implementation. It would be designed to ensure that the first experience every young person might have after leaving full-time education would be that of making a contribution to meet a community need. During the six or twelve months of service, the young person, or indeed, the young retiree would, as a by-product, be fed and housed and have some spending money left over. But the overwhelming testimony of those who have participated in such schemes has been the thrill of discovering new things that they are good at, or finding new customers for long-established skills, and, in both cases, the sense of self-worth that comes from making a contribution and being needed. It is not for businesses to start such schemes. But it is in partnership with businesses that such schemes will achieve their full potential, and help to break down the idea that a waged or salaried job is the only way to be useful or valued. Ironically, such experiences in the non-economic part of life actually serve to equip people with more entrepreneurial skills.

Textbox 9.5   Work, wealth and worth: government

From job creation to opportunities for growth

The society we want to encourage is one in which some contribute through waged work. Many more will live a portfolio life. Some of their time will be spent learning; some will be spent earning; and some will be spent contributing.

  The state can help: here is a simple three point plan.

- Stage one is to ensure that during the years of compulsory education, every person is exposed to experience of what they are good at. My rule of thumb would be two weeks of work experience at the age of 12, increasing by two weeks every year to eight weeks by the age of 16. The aim of that would be to force on all pupils a far greater exposure to the range of possible skills and careers.

To make this possible, redefine the curriculum so that work experience is properly recognised as the practical application of what had been learned, just as a period in France is the logical accompaniment to the textbook curriculum of every pupil of French.

- Stage two is to provide a simple two way agreement or contract for school leavers. Under this contract, the community guarantees the pupil one year's placement backed by suitable training. No-one at all leaves school to go straight into unemployment. During the six or twelve months of service, the young person, or indeed, the young retiree would, as a by-product, be fed and housed and have some spending money left over. Offer option of doing it after a later school-leaving date, or after finishing a degree. To qualify for the full range of state benefits the year of training-backed service would have to be completed before the age of 23.

- Stage three is to introduce a form of national learning insurance. This would provide everyone who lost their job with a 'deposit account' of training credits. Anyone who had been working for a year would be entitled to three months training. Those who had longer periods of work behind them would be entitled to a longer spell of retraining. After five years in a job the learning insurance could be used to pay for a retraining sabbatical, helping people who felt they were in a rut to learn new skills.

Human beings need to be needed. They cannot belong unless they feel needed. They cannot grow unless their talents are used. Just as companies have been held back from delivering the shareholder value of which they are capable by a narrow view of success, so communities today are held back from developing their full potential by the same obsolete view which sees resources only as paid resources and results only as money spent.

All over the world, societies face the struggle to prevent the realisation of the 'rough neighbours' scenario. The deciding factor for many of those societies will be how they handle the issue of worth. Businesses of all shapes and sizes will gain directly – through an enhanced licence to operate and increased goodwill – and indirectly – through the strengthening of the communities on which they depend – by investing in the self-worth of many people whom they will never, directly, employ. Their neighbours – and our neighbours – will be 'rough neighbours' unless they are neighbours with some work, wealth and worth.

The more entrepreneurial of our business leaders will be the first to re-position their businesses – as Monsanto is doing – so that they find new business ways of meeting human need which directly or indirectly rebound to the long-term benefit of their shareholders. They will be rigorous in measuring their impacts; they will never lose sight of their prime duty to be stewards for the long-term health of the business: but they will manage their businesses not as sealed cylinders but as living organisms – which feed and are fed by the other forms of life around them.

The most successful will have found new ways of doing business that simultaneously create shareholder and social value – demonstrating afresh that business success is only ultimately sustainable where the company is meeting human needs, and that values are inextricably linked with the creation of value.

10 DIVINE DISCONTENT

> **Textbox 10.1   Honda**
>
> *Mr. Hori: In the past Honda Motor Co. Ltd has been held up as an example of a truly excellent company. Do you agree with this evaluation of Honda?*
>
> Mr. Kawamoto: Today, I definitely do not think that Honda is an excellent company. In fact, the present Honda is ill. Twenty years ago, when the company's founder Soichiro Honda was president, I think the company was excellent. Twenty years ago Honda's competitiveness, growth plans, and drive to press forward fit perfectly with what the market demanded. When the fit is perfect, then a company can be called excellent. At that time, Honda was very productive and benefited both its shareholders and the world.
>
> But it has been 43 years since Honda was first established. People, when they reach the age of 40, complain of back pain and ask for a massage when they get home at night. When companies grow old, they too accumulate marks of experience. This experience becomes the criterion for judging past successes and the starting point for future developments. Over time successes become constraints to freedom of action. This leads to the development of 'large company disease' which diminishes a company's ability to respond to change.
>
> This is what happened to Honda. Honda has developed a tendency to base value judgments on past successes. We insist that tasks be handled within the parameters of existing organizations, even when these organizations fail to serve the customers for whom we work. You can even hear responses such as, 'No, it can't be done,' or, 'It's not necessary,' when people make suggestions or requests. This is a sign of company illness. The way to make Honda healthy again is to apply what the company has learned from its past mistakes to the new age, with its range of values.[1]

It doesn't take long to identify a company which is on the inclusive journey. You can feel it in the atmosphere – a current of excitement and commitment. On your way there the taxi driver has positive comments. The receptionist treats you like a guest; the people in the offices and production areas can talk in a lively and intelligent way about the company and its progress, and the leaders of the organisation (which means a considerable number of people, not just the chief executive) are notable for their belief in the company and its goals, their openness, their dedication, their insistence on measurement and their relentless self-criticism. Everywhere, you meet perfectly normal people who each radiate just that fraction of extra spirit, competence, and self-belief. There is a humanity about the way individuals are treated, allied to a steely determination to achieve results. You come away wishing you could bottle the spirit of the place and take it back with you.

In times of uncertainty it is the leader's job to give people some certainty: when things seem settled it is the leader's job to unsettle them with questions to which she or he probably does not know the answers. And it is the task of all who work in the organisation to ask questions too.

That is the spirit which inspired the RSA *Tomorrow's Company* Inquiry and it is the spirit which is needed to regenerate the entrepreneurial qualities in a settled organisation. Already, in the short time since the Centre for Tomorrow's Company was formed in 1996, we have learned the value of a forum which allows leaders to fuel their restlessness and to indulge their thirst for new ideas. We are creating opportunities for local companies to share with each other the tales from their own journey. We are working to embolden the investment community to develop more stimulating and forward-looking methods for analysing and questioning companies. We want to encourage researchers to probe, and business schools to stimulate their students' thinking about the principles which lie behind lasting success in business. It would be a measure of the Centre's success if the contents of this book soon became outdated.

LEADERSHIP AND THE UNEXPECTED

Imagine a company which has, apparently, done it all. It has faced the prospect of extinction, and it has pulled through. It has cut its costs, re-engineered its operations, turned its processes upside down, developed new relationships with suppliers, gone through the stage of cut-back. It has involved everyone in generating a sense of common purpose: it is true to some enduring values. It has started a revolution in its supplier relationships and unleashed the abilities of its management team. What is there left to do?

I was visiting such a business recently. The chief executive told me that he did not know what the next external crisis might be – it might come from competitors, environmental pressures, international tension. Whatever it might prove to be, he wanted the business to anticipate it. With his team he was mentally turning the whole beautifully functioning organism upside down and shaking it. 'Why do we need a corporate HQ?' 'Why have artificial boundaries in the value chain?' 'How do we get nearer to the real customer?' 'How do we disturb our settled assumptions about what makes us successful?'

This was divine discontent, at once uncomfortable and invigorating. It's rather like the feeling the author has when he completes the last chapter . . . and he suddenly realises that that is only the beginning!

APPENDICES

APPENDIX 1: Agendas for action

Agenda for action: directors

1 **Company purpose and values** – Have we adopted a clear statement of purpose? Have we adopted an explicit statement of values which indicates how the company will conduct business and behave in its key relationships?

2 **Key relationships** – Do we know which relationships are crucial to the success of the business? How do we ensure that the company is maintaining consistent and open two-way communications with people in all its key relationships? Have we anticipated the consequences of failure in key relationships? How do we ensure that the risk of failure is being managed?

3 **Success model** – Have we adopted a success model for the company which demonstrates how value is added?

4 **Measurement** – Do we review the company measurement system annually, against its ability to support our goals, purpose, values and key relationships? Do we measure outcomes as well as outputs? Is sufficient time spent reviewing relationships? Do we receive a regular report on issues such as reputation, *licence to operate* and environmental impact?

5 **Reward system** – Do we review the reward system against its ability to reinforce business goals and motivate the right behaviours? Do we monitor positive behaviours such as teamworking and empowering? Do we seek reports on levels of behavioural risk in key areas of the business?

6 **Learning organisation** – Do we accept that the company has the primary responsibility for providing a framework for learning? Which of us champions learning issues? How do we ensure that the company has a systematic approach to learning and resources to support it?

7 **Fiduciary responsibilities** – Are we satisfied as fiduciaries that we are acting in the interests of the general body of shareholders as it exists from time to time, and not simply current shareholders?

8 **Business renewal** – What steps do we take to review and obtain continued commitment to the company's long-term strategy?

9 **Climate for success** – What initiatives and partnerships are we involved in aimed at improving the climate for success? How do we make known our views on competitiveness issues? Have we reviewed the capabilities

of our representative bodies against a backdrop of global competitiveness?

10 **Raising performance standards** – What networking activities do we
participate in aimed at spreading best practice? Are we part of a supply
chain in which all participants acknowledge their membership and work
jointly on reducing costs and raising performance standards through a
focus on meeting customer needs?

Agenda for action: managers

1 **Purpose** – Do we articulate the company's purpose consistently? Does the company's purpose serve to inspire commitment?
2 **Values** – Are we clear and consistent about values? Are those values explicit? Do we practise what we preach on openness, fairness and diversity?
3 **Success model** – Can we articulate the company's success model to key groups? Can they describe the model to us? Do they understand their part in adding value to the business?
4 **Leadership** – How successful are we in gaining the commitment of those whose contribution is crucial to the sustainable success of the business? How do we know about their level of commitment?
5 **Communication and involvement** – Is our communication process aimed at raising levels of understanding on all sides and aligning the interests of those important to the success of the company? Do we adapt the company as a result of communication? What programmes have we put in place aimed at enhancing the company's key relationships? For example, do we participate in any community/government partnerships? Do we have any supplier programmes? Do we have a programme for educating investors about the company? What kind of dialogue do we have with our customers?
6 **Reward system** – How do we ensure the company behaves successfully? Do we use a success language and operate a reward system which encourages behaviours that drive performance?
7 **Measurement** – Do we have a useful overall measure of management effectiveness? Do our measures match our success model? Are they applicable to the context of our business? Do we measure progress in each relationship? Are we fully reflecting the level of public interest in our business in terms of measuring our *licence to operate*?
8 **Organisation** – Does our structure match our sources of success? Is it flexible enough to adapt to change? How do we identify organisational barriers to flexibility and to the achievement of our company purpose?
9 **Learning organisation** – Do we inspire our people to learn? Is our appraisal system effective in linking personal development and learning with business goals? Do we have a systematic approach to becoming a learning organisation? Do our key people have personal development plans? Do we equip our people with transferable skills?

Agenda for action: the investment community

Analysts and fund managers

1 **New success criteria** – Have we developed appropriate success criteria for assessing companies? Have we based them on *all* the company's key sources of sustainable value, such as the commitment and capability of its people, or the risk of key relationships failing?

2 **Promoting understanding** – Do we articulate investment objectives to corporate management in order to facilitate mutual understanding of expectations? Do we promote better industry knowledge through our training programmes?

Pension fund trustees and actuaries

3 **Creating a proper time-frame** – Have we set a time-horizon over which the investment performance of fund managers is to be assessed? Was this agreed at the outset, on their appointment? Is the time allowed long enough to allow reliable conclusions to be drawn?

4 **Consistency of judgement** – Have we set out the criteria by which we and our fellow trustees will judge a fund manager's performance? Have we set out the objectives of each investment fund?

5 **Assessing our own performance** – Have we made formal choices on investment strategy issues such as risk tolerance? Is the risk level of the portfolio appropriate to the interests of the ultimate beneficiaries? Have we properly balanced income and capital growth? Is our time-horizon short or long?

Finance directors, accountants and auditors

6 **Measuring success** – What success model is the company using? Do our performance indicators for each key relationship correlate with it? Do our measures balance historic financial performance against the strategic health of the business and its future prospects? Are we measuring risk on the right parameters? Does our measuring and reporting reflect the full context of the company's business operations?

7 **Helping to widen perspectives** – Does our framework of key measures cover values, behaviours and outcomes, the health of key relationships, and competitive performance levels in key processes, as well as the financial components?

8 **Providing the context** – Does our financial reporting provide a wider view, through appropriate information covering corporate purpose and values, and giving a relevant context for the business?

Agenda for action: learners and educators

Learners and parents

1. **Developing awareness** – Are we aware of the realities of global competition and what the implications are for future working lives?
2. **Getting involved** – Are we aware of the skills and capabilities required by Tomorrow's Company? Do we require of education and training that it promotes self-reliance, flexibility and breadth?
3. **Learning to learn** – Have we acquired the *learning habit*? What have we done about a personal learning plan? Does our plan match likely market needs?

Schools and career advisers

4. **Our role** – What part do we play in meeting the UK National Education and Training Targets (or their equivalent)?
5. **Matching real needs** – How do we know our current educational approach, and our curriculum material, are adequate to prepare people for tomorrow's business world? Do we include students, parents, employers and the wider community in our efforts to bridge the academic and vocational divide? Do we link the concept of employability with life-long learning? Do we reflect the need for multi-skilling, rather than for qualifications matched to particular industries?
6. **Examining assumptions** – What are the preconceptions of our students about companies' future requirements and about the growth of self-employment? What assumptions do they make about their own potential?
7. **Altering perspectives** – Have we asked our students to read about the *Tomorrow's Company* findings? Does it alter their views?
8. **Setting personal goals** – Have we encouraged them to have a personal development plan, setting out their goals, achievements and development actions?
9. **Valuing partnerships** – Do our partnerships with businesses deliver as much as they should?

Management educators

10. **Assessing the curriculum** – How do we know our curriculum meets the needs of *Tomorrow's Company*? Is it sufficiently *inclusive*? Is it focused on helping us improve our international competitiveness and speed up our response to change?
11. **Promoting the learning habit** – Do we encourage all our students to have personal development plans and our corporate supporters to create a framework for learning?

APPENDIX 2: Building a framework for success

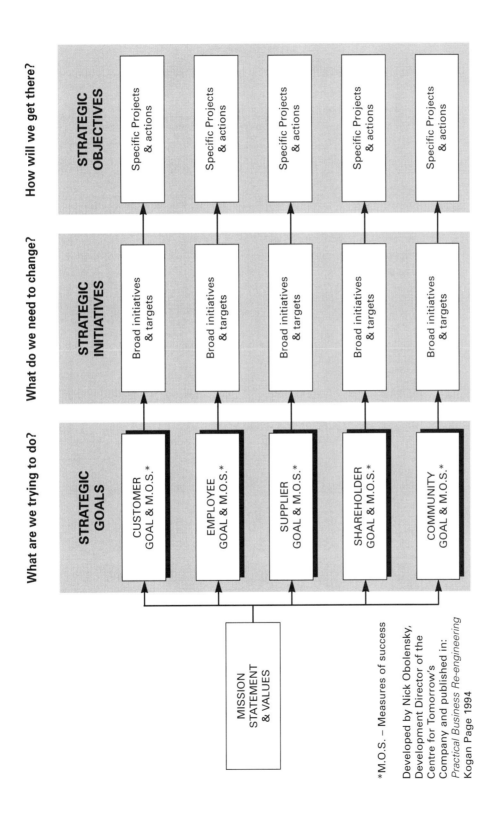

How will we get there?

STRATEGIC OBJECTIVES

Specific Projects & actions

Specific Projects & actions

Specific Projects & actions

Specific Projects & actions

Specific Projects & actions

What do we need to change?

STRATEGIC INITIATIVES

Broad initiatives & targets

Broad initiatives & targets

Broad initiatives & targets

Broad initiatives & targets

Broad initiatives & targets

What are we trying to do?

STRATEGIC GOALS

CUSTOMER GOAL & M.O.S.*

EMPLOYEE GOAL & M.O.S.*

SUPPLIER GOAL & M.O.S.*

SHAREHOLDER GOAL & M.O.S.*

COMMUNITY GOAL & M.O.S.*

MISSION STATEMENT & VALUES

*M.O.S. – Measures of success

Developed by Nick Obolensky, Development Director of the Centre for Tomorrow's Company and published in: *Practical Business Re-engineering* Kogan Page 1994

APPENDIX 2 (continued): An example

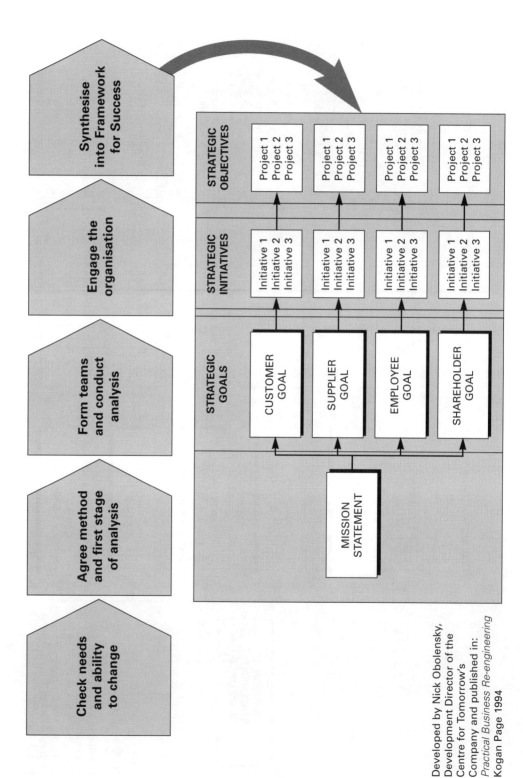

Developed by Nick Obolensky,
Development Director of the
Centre for Tomorrow's
Company and published in:
Practical Business Re-engineering
Kogan Page 1994

APPENDIX 3: Grand Metropolitan Report on Corporate Citizenship 1997 – community measurement and reporting*

This report would be incomplete without feedback on what objective yardsticks exist or are being developed to measure attitudes to key aspects of community involvement and our own performance as a corporate citizen.

Although we recognise that we have a long way to go, we are striving for systems reflecting the model described in the RSA's Tomorrow's Company report, which 'matches performance measurement to (the company's) purposes and success model, so that it can assess areas of risk, the health of relationships and the degree of renewal, and can anticipate fully its opportunities'.

LEARNING AND CONSTANT EVOLUTION

In line with the 'Managing for Value' principle being applied throughout GrandMet, measurement and benchmarking have become vital parts of our community relations process. We are constantly seeking, piloting and testing new measurement and evaluation methods to help ensure continuous improvement. We believe systematic evaluation and monitoring are essential if we are to remain effective and develop as a socially responsible learning organisation.

Our community relations team reviews the literature – books, articles, external surveys and statements by governmental and other bodies – on corporate social responsibility, and actively seeks out information about local community concerns and GrandMet's effectiveness in addressing them, with surveys and other measurement techniques.

MEASUREMENT OF IMPACT

As reported in the case studies, evaluation against defined objectives is built into every project we undertake. We measure both community and business impact and believe this helps us to design more effective programmes, ensuring our limited resources achieve maximum beneficial impact.

* This is an extract from Chapter 4 of the Report

BENCHMARKING

GrandMet is a member of the London Benchmarking Group. This consists of six major UK companies seeking to develop and expand the reporting of community involvement activities so that they are more transparent and can be judged by the total impact they achieve.

The following tables and charts should help to give an idea of the scale, nature and effectiveness of GrandMet's corporate citizenship activities.

LEVEL OF SPEND AND IMPACT

Table 1
Summarises the key statistics of GrandMet's £13million community investment programme. The diagram indicates how this is divided between cash donations, product donations and social sponsorship.

Table 2
Analyses GrandMet's contributions within a new template designed by the London Benchmarking Group, which defines more broadly overall corporate community involvement (CCI) spend or 'input'. It includes our additional £4million direct community input arising from commercial initiatives.

Table 3
Expands the template by showing examples of 'output' measures for a number of different programmes. The diverse nature of our activities and the resources deployed, means it is not possible to aggregate output measures.

FEEDBACK AND EFFECTIVENESS

Table 4
Summarises the results of surveys conducted in 1994 through Pillsbury's consumer relations free phone number and Cone/Roper study with US consumers.

Table 5
Summarises the results of a UK CCI survey of Opinion Leaders conducted in 1996 by MORI, in association with Bruce Naughton Wade.

Table 6
Reports on a study of GrandMet employee volunteering in the US and summarises the results of a 1992 Points of Light Foundation survey of 2,500 business executives employed by America's top 1,800 public companies.

Table 7
Benchmarks the company's community involvement effectiveness by developing a best practice model (based on the European Quality Model) and an assessment process verified by an independent panel. GrandMet is one of a group of seven companies piloting a CCI index with consultants Bruce Naughton Wade.

Table 1 Total 1996 GrandMet community investment spend: £13 million

GrandMet spends approximately 1.5% of world-wide trading profit less interest costs on community investment

Sector Analysis

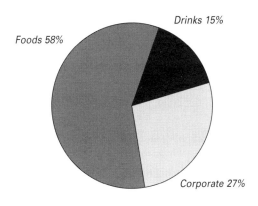

Foods 58%   Drinks 15%

Corporate 27%

Geographical Analysis

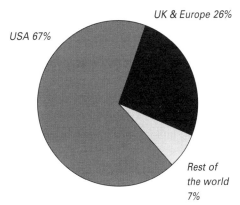

USA 67%   UK & Europe 26%

Rest of the world 7%

Programme Analysis

	Cash Donations and Costs	Social Sponsorship	Product Donations	Total Spend
Type of Spend (1)	£8,049,000	£2,025,000	£2,802,000	£12,876,000
	63%	16%	21%	100%
Project Classification				
Education	36%	15%	0%	25%
Youth	15%	12%	1%	12%
Homeless & Health	7%	26%	4%	9%
Economic Regeneration	2%	4%	0%	2%
Environment	1%	3%	0%	1%
Disability	1%	0%	0%	1%
Arts	2%	11%	0%	3%
Employee Matched Giving (2)	11%	0%	0%	7%
Relief of Poverty (3)	1%	0%	92%	20%
Other	24%	29%	3%	20%
Total (4)	100%	100%	100%	100%

Source: 1996 World-wide Group Community Survey

Notes

(1) Excludes externally generated funding, employees' and retirees' volunteering time.

(2) Excludes employees' own giving and fund-raising.

(3) Includes Second Harvest in USA.

(4) Excludes commercial initiatives as defined in London Benchmarking Group Reporting.

Table 2 Total 1996 GrandMet community spend based on the London Benchmarking Group's template for reporting community involvement

Activity	Abbreviated Definitions	INPUT Programme Costs in £000
1 Charity	**Responding to appeals from the community**	
Donations	Cash given to national and local appeals	1,513
Social Sponsorship	Support to causes or events with name recognition, but the activity is not part of a company's marketing strategy, it is to benefit the charity	2,025
Secondments & Consultancy	The service of employees provided by the company	not quantified
In-kind Giving	Gifts of product and equipment or use of company premises	554
Employee Matched Giving	Matching the cash gifts of employees to charities of their choosing	799
Employee Volunteering	Cash granted to support employees in community activities of their own choosing (GrandMet does not quantify 'time off')	17
Facilitating Giving	Companies using their relationships with customers and consumers to collect for good causes	53
Sub Total		**5,021**
2 Social Investment	**Sustained involvement in issues important to the company**	
Grants	Cash invested in programmes to achieve specific agreed goals	4,350
Secondments & Consultancy	The loaning of employees to community organisations on a full time, long term or part-time basis to achieve mutually agreed goals	335
In-kind Contributions	Gifts such as product and equipment that are central to the success of a focused programme	2,586
In-house Training	Work experience and training opportunities for young people or representatives from the public and non-profit sectors	not quantified
Supplier Development	Additional costs associated with creating jobs for disadvantaged groups as suppliers to the company	2
Sub Total		**7,273**
3 Management Costs		
Charity & Social Investment Costs	The salaries, benefits, overheads and operating budgets of the company's community support activities	582
4 Commercial Initiatives	**Partnerships to promote and protect commercial interests**	
Sponsorship	The amount of a sponsorship given to a charity or non-profit organisation	282
Cause-Related Marketing	The funds raised for a charity and other funds or assistance given	353
Strategic Contributions	Gifts to universities and trade related organisations whose activities support the success of the business, its employees and retirees	3,232
Staff Training	Community assignments as part of company's training plan	not quantified
Sub Total		3,687
Total		**16,743**

Table 3 Measuring the impact of corporate community involvement

The London Benchmarking Group's input/output matrix

Activity	Input GrandMet Example	Cash Value	Outputs Leverage/Matching	Social Impact (Annual)	Business Impact (Annual)
1. Charity					Philanthropic
Donations	Mencap Blue Sky Appeal	£33K	Employee-led fund-raising activities	Setting up of Family Volunteer Advice Service throughout UK	
Social Sponsorship	Gilbey's Adult Literacy Awards	R250K	South African government may match funding in 1997	Bringing PR and motivation to adult achievement in literacy and basic education. It has directly reached 131 centres, 2,955 practitioners, 48,930 learners and their extended families	Trade and government relations Consumer and employee 'feel good' factor
Employee Matched Giving	BK, Heublein, Pillsbury United Way	$1.25m	$1.25 million donated by employees matched by companies	$2.5 million to not-for-profits each year. Aggregate impact unquantifiable	Helps attract, retain and develop great people. Enhances morale, teamwork, creativity, pride in company, community and diversify awareness
Employee Volunteering	Pillsbury - REACH and Golden Ambassadors	$20K	1,200 volunteers 11,000 hours supported by Pillsbury	193 community projects received direct help	
2. Social Investment					
Grants/Donations	GrandMet - Tomorrow's People	£1m	Other companies and government agencies fund £10m pa	Over 25,000 young and unemployed helped each year. Added value to UK economy over £150m (taxes paid less welfare costs)	Positive impact on social issues which can adversely affect business environment. Corporate reputation and government relations. Learning platform for other social investment programmes
Secondments and Consultancy	GrandMet - Community Assignments	not quantified	Volunteers' time external funding	Business and technical skills to charities	Enhances morale, teamwork, creativity, pride in company, community and diversity awareness
In-kind Contributions	Pillsbury - Second Harvest	$4m	Distribute via established national network	Food for 15,000 children and families	Distribution for surplus product and off-peak use of production facilities
3. Commercial Initiatives					
Sponsorship	Malibu - Surfers Against Sewage	£27K	Malibu sponsorship has helped to recruit 3,000 new members	Campaign for cessation of raw sewage in seas around UK has received national radio and newspaper coverage	Brand integrity and PR. Surfers are the leading edge in style amongst Malibu's consumers. National media described Surfers Against Sewage as the 'coolest pressure group in the UK'
Cause-Related Marketing	J&B - Care for the Rare (see also Pillsbury Customer Partnership case study)	£350K	Consumers contribute per bottle. Employees contribute via fund-raising	The programme has helped over 22 different species, working with conservation organisations and governments around the world	Duty free litre sales increased by 37%. Favourable trade and consumer response. PR spin offs include TV documentary film
Strategic Contributions	ID Mauritius - Drinks Industry Action Group	£4K	Joint partnership with 3 other drinks companies, police force and government	Sponsored drink/drive TV campaign with police force. Actively involved with Ministry of Youth and Education in school seminars on danger of alcohol abuse	Seen to be proactive and self-regulating in encouraging responsible consumption
4. Business Basics	A Social Audit	not quantified	In addition to on-going process controls such as environmental audits, GrandMet is piloting social audits with its food and drinks businesses to create a model for broader	measurement and evaluation reporting, by producing a host country 'balance sheet' of activities and impacts. Phase 1 is to develop and use quantifiable measures of activity and performance in a manner analogous to financial accounts. Phase 2 to provide a means similar to financial audit to give an independent assessment and evaluation of that performance by respected outsiders	Measuring Corporate Citizenship Study developed by Walker Research on a sample of US corporations using impact coefficients and regression analysis demonstrates a correlation between quality community involvement and bottom line profitability

From GrandMet Report on Corporate Citizenship 1997

Table 4 US consumer survey

Pillsbury's consumer relations free phone number conducted a survey in 1994 with 591 callers who were consumers or interested in the company's brands.

Community involvement

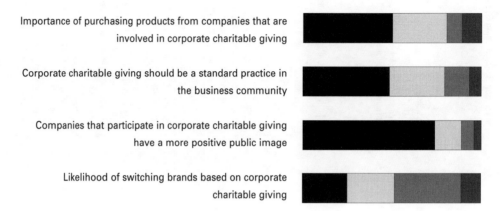

Cause-related marketing

Cone/Roper conducted a study of US consumer attitudes towards cause related marketing in 1994 with 2,000 adults set a national benchmark to this strategic positioning/marketing practice.

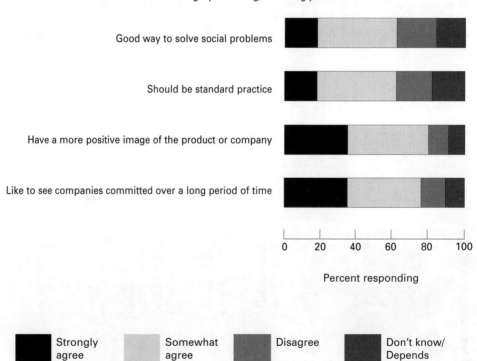

Percent responding

■ Strongly agree	▨ Somewhat agree	▨ Disagree	■ Don't know/ Depends

Table 5 UK Opinion Leader Survey

Level of endorsement of key benefits to be derived from corporate community involvement (CCI).

- When opinion leaders were asked to rate a number of possible benefits that companies may derive from being involved with corporate community involvement, the results were very consistent with spontaneous benefits mentioned – ie primarily relating to corporate image, supported by benefits in terms of employee motivation.
- GrandMet was rated third amongst leading companies mentioned as performing well in CCI in the UK.
- Respondents were asked to indicate, using a scale of 1-10, the extent of each of the following potential benefits for a company:

Top 10 perceived company benefits of CCI (mean source)

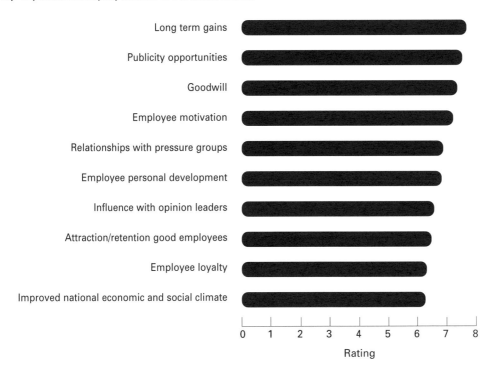

The Opinion Leader Survey conducted July 1996 by MORI in association with Bruce Naughton Wade

The sample

101 opinion leaders were interviewed, drawn from different spheres of influence:

- Government and politics.
- Voluntary sector.
- Media, academia, education, think tanks.
- Business and city

Table 6 Employee response and volunteering

Employee surveys

GrandMet's annual world-wide internal Community Survey, together with a series of GrandMet employee communication focus groups, independently run in 1996, indicated strong support for community involvement and requests for more feedback on our activities.

Employee doing and giving

A survey amongst our US employees revealed increased volunteering from 30% to 48%.
Payroll giving increased during the year by 37%.

US business executive survey on corporate volunteer programmes

The US Congress Board, in conjunction with the Points of Light Foundation, surveyed 2,500 targeted executives in the 1,800 largest US public companies in May 1992.

Benefits for employee volunteer programmes

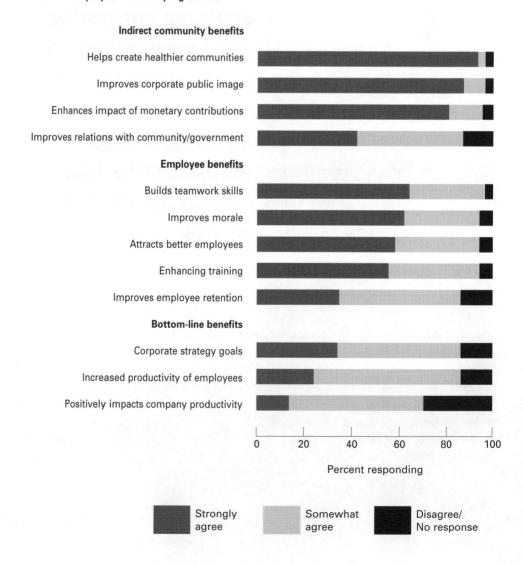

Peer company measures
Table 7 Benchmarking the effective use of funds and resources

GrandMet is piloting a CCI index with other companies to benchmark effectiveness by developing a best practice model (based on European Quality Model) and an assessment process verified by an independent panel. Our comparative score in all the eight categories indicates both effective performance across the board and further room for improvement, as shown below.

1996 pilot assessment

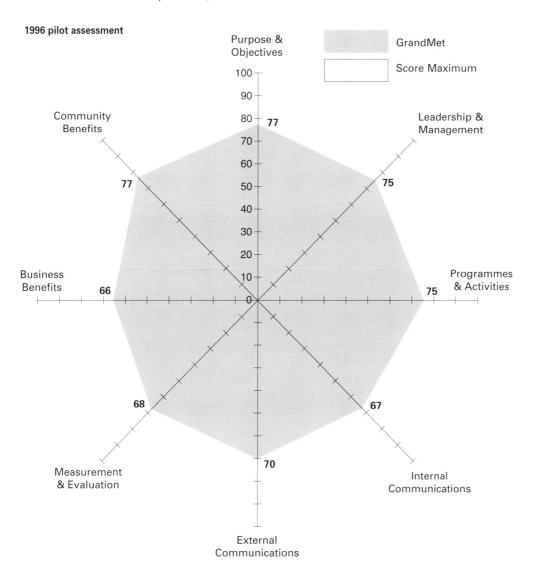

In the Bruce Naughton Wade 1996 'Peer Group' Study, CCI heads of a sample of major companies provided qualitative data which rated GrandMet the highest overall aggregate for the second year running. The Study also incorporated the views of key voluntary sector leaders and civil servants in government departments.

NOTES

PREFACE

[1] Goyder, George (1992), *The Just Enterprise*, Adamantine Press.

CHAPTER 1

[1] Mill, John Stuart (1859), *On Liberty*, Chapter 1, quoted in *Utilitarianism*, edited by Mary Warnock, Fontana Library 1962, p.127.

CHAPTER 2

[1] Casson, Mark (1991), *The Economics of Business Culture*, Oxford Clarendon Press.

[2] Smith, Adam (1790), *Wealth of Nations*, Penguin English Library Edition, Introduction, p.17.

[3] J. Willard Marriott, Snr quoted in *Built to Last: Successful Habits of Visionary Companies* by James C. Collins and Jerry L. Porras, Century Business Books, 1995, p.83.

[4] Robinson, Peter (1994), *Snapshots from Hell: The Making of an MBA*, Nicholas Brealey, pp.224-225.

[5] Ibid. The quotation within this extract is from Joseph Schumpeter (1911), *The Theory of Economic Development*.

[6] John Gardner quoted in *Leadership* by Philip Sadler, Kogan Page, 1997, p.21.

[7] Robinson, Peter (1994), *Snapshots from Hell*, pp.187-188.

[8] I am indebted to Professor John Kay for this phrase.

[9] Taggart, James, Kontes, Peter and Mankins, Michael, (1994), *The Value Imperative*, Free Press, p.205.

[10] Chatham House Forum Report (1996), *Unsettled Times*, Royal Institute for International Affairs, p.20.

[11] Plender, John (1997), *A Stake in the Future – The Stakeholding Solution*, Nicholas Brealey, pp.23-25.

[12] *Financial Times* (1996) 'Employers' body says German-style two-tier boards not the answer to reform needs: CBI turns its back on stakeholder plans', 1 November.

[13] Wheeler, David and Sillenpää, Marian (1997), *The Stakeholder Corporation – A Blueprint for Maximising Stakeholder Value*, Pitman, pp. 167-168.

CHAPTER 3

[1] *Shorter Oxford English Dictionary*, Oxford University Press.
[2] Onians, Richard (1995), 'Making small fortunes: success factors in starting a business', *RSA Journal*, May, p.20.
[3] From *Dr Johnson's Dictionary* quoted in *The Just Enterprise* by George Goyder, 1993, p.15.
[4] *Shorter Oxford English Dictionary*, OUP.
[5] *Financial Times* (1995), July 1, p.1.
[6] Grisham, John (1993), *The Firm*, Arrow, p.51.
[7] The Inclusive Approach and Business Success: The Research Evidence, An Interim Report by the Centre for Tomorrow's Company.
[8] Kotter, John P. and Heskett, James L. (1992), *Corporate Culture and Performance*, Free Press, p.11.
[9] Geus, Arie de (1995), 'Companies: what are they?', *RSA Journal*, June p.26.
[10] Collins, James C. and Porras, Jerry L. (1995), *Built to Last*, Chapter 1.
[11] Pettigrew, Andrew and Whipp, Richard (1991), *Managing Change for Competitive Success*, Blackwells.
[12] Kim, W. Chan and Mauborgne, R. (1997), 'Value innovation: the strategic logic of high growth', *Harvard Business Review* January–February. As summarised in the *Financial Times*, 7 April 1997, p.14.
[13] Rajan, Amin (1996), Manufacturing Winners: Becoming World Class in an Anti-Manufacturing Culture, *RSA Journal*, May, pp.32-39.

CHAPTER 4

[1] Negroponte, Nicholas (1996), *Being Digital*, Coronet Books, p.5.
[2] *Financial Times*, 5 April 1997, p.20.
[3] *The Economist*, 30 September 1995, p.107.
[4] *Financial Times*, 24-25 August 1996.
[5] Chatham House Forum Report, (1996), *Unsettled Times*, p.9.
[6] *Fortune*, 27 June 1994, p.20.
[7] Nairn, Geoffrey, (1997), 'The Future of Work', *Financial Times New Year Review: The Shape of Things to Come*, 8 January, p.10.
[8] Mulgan, Geoff (1994), *The end of unemployment: bringing work to life*, Demos, p.6.
[9] Ibid., p.22.
[10] The Henley Centre for Forecasting, Planning for Social Change Survey, 1993.
[11] RSA/Inquiry Tomorrow's Company *Report*, Gower, 1995, p.14.
[12] Herkstroter, C.A.J., 'Dealing with contradictory expectations: the

dilemmas facing multinationals', Amsterdam, 1996, from Group External Affairs, Shell Centre, London SE1 7NA.

[13] *European Values Study 1981-1990*, published by the Gordon Cook Foundation on behalf of the European Values Group.

[14] Robert Shapiro, interviewed in *Harvard Business Review*, January–February 1997, pp.80-81.

[15] Chatham House Forum Report (1996), *Unsettled Times*, p.92.

[16] McRae, Hamish (1995), *The World in 2020*, HarperCollins, p.103.

[17] Goodman, Alissa, Johnson, Paul and Webb, Steven (1997), *Inequality in the UK*, Oxford University Press.

[18] United Nations Development Programme, *Human Development Report*, summarised in the *Independent on Sunday*, 21 July 1996, p.l9.

CHAPTER 5

[1] All references in this chapter to MORI research were obtained by the author direct from the organisation. The MORI Excellence Model was developed by Peter Hutton of MORI and draws on the Business Excellence Model of the European Foundation for Quality Management and the RSA Inquiry Tomorrow's Company.

[2] Frederick F. Reicheld (1996), *The Loyalty Effect: The hidden force behind growth, profits and lasting value*, Harvard Business Press.

[3] Feldman, Stanley J., Soyika, Peter A. and Ameer, Paul, 'Does improving a firm's management sytem and environmental performance result in a high stock price?', survey conducted by ICF Kaiser, Fairfax, Virginia, January 1997.

[4] *Financial Times* (1996), 'Brand new look at loyalty', 19 September, p.2.

[5] Conference board of America Study quoted in 'Guide to Business in the Community', *Financial Times* 1996, p.5.

[6] *Innovation – Breakthrough Ideas*, MIT News Office, Cambridge, MA.

[7] *Harvard Business Review*, January–February 1997, pp.81-82.

[8] Cleaver, Anthony B. (1987), 'The social responsibilities of business', Canor Lecture, *RSA Journal*.

[9] Portway, Sarah (1995), 'Corporate social responsibility: the case for active stakeholder relationship management' in *Strategic Public Relations* by Norman A. Hart (ed.), Macmillan Press.

[10] Fogarty, Michael and Legard, Robin (1993), *More than Money*, Rowntree Foundation, p.12.

[11] London Benchmarking Group (1997), 'Companies in Communities: Getting The Measure' obtainable from Corporate Citizenship International, 1 Russell Chambers, Covent Garden Piazza, London WC2E 8AA.

[12] Adams, *Financial Times*, 15 September 1995

[13] Hark, Heskett and Saffer (1990), 'The Profitable Art of Service Recovery', *Harvard Business Review*, July–August.

[14] Mutter, Peter (1997)7 'Working together for a secure future', *Croners*

Journal of Human Resource Management, July 1997.

[15] Ibid.

[16] Cave, Alan (1994), *Managing Change in the Workplace*, Kogan Page, p.204.

[17] Iwasaki, Yoshio and Nakane, Jinichiro (1995), 'Downscaling to adapt to your environment', *Target,* Vol.11, No.4 July–August.

[18] Ibid.

[19] Institute for Employment Research, University of Warwick, 'Review of the Economy and Employment', *Financial Times* October 1995.

[20] Gapper, John and Denton, Nicholas (1996), *All That Glitters*, Hamish Hamilton, quoted from serialised extracts in *Financial Times* 19 September 1996.

[21] *Financial Times*, 29 July 1996, p.8.

[22] *Financial Times*, 2 October 1995, p.14.

[23] *Making International Strategic Alliances Work*, Conference Board Europe 1995, quoted in *Financial Times* 2 October 1995, p.14.

[24] Rosabeth Moss Kanter quoted in *Financial Times* 2 October 1995, p.14.

[25] Womack, James and Jones, Daniel T. (1996), *Lean Thinking*, Simon & Schuster, pp.113-115.

[26] *Financial Times*, 16 October 1995, p.7.

[27] *Logistics Excellence in Europe*, published by A. T. Kearney 1996, quoted from extracts in *Financial Times*, 'Logistics Survey' 15 October 1996, p.3.

CHAPTER 6

[1] Doyle, Peter (1994), 'Britain's Top Companies: Setting Business Objectives and Measuring Performance', *Journal of Marketing Management*, Vol.20 No.2, Winter.

[2] Collins, James C. and Porras, Jerry L. (1995), *Built to Last*, p.54.

[3] Ibid., p.55.

[4] Ibid., p.489.

[5] This summary is taken from a case study in Nick Obolensky, *Practical Business Re-engineering: Tools and Techniques for Achieving Effective Change*, Kogan Page, 1994, pp.218-227.

[6] Kaplan, Robert S. and Norton, David (1996), 'Using the balanced scorecard as a strategic management system', *Harvard Business Review*, January–February.

[7] 'Transforming the organisation: new approaches to management, measurement and leadership' by Keith Ruddle and David Feeny, Templeton College Oxford 1997, quoted in *Financial Times* 18 July 1997, p.12.

[8] The Inclusive Approach and Business Success: The Research Evidence, An Interim Report by the Centre for Tomorrow's Company.

[9] Waterman, Robert (1995), *Frontiers of Excellence*, Nicholas Brealey, pp.87-110.

CHAPTER 7

[1] Votaw, Dow (1965), *Modern Corporations*, Prentice Hall, pp.96-97, quoted in Margaret Blair, *Ownership and Control*, Brookings Institution 1995, p.224.

[2] One of the differences between corporate governance in the UK and the USA is that in the USA there is a whole history of litigation – from Dodge *vs.* Henry Ford in 1919 to Paramount Communications Inc. *vs.* QVC Network Inc. in 1994 – in which the concept of shareholder value is asserted as being distinct from the long-term value of the company. Cf. Margaret Blair, *Ownership and Control*, 1995, pp.209-222.

[3] The distinction between 'accountable to' and 'accountable for' was suggested to me by Michael Nisbet who chaired the Corporate Governance Working Group as part of the RSA Tomorrow's Company Inquiry. It has also been widely used by Alistair Ross Goobey.

[4] 'Neglect of the new addition' by Duncan Angwin and Robin Wensley, University of Warwick, quoted in *Financial Times* 5 February 1997, p.2.

CHAPTER 8

[1] Creighton, Louise (1917), *Life and Letters of Thomas Hodgkin*, Longmans & Co.

[2] 'Survey of the World's Economy', *The Economist* 28 September 1996, p.4.

[3] Diana Farrell, McKinsey Global Institute, presentation to the Investor Relations Conference 23 June 1995, *Journal of the Investor Relations Society*, July 1995, pp.6-7.

[4] 'Artificial intelligence: the model fund manager', *The Economist*, 15 September 1995, p.103.

[5] Research obtained by the author from the Institutional Fund Managers Association.

[6] In the UK, a DTI-sponsored committee, chaired by Paul Myners, produced a report entitled, *A Winning Partnership*, with model guidelines for companies and investors. In the USA, the conference produced a report entitled, *Communicating Corporate Performance: A Delicate Balance for Managements, Shareholders and Boards of Directors*, Conference Board, New York, 1997.

CHAPTER 9

[1] Geoff Mulgan and Charles Leadbetter, 'The end of unemployment: bringing work to life', Demos 1994, p.23.

[2] Chatham House Forum Report (1996), *Unsettled Times*, pp.121-130.

[3] Ibid., p.121.

[4] *Harvard Business Review*, January–February, 1997.

[5] Ibid., pp.86-7.

[6] Knight, Alan, *Green Futures*, No.2, December, 1996, p.28.

[7] *Tomorrow Magazine*, January–February 1997, pp.22-37.

[8] The phrase 'work, wealth and worth' was introduced to me by Common Purpose, a UK organisation which brings business and community leaders together and stimulates them to develop a shared vision for the future.

[9] Robinson, Steve (1996), *Out of the Twilight Zone: Managing threats and opportunities of an environmentally sustainable business*, The Environment Council.

CHAPTER 10

[1] From *Perspectives*, published by Boston Consulting Group. Interview between Mr Koichi Hori, President BCG Japan and Mr Nobuhiko Kawamoto, President Honda Motor Company Ltd.

INDEX